n or before

THE COMPLETE
BARTENDER'S
GUIDE

First published in 2003

Reprinted with updates in 2010

Second edition 2013

Copyright © Carlton Books Limited 2003, 2013

A CIP catalogue record for this book is available from the British Library

ISBN 978-1-78097-390-6

Printed in China

Publisher's note:
Please use caution when using raw eggs in any of the recipes included in this book. Raw eggs have been known to cause salmonella poisoning and should not be consumed by infants, young children, pregnant women, mothers who are nursing, the elderly, or anyone with a weakened immune system. Readers who are pregnant or nursing children are strongly recommended to avoid any alcohol consumption.

All instructions and warnings given in this book should be read carefully. The author and publisher have made every effort to ensure that all information is correct and up to date at the time of publication.

Neither the author nor the publisher can accept responsibility for, or shall be liable for, any accident, injury, loss or damage (including any consequential loss) that results from using the ideas, information, procedures or advice offered in this book.

Cocktail Glasses: Key

A) Old-Fashioned	H) Coffee Liqueur
B) Highball	I) Champagne Flute
C) Collins/Tumbler	J) Martini/Cocktail
D) Shot	K) Champagne Saucer
E) Collada	L) Goblet/Wine
F) Brandy	M) Margarita
G) Parfait	See pages: 12-13

THE COMPLETE
BARTENDER'S
GUIDE

SECOND EDITION

DAVE BROOM

CARLTON
BOOKS

Contents

Chapter 5: Tonics and Juices — 372

Introduction

The sound is spreading around the globe. A rasping, crunching noise, like someone sprinting up a gravel path. It is a sound which had almost disappeared until recently, a black and white sound that triggered a vague memory of Hollywood movies and 1950s sitcoms, a sound made by clean-cut people enjoying each other's company, or by uniformed bartenders who knew every customer's secrets and never divulged their own. It is the sound of ice and spirits dancing together in a shaker to make a fantastical new product. It is a cocktail being born. Cocktails and cocktail bartending had almost died out in the 1970s and '80s. There were a few great hotels with top-class bartenders and a few young acolytes who keep the tradition alive in small, often private, clubs.

Cocktails were still being made, but they had slipped from mass-market consciousness along with tailfins on Cadillacs. The three Martinis sipped over a long lunch had been replaced with three mineral waters and a plate of sushi.

Thankfully, fashion is a cyclical thing and at the height of the neo-Prohibitionist movement at the start of the 1990s (it happened) a new generation began to rebel. They spurned the health fascists, demanding red meat and strong alcohol, puffing on smuggled Cuban cigars, and quaffing red wine. This is – was – a generation who want flavour, prefer to relax in quality bars, and drink quality drinks. The sound of the shaker began to get louder once more.

This book celebrates the rebirth of the cocktail. It shows that its history is one of continual evolution and re-invention and gives recipes for old classics and new drinks. Over the past 200 years a few cocktails have achieved classic status. These are described in more detail because their stories are interesting. If they can be made well, then there'll be no problem making any of the drinks in this book.

Making is the important word. This isn't just a book to flick through, but one to be used – so we look at what equipment the home bartender (on any budget) will need and how to use it. It doesn't stop there. You also have to know what ingredients go into these magical potions, not just juices, water and ice, but the whole world of alcoholic drinks.

One thing is clear when you talk to any top bartender. You can't make a great drink from cheap ingredients. The cocktail revival has, not altogether surprisingly, heralded a revival in premium spirits. Small batch bourbon, malt whisky, top-end gins, tequilas and vodkas have all appeared on the back of this. Each one of those categories is looked at in detail with explanations on how each spirit is made and also what they taste like.

Wine, too, is part of a drink-lover's repertoire today and while you might not want to experiment with some Zinfandel in a shaker, every home bartender should have wine knowledge as well – after all there are times when a glass of chilled white, or a warming red is the only thing which will do. The 21st century drinker is unlike their 1950s counterpart. Then, if you liked one type of drink you stuck with it; now, people flit from one spirit to another; from wine to beer. The only criterion is that whatever the drink, it should be the best quality.

This is a wonderful time to be a cocktail lover. Now, get shaking!

Equipment

You can make drinks with virtually no bar equipment, but it's difficult to make great drinks with little more than the basics. You don't need to transform your living room into a proper bar, but if you want to make a good impression then it's worth investing in the essentials: a shaker, for example, the right glasses, a good range of spirits, liqueurs and bitters.

You'll want to know how to open a bottle of Champagne, how to cut a twist and flame a bit of orange peel. In time you'll realise that what turns an ordinary drink into a work of art is simply attention to detail: using orange or Peychaud bitters instead of Angostura, even just knowing how important good quality ice is. Small and inexpensive touches that make all the difference.

Cocktail Shakers

Shakers come in a mass of shapes and sizes and while it might seem like a good idea to invest in a novelty one, run three simple checks before you part with your money. Firstly, is it easy to hold? It's pointless having a baroque instrument on the bar if you drop it all the time. Secondly, is it easy to use? Does the lid get stuck, or fall off, and can you strain easily? Thirdly, is it made from stainless steel or glass? If it isn't, don't buy it.

Many bartenders use a Boston shaker. This comes in two parts: one a tall thick glass, the other similarly shaped but slightly smaller and made of stainless steel. This part fits inside the top of the glass part, allowing you to shake the ice and liquid between the two. You can also use the glass part for stirring drinks and, because it's clear, it allows you to see if your proportions are correct. Be warned, Boston shakers can be tricky to separate.

Juggling

You may, in time, decide to try and copy that hotshot barkeep you saw working the crowd in Las Vegas with his juggling tricks. My advice is DON'T. Flair bartending – as juggling bottles, glasses and shakers is known – is great fun to watch but, without wishing to be too much of a killjoy, the most important element in making a drink is making sure the drink is made correctly and tastes good. Anyway, it can make a dreadful mess of the carpet.

Glasses

There are eight glass shapes which are most widely used.

A) Shot It's fairly obvious what this glass is for. Small shots of the hard stuff intended to be drunk quickly, frozen vodka, tequila, etc. They can double up as measures if yours is lost in the fridge.

B) Old Fashioned Great for the eponymous cocktail (or variants thereof) which can be built in the glass or for old-fashioned drinks like whisky and soda.

C) Collins (Tall) The shape shows that this is a glass intended for long drinks, not just members of the **Collins** family but **Gin & Tonic** is perfect in this as are **Mojitos** and **Mint Juleps**.

D) Champagne flute The only glass for Champagne. Its shape encourages a regular, prolonged, stream of bubbles.

E) Wine glass Red wines and great whites need to breathe in the glass to release its aroma. A wide mouthed goblet not only does this but also allows you to swirl the wine to see the colour.

F) Champagne saucer A variant on the glass that is erroneously used for Champagne. Use this for any short mixed drink: **Daiquiri**, **Sours**, etc.

G) Highball Use this for making long drinks, modern, fruity cocktails, **Bloody Mary**, etc.

H) Martini (Cocktail) The classic shape for all short mixed drinks, such as **Martini** and **Manhattan**. Three rules: (1) make sure they are cold; (2) hold them by the stem while drinking (or the drink will heat up); (3) buy smaller rather than larger examples.

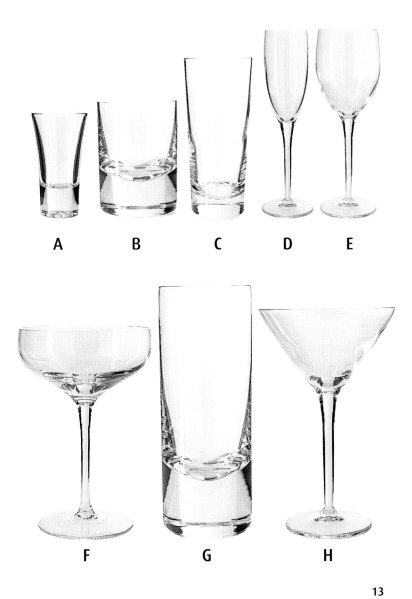

A   B   C   D   E

F   G   H

Blenders

Think of bartending as being like a chef. You are working with flavours, combining different ingredients to create a satisfying dish. You use knives and chopping boards. You sift, chop, strain and stir. No surprise then that many other kitchen appliances are shared by bartenders. Juicing machines are essential, while electric blenders are used for a large range of drinks: frappés for example, or frozen daiquiris. The former is served with all the ice, the latter can be served either with the ice or strained. Once you get used to making drinks in the blender another new world of flavour opens up.

It was the arrival of the electric blender that kicked off the daiquiri boom in Havana in the 1930s. It continues even today. Tony Conigliaro, one of London's top bartenders, has created a frozen gin & tonic (2 shots Tanqueray, zest of a lemon, and a splash each of tonic water, simple sugar and Cointreau) which works superbly well.

Blenders have a stainless steel cutting blade, which rotates at very high speeds meaning that you can crush ice easily (though low power domestic appliances may not be able to do this. Please check!) and also blend in fruit: strawberries, banana, melon, along with the ice and the alcohol. You could even use the blender to zap the fruit on its own. It makes a thicker drink than a juicer. There are many different brands on the market ranging in price from £29–£139 ($40–$200) and made by the majority of kitchen equipment specialists.

Fresh is best

Soda siphons, and syrup concentrates, while an integral part of American culture, are not necessary for the home bar. The key to modern cocktails is freshness, rather than concentrates and syrups, and while the addition of syrups to carbonated/"charged" water brought pleasure to not only generations of American children – and teetotallers in the nineteenth and twentieth centuries – a juicer and blender are both better for making cocktails. Bars are bars, soda siphons are soda siphons. Never the twain should meet.

Corkscrews

Like shakers these come in a bizarre range of shapes and sizes, however the simplest designs tend to be the best. Stick to the good old-fashioned corkscrew, known as the waiter's friend (far right, opposite page). It has a knife on one side for cutting the foil and a spiral and lever on the other. It works a treat, doesn't break the corks and fits neatly into your pocket.

Bar Accessories

▼ Mixing Glass This is an essential piece of kit you can't be without.

▲ Strainer To ensure that no bits of ice end up in the drink.

▼ Measuring spoons
To gauge those vital small additions.

▼Measure Use a measure until you feel confident to measure by eye.

▼ Ice bucket
Keep it full.

▼ Ice scoop To ladle in the ice when making frozen drinks.

▲ Chopping board Use as a preparation surface when making drinks, chopping up fruit, herbs and other garnishes.

▼ Straws These come in different lengths and widths, depending on the type of drink being served. They are necessary for longer drinks.

▲ Sharp knife Especially important for preparing garnishes.

▼ Cocktail sticks Handy for securing olives, onions, cherries and other fruit.

▲ Swizzle sticks Useful for stirring long drinks.

▼ Ice tongs Use tongs instead of your hands to pick up ice, otherwise it will melt.

Bartending at home

Once you've developed a passion for mixing drinks, the next thing you'll need is a home bar for assembling drinks. The days of improvizing in the kitchen will become a thing of the past and you'll want to perform your mixing skills in front of your friends. The area you choose to set up a home bar will depend on the layout of your house, the space available and your budget! Usually the room you use for social gatherings – the living room or den – tends to be the obvious choice for the home bar. It is entirely up to you, however, there are some practicalities to bear in mind before you set up. A large home bar is more than just a collection of bottles and glasses: it is, to all intents and purposes, a scaled- down version of a professional bar. It is up to you how much money you invest, but there are some essentials for which you will have to budget.

Case the Joint

Visit a few bars and study how they are set up. They allow bartenders to mix different drinks at the same time, without searching for ingredients. There will be a fridge under the bar top, alongside the sinks and an area for commonly used spirits.

All Mod Cons

A sink You'll need at least one, preferably two. One for washing your hands and washing up glasses, knives, chopping boards and other equipment; the other for rinsing fruit, chilling down glasses, etc.

A fridge (or, space allowing, a fridge-freezer). In this you'll keep the ice, white spirits, fruit juices, Champagne, white wine and beer.

An ice-making machine Although not essential is very useful because of the volumes of ice needed when making drinks.

A non-slip floor surface This is also advisable. Liquids tend to be spilled when making drinks and can cause accidents.

Stainless steel The best material for the bar top because it is not only easy to clean but also looks impressive. On top of the bar you should have your shakers, measures, a full basket of fruit, a blender and a juicer.

Following this principle, keep the spirits which you use the most frequently within easy reach. Store the fancy drinks, such as bourbons, tequilas, liqueurs and so on, on higher shelves and in groups. Arrange your glasses in order of use as well, storing those you require most often in the most accessible places.

Setting up your own Minibar

Not all of us have the space to dedicate a corner of a room, let alone an entire room, to mixing drinks. In any case, you can have as much fun making cocktails from a small cocktail cabinet. Look around in car-boot sales or antique shops for them; it is amazing what you can find.

The key here is to choose your spirit brands carefully and only buy the spirits and liqueurs which you know you'll use regularly. Because space is limited, restrict the number of spirits to those that work the best with the widest range of cocktails: a good quality silver, or reposado tequila will be more versatile than an expensive anejo, for example.

Store your most useful spirits in the cabinet along with your shaker, strainer, measures, and so on, and keep other less used spirits and liqueurs close by in a cupboard where you keep your glasses. Store vodka and gin in the fridge so that you also have space in your cabinet for bitters, rum, bourbon/Scotch and tequila.

In a large home bar it is possible to mix a variety of different drinks for your guests, but with a smaller set up it might be best

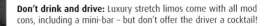

to decide what you are going to make and give everyone the same. It makes life easier and allows you to concentrate on the most important aspect of mixology, which is making a good drink. The downside of having a small bar is that it can take a little more time. If you are making a round of martinis, you'll have to go to the kitchen to get the ice, gin, vermouth and cold glasses, so ensure that these are all ready and waiting for collection before your guests arrive. The last thing you want to be doing is rattling around in the fridge for that bottle of gin. Then, when you get back, you can amaze your friends with your dexterity.

Don't drink and drive: Luxury stretch limos come with all mod cons, including a mini-bar – but don't offer the driver a cocktail!

Principles of storage

Apart from having the right bottle in the right place at the right time, good storage also involves knowing the best way to preserve a drink's freshness and character.

Spirits

Spirits are less sensitive than wines, but even they have their own peculiarities. White spirits, especially vodka and gin, should be kept in the fridge, or better still in the freezer. The cold temperature gives them a rich texture and, since cocktails are cold drinks, improves the quality of your mixed drink. Remember to stick to brands at 40% ABV and above; anything below that will freeze. Brown spirits, such as brandy, Scotch/bourbon and dark rum can be kept at room temperature.

Unlike wine, spirits do not improve in the bottle, although there are some people who claim that Chartreuse does. Usually a spirit will start to deteriorate if the bottle has been opened months or years before. This is because when air is let into the bottle the spirit starts to oxidize, the aroma flattens and loses its vibrancy. If you do have a half-full bottle of precious malt, cognac or bourbon then simply decant it into a smaller bottle. Brown spirits in clear glass bottles will lose their colour if stored for long periods in direct sunlight.

Wine

Wine storage is a slightly more complex issue. Many wines will improve in the bottle and ideally should be stored in a cellar. That said, most of us tend to drink wine soon after we buy it, which is why many wines are made to be drunk when young. Speak to your wine merchant and find out what wines will benefit from some ageing: these will include quality claret, some Californian and Australian Cabernet and Merlot, Burgundy (red and white) top German Riesling, Loire Chenin Blanc and Cabernet Franc, Rhône reds, Chianti Riserva, Barolo/Barbaresco. The same goes for Champagne, including most non-vintage brands. It really is a good idea to buy Champagne by the case and store it for a few months.

In the unlikely event...

There are many devices available which aim to preserve wine, but if you are going to finish off a bottle the next night, just replace the cork in the bottle. The Vacuvin system which sucks the air out of the bottle might save the wine from oxidizing but it also sucks the life and aroma out at the same time. Wine bars use a system which pumps nitrogen into the bottle, sealing it from the worst effects of the air, but while it is quite efficient this method is expensive.

There many myths about how to keep Champagne, such as putting a silver spoon in the neck of the bottle in order to preserve the bubbles. This is just a myth. Champagne should be sealed with a stopper and put in the fridge. The stopper won't prevent the gas from escaping – the bubbles remain in the wine for a day or so – but it does stop any odours from the fridge seeping into the wine.

What a corker

If a wine smells of wet newspaper it is corked. This is not your fault, it is not the wine merchant's fault or even the winemaker's. It is caused by a chemical (TCA) in the cork infecting the wine.

Racks and Cellars

Even if you are not intending to store wine for a long time you will need somewhere to keep the bottles. Although to begin with you may have no intention of creating a cellar, you may change your mind once you have been bitten by the wine bug. Then you'll make the big leap and be persuaded by your friendly wine merchant that you should invest in a case or two of high quality wine which needs to be aged, then comes the vintage port and, before you know it, you need a proper cellar. But before that day arrives, all you need to start with is a wine rack. You don't need to buy an expensive one, particularly since it won't be seen in a dark, cool storage place.

All you need is a simple self-assembly rack which stores the bottles on their sides. This is especially important if you are keeping the wine for a long time because you don't want the corks to dry out. It's always worthwhile asking a hotel or restaurant which is being refurbished or closed down whether they are willing to sell a wine rack to you at a good price.

If you do decide to set up a proper cellar there are certain key rules to bear in mind in terms of temperature and humidity. Wine doesn't store well in hot conditions and should be stored at temperatures below 25°C (77°F). Similarly, your cellar should not be too cold. If the temperature drops below freezing, not only could the wine freeze but also the corks may burst out of the bottles. Aim for a temperature range between 10°C (50°F) and 15°C (59°F) and avoid extreme swings in temperature. A humid cellar is vital as well. Dry conditions mean dry corks and dry corks lead to oxidized wine. If you aim for a level of around 75 per cent humidity you won't have too many problems.

All in all, you need to choose your location carefully. It's all very well already having a cellar under the house, but if it also contains your boiler then it won't be any good for storing wine. The garage may be the right size for a cellar, but it's unlikely to be sufficiently humid. A large cupboard in a spare room or study may be the right size, but check whether there are any hot water pipes running in the wall behind it because these will make the storage space too hot.

You can hire the services of a specialist firm to design and install a cellar, but first decide whether you could do it yourself by insulating a cupboard or box-room. Your trusty wine rack can be pressed into service again, although if you have large quantities of the same wine it might be easier to store them together in larger boxes or bins. Try and arrange the storage so that the wines that need the longest time to mature, such as vintage port, are positioned furthest away from the door. Those which are ready to drink should be the easiest to lay your hands on. Use your wine rack for everyday, ready-to-drink wines, and the cellar for the bottles you want to keep for years.

Bar Craft

A cocktail is a mixed drink. Classically it contains three broad parts: a base spirit which makes up the bulk of the volume and gives the drink its main flavour; a mixer, which binds it together; and the flavouring, which could be a dash of bitters, a drop of liqueur, or a squeeze of juice. Of course, it's slightly more complex than that, but the point is that a cocktail should be a balanced drink, where no single element dominates. In short, a cocktail is a drink which is greater than the sum of its parts.

Techniques and craft

Shaking

Shaking is the most effective way of mixing the ingredients, while simultaneously chilling the drink and diluting it slightly. Dilution helps to release flavours allowing them to blend together. Never fill the shaker more than halfway with ice. Shake the drink until the outside of the shaker is freezing to the touch. Cocktails should be very cold. Use ice cubes, not crushed ice, unless otherwise stated in the recipe because a drink shaken over crushed ice can quickly become too diluted.

Stirring

In general, stirring is used to marry flavours which go together easily, without making the drink cloudy, which is what happens when you shake. The principle is the same as shaking: a way to mix the ingredients together, chill a drink quickly and dilute it slightly. Half fill a shaker with ice and stir for about 20 seconds, or until the outside is chilled, then strain into cocktail glasses. Some recipes, for example the Old Fashioned, suggest the drink is stirred in the serving glasses.

Mine host: The barman is king of all he surveys and purveys to customers.

Blending

This is a good way to make long, thirst-quenching drinks. Simply whizz up the ice with the spirit ingredients and serve unstrained in the glass. Because the ice is crushed it melts more quickly and produces a fairly dilute alcoholic slush in the glass. It's a matter of personal preference. I like to taste the alcohol in the drink, but I can see the advantage of a frozen blended drink when you have a long, hot summer's afternoon ahead of you, hence the **Frozen Daiquiri.**

Muddling

Some recipes, such as **Caipirinha**, p. 74, and **Old Fashioned**, p. 158, call for "muddling" to take place. This involves pressing and mixing ingredients: mint, fruit, peel etc., in the bottom of the glass, often with bitters and over bar sugar. The rough surface of the sugar helps break up the ingredients easily. You can use the back of a spoon if you don't own a proper muddler, an implement similar to a pestle.

Layering

This process involves introducing the heaviest part of the drink first, followed by a succession of progressively lighter layers. The layers are carefully poured over the back of a spoon to sit one on top of the other. (See the **B52**, p. 51, or **Traffic Light**, p. 199).

Salting and Sugaring

The intention here is to coat the outside, not the inside, of the rim. Don't, therefore, bury the rim in a pile of salt or sugar.

Instead, moisten the outside rim with lime or lemon juice and then carefully turn the glass, side on, in a saucer of salt or sugar. Alternatively, you can sprinkle the salt or sugar onto the rim while rotating the glass, although this is a messier method.

Fruit

When using fruit for a garnish, make sure it is fresh and has been thoroughly washed. Try rolling limes and lemons before you cut them as this starts to release their juices. To cut a twist, pare small strips from a lemon ensuring there is some white pith attached. Holding the peel between thumb and forefinger give it a quick twist so that it sprays some of its oil on the surface of the drink. Run the twist round the rim of the glass and gently drop in.

Flaming

The secret of flaming brandy is to warm the glass first, either over a hot coil on the stove or by holding it under a hot tap. Pour in the brandy and ignite. To light absinthe, or high-proof vodka, hold the flame at the edge of the glass until the alcohol catches. Be aware that the flames can flare up, so ensure that your hair is not hanging over the glass.

Party Trick

One crowd-pleasing technique is to cut a section of orange peel about the size of a 10p piece. Now light a match. Hold the peel over the drink between thumb and forefinger and half snap, half flex it outwards. The spray of oils will ignite and settle on the drink giving it a wonderfully exotic flavour.

Home flavoured spirits

To flavour spirits yourself, simply add the flavouring of your choice, for example fruit, nuts, peel, chillis, garlic, chocolate or herbs and leave to stand. Vodka is the most widely used base spirit for infusion and since it is light in character allows the flavours to show themselves fully. That said, gin is wonderful (think sloe and damson) as is tequila (chilli, even lemon) and overproof rum. You can even use a moscato grappa for a walnut-based infusion and it works well. If you can find high-strength Polish Pure Spirit use it. The high level of alcohol means extraction is quicker. Dilute the result with standard strength vodka. Overproof rum works on the same principle.

You can use sweet or savoury ingredients as flavourings. Do not fall into the trap of using only sweet ingredients: chocolate vodka, for example, is fun the first time you try it, but the novelty soon wears off. Savoury/fresh fruit infusions tend to be more versatile and interesting.

Only you can tell when the infusion tastes as you want it, so it is difficult to give precise timings here. Keep on trying the infusion at regular intervals, then remove the flavouring agents when you have achieved the taste you want. In general, strongly flavoured herbs and pods only need a few days, chillis need around a week (though this depends on how hot you want your spirit to be and what type of chilli you use). Citrus zest can

take up to a month. Soft fruits, such as raspberry, infuse flavour quickly while sloe berries take their time.

Complex infusions using a large number of ingredients may need months. You can dare to experiment, using anything you can lay your hands on, or go seasonal. Make gooseberry vodka when they are fresh and rosehip vodka when they are in season. This will give you a wide range of flavours to play about with.

Chilli Vodka: Chillis can give plain vodka a very special kick in little more than a week.

Simple Sugar

Many recipes call for simple sugar. You can use sirop de gomme but it's easy to make your own. Take equal parts of white sugar and cold water and bring to a gentle boil stirring occasionally. When all the sugar has dissolved and the liquid is clear, remove from the heat and do not allow to brown. Seal in a jar and store in the fridge. An even easier method is to take a clean, preferably clear, empty 75cl bottle and fill it halfway with sugar. Top up with water and allow the sugar dissolve. You can add mint, lemon peel or any other flavouring of your choice to the syrup.

Bartenders Checklist

Alcohol

Gin (kept in fridge or freezer)
Vodka (kept in fridge or freezer)
Bison Grass vodka
Homemade flavoured vodka
White rum
Gold/aged rum
Tequila (100% blue agave
  silver/reposado)
Bourbon
Rye whiskey
Blended Scotch
Cognac
Noilly Prat
Red vermouth
Punt e Mes
Cointreau/curacao
Campari
Maraschino liqueur
Absinthe
Green Chartreuse
Kahlua
Champagne

Port
Fino sherry
Selection of liqueurs (amaretto,
  crème de cacao/menthe, etc.)
Angostura bitters
Peychaud bitters
Orange bitters
Underberg (for hangovers)

Others

Fresh limes, lemons, oranges,
  kumquat
Orgeat syrup
Grenadine
Freshly squeezed fruit juices
Maraschino cherries
Caster sugar
Maldon salt
Lime cordial
Tabasco
Worcestershire sauce
Horseradish
Mixers (tonic, soda, ginger ale)

A–Z of Cocktails

Here's the fun section, where all the simple, classic, exotic, and indulgent cocktails from all over the world are listed for your perusal. On the following pages you will discover tart temptations such as a Pisco Sour, sweet sensual sippers such as Bellini, and mind-how-many-you-have martinis, both classic and nouveau pretenders to the title. Feature cocktails focus on classics.

Should you decide to make one or two of them, you will find the exact measurement for each ingredient and clear instructions on how to create a professional looking cocktail, shimmering and inviting in its appropriate glass.

Some cocktail names are shared by similar or completely different recipes. The variations are marked as (alt).

Cocktail Recipes

21st Century (Jim Meehan)

2 oz (60 ml/4 tbsp.) Siete Leguas Blanco tequila
¾ oz (22 ml/1½ tbsp.) lemon juice
¾ oz (22 ml/1½ tbsp.) Marie Brizard white creme de cacao
Pernod rinse
Shake all and strain into a Pernod-rinsed cocktail glass.

57 T-Bird

1 oz. (30 ml/2 tbsp.) vodka
⅔ oz. (20 ml/1⅓ tbsp.) amaretto
⅔ oz. (20 ml/1⅓ tbsp.) melon liqueur
⅔ oz. (20 ml/1⅓ tbsp.) peach schnapps
1⅔ oz. (50 ml/3⅓ tbsp.) fresh orange juice
Shake the ingredients, then strain into an ice-filled old-fashioned glass and serve.

Absolut Hero

1 oz. (30 ml/2 tbsp.) blackcurrant vodka
1 oz. (30 ml/2 tbsp.) lemon vodka
1 oz. (30 ml/2 tbsp.) melon liqueur
⅔ oz. (20 ml/1⅓ tbsp.) fresh lime juice
⅔ oz. (20 ml/1⅓ tbsp.) egg white
club soda
lime wedge to garnish
Shake the ingredients, except club soda. Strain into an ice-filled highball glass. Fill with soda and stir. Garnish with the lime wedge and serve.

Acapulco

1 oz. (30 ml/2 tbsp.) gold tequila
1 oz. (30 ml/2 tbsp.) gold rum
2 oz. (60ml/4 tbsp.) grapefruit juice
3 oz. (90ml/6 tbsp.) pineapple juice
Shake the ingredients, then strain into an ice-filled highball glass.

Adam and Eve

1 oz. (30 ml/2 tbsp.) cognac
1 oz. (30 ml/2 tbsp.) gin
1 oz. (30 ml/2 tbsp.) Forbidden Fruit liqueur
Shake the ingredients, then strain into a martini glass and serve.

Affinity

2 oz. (60 ml/4 tbsp.) Scotch whisky
1½ oz. (45 ml/3 tbsp.) sweet vermouth
1½ oz. (45 ml/3 tbsp.) dry vermouth
2 dashes Angostura bitters
twist of lemon to garnish
**Stir the whisky and vermouths in
a mixing glass, then strain into
a martini glass and serve with
the lemon twist.**

After Eight

Affinity

1 oz. (30 ml/2 tbsp.) Kahlua
1 oz. (30 ml/2 tbsp.) crème de menthe
1 oz. (30 ml/2 tbsp.) crème de cacao (brown)
dash cognac
Shake the ingredients, then strain into a martini glass and serve.

41

Afternoon Delight

1 oz. (30 ml/2 tbsp.) dark rum
1 oz. (30 ml/2 tbsp.) fresh orange juice
1 oz. (30 ml/2 tbsp.) coconut cream
½ oz. (15 ml/1 tbsp.) crème de fraise
½ oz. (15 ml/1 tbsp.) heavy (double) cream
6 strawberries

Place the ingredients into a blender. Add crushed ice and blend. Pour into a goblet and serve.

Alabama Fizz

2 oz. (60 ml/4 tbsp.) gin
1 oz. (30 ml/2 tbsp.) fresh lemon juice
dash gomme syrup
club soda

Shake the ingredients, except the soda, then strain into an ice-filled highball glass. Fill with soda, stir, and serve.

Alabama Slammer

1 oz. (30 ml/2 tbsp.) amaretto
1 oz. (30 ml/2 tbsp.) Southern Comfort
1 oz. (30 ml/2 tbsp.) sloe gin
dash fresh lemon juice

Stir the amaretto, Southern Comfort, and gin in a mixing glass, then strain into a shot glass. Add the lemon juice and serve.

Alaska

2 oz. (60 ml/4 tbsp.) gin
splash yellow Chartreuse
dash Angostura or orange bitters
lemon twist to garnish

Alaska

Shake the ingredients, then strain into a martini glass. Add the twist and serve.

Alcazar

2 oz. (60 ml/4 tbsp.) Canadian Club
1 oz. (30 ml/2 tbsp.) Benedictine
dash orange bitters
Shake the ingredients, then strain into a martini glass and serve.

Alcazar (alt)

1 oz. (30 ml/2 tbsp.) vodka
1 oz. (30 ml/2 tbsp.) apricot purée
dash apricot liqueur
champagne
**Shake the ingredients, except the champagne. Strain into a champagne
flute. Fill with champagne, stir, and serve.**

Alexander Baby

1 oz. (30 ml/2 tbsp.) Navy rum
1 oz. (30 ml/2 tbsp.) brown crème de cacao
1 oz. (30 ml/2 tbsp.) heavy (double) cream
Shake the ingredients, then strain into a martini glass and serve.

Alexander's Brother

1 oz. (30 ml/2 tbsp.) gin
1 oz. (30 ml/2 tbsp.) white crème de menthe
1 oz. (30 ml/2 tbsp.) heavy (double) cream
Shake the ingredients, then strain into a martini glass and serve.

Alexander's Other Brother

1 oz. (30 ml/2 tbsp.) gin
1 oz. (30 ml/2 tbsp.) white crème de menthe
1 oz. (30 ml/2 tbsp.) heavy (double) cream
grated nutmeg to garnish
Shake the ingredients, then strain into a martini glass. Sprinkle with nutmeg and serve.

Alexander's Sister

1 oz. (30 ml/2 tbsp.) gin
1 oz. (30 ml/2 tbsp.) green crème de menthe
1 oz. (30 ml/2 tbsp.) heavy (double) cream
Shake the ingredients, then strain into a martini glass and serve.

Alfonso

1 oz. (30 ml/2 tbsp.) Dubonnet
1 sugar cube
2 dashes Angostura bitters
champagne
Place the sugar cube in a champagne flute and soak with the Angostura bitters. Add the Dubonnet, fill with champagne, then stir.

Alfonzo

2 oz. (60 ml/4 tbsp.) Grand Marnier
1 oz. (30 ml/2 tbsp.) gin
1 oz. (30 ml/2 tbsp.) dry vermouth
½ oz. (15 ml/1 tbsp.) sweet vermouth
dash Angostura bitters
Shake the ingredients, then strain into a martini glass and serve.

Algonquin

2 oz. (60 ml/4 tbsp.) rye whiskey
1 oz. (30 ml/2 tbsp.) dry vermouth
1 oz. (30 ml/2 tbsp.) pineapple juice
dash of Peychaud bitters
Shake the ingredients, then strain into a martini glass and serve.

Allies

1 oz. (30 ml/2 tbsp.) dry vermouth
1 oz. (30 ml/2 tbsp.) gin
1 oz. (30 ml/2 tbsp.) kummel
Stir the vermouth, gin, and kummel in a mixing glass, then strain into a martini glass and serve.

Algonquin

Amaretto Comfort

2 oz. (60 ml/4 tbsp.) amaretto
2 oz. (60 ml/4 tbsp.) Southern Comfort
1 oz. (30 ml/2 tbsp.) heavy (double) cream
Stir the amaretto and Southern Comfort in a mixing glass, then strain into a large martini glass. Float the cream on top and serve.

Amaretto Tea

6 oz. (180 ml/12 tbsp.) hot tea
2 oz. (60 ml/4 tbsp.) amaretto
whipped cream for topping
Place a spoon in a parfait glass, then pour in the hot tea. (The spoon prevents the glass from cracking.) Add the amaretto, without stirring, and top off with the whipped cream and serve.

Ambrosia

1 oz. (30 ml/2 tbsp.) calvados
1 oz. (30 ml/2 tbsp.) cognac
dash curaçao
chilled champagne

Shake the calvados, cognac, and curaçao, then strain into a champagne saucer. Fill with champagne and serve.

American Beauty

½ oz. (15 ml/1 tbsp.) brandy
¼ oz. (8 ml/½ tbsp.) dry vermouth
¼ oz. (8 ml/½ tbsp.) sweet vermouth
¾ oz. (22 ml/1½ tbsp.) fresh orange
dash grenadine
dash Crème de Menthe [optional]
½ oz. (15 ml/1 tbsp.) port

American
Beauty

Shake the ingredients, except the port, strain into a martini glass, float the port, and serve.

American Coffee

1 oz. (30 ml/2 tbsp.) bourbon
6 oz. (180 ml/12 tbsp.) hot black coffee
2 tsp. raw sugar
heavy (double) cream

Pour the bourbon and black coffee into a liqueur coffee glass, then add the sugar. Float the cream on top and serve.

American Fizz

1 oz. (30 ml/2 tbsp.) dark rum
1 oz. (30 ml/2 tbsp.) banana purée
1 oz. (30 ml/2 tbsp.) pineapple juice
champagne

Shake the ingredients, except the champagne. Strain into a champagne flute. Fill with champagne, stir, and serve.

American Grog

2 oz. (60 ml/4 tbsp.) dark rum
½ oz. (15 ml/1 tbsp.) fresh lemon juice
1 sugar cube
Place the ingredients into a goblet. Top with hot water, stir, and serve.

Angel Face

1 oz. (30 ml/2 tbsp.) gin
1 oz. (30 ml/2 tbsp.) apricot brandy
1 oz. (30 ml/2 tbsp.) calvados
Shake the ingredients, then strain into a martini glass and serve.

Angel's Kiss

¼ oz. (8 ml/½ tbsp.) white crème de cacao
¼ oz. (8 ml/½ tbsp.) sloe gin
¼ oz. (8 ml/½ tbsp.) brandy
¼ oz. (8 ml/½ tbsp.) light (single) cream
In a shot glass, layer each of the ingredients in turn and serve.

Angelic

3 oz. (90 ml/6 tbsp.) bourbon
1 oz. (30 ml/2 tbsp.) crème de cacao
1 oz. (30 ml/2 tbsp.) Grenadine
1 oz. (30 ml/2 tbsp.) heavy (double) cream
Shake the ingredients, then strain into a double martini glass. Sprinkle on the nutmeg and serve.

Anglo Angel

1 oz. (30 ml/2 tbsp.) vodka
1 oz. (30 ml/2 tbsp.) Mandarine Napoleon
1 oz. (30 ml/2 tbsp.) mandarin juice
2 dashes Angostura bitters
Shake the ingredients, then strain into a cocktail glass and serve.

Anisette

1 oz. (30 ml/2 tbsp.) anisette
½ oz. (15 ml/1 tbsp.) Benedictine
2 dashes Angostura bitters
water

Shake the ingredients, except the water, then strain into a frosted martini glass and serve. Fill up with water poured through crushed ice. (You can use a sieve for this.)

Anita's Attitude Adjuster

¾ oz. (22 ml/1½ tbsp.) light rum
¾ oz. (22 ml/1½ tbsp.) vodka
¾ oz. (22 ml/1½ tbsp.) gin
¾ oz. (22 ml/1½ tbsp.) tequila
¼ oz. (8 ml/½ tbsp.) triple sec
juice of half a lime
sparkling white wine
¾ oz. (22 ml/1½ tbsp.) orange juice

Squeeze the lime into a highball glass, add ice cubes and spirits. Stir, fill up with sparkling white wine, and serve.

Ante

1 oz. (30 ml/2 tbsp.) calvados
1 oz. (30 ml/2 tbsp.) Cointreau
1 oz. (30 ml/2 tbsp.) Pernod or Dubonnet

Shake the ingredients, then strain into a martini glass and serve.

Apple Blow Fizz

⅓ oz. (10 ml/⅔ tbsp.) apple schnapps
⅓ oz. (10 ml/⅔ tbsp.) cranberry juice
champagne

Pour the schnapps and juice into a champagne glass and stir. Fill with champagne and stir again.

Apple Colada

1 oz. (30 ml/2 tbsp.) white rum
⅔ oz. (20 ml/1⅓ tbsp.) apple schnapps
1 oz. (30 ml/2 tbsp.) coconut cream
2 oz. (60 ml/4 tbsp.) apple juice
½ tsp. superfine (caster) sugar
half an apple, peeled
**Blend the ingredients. Add crushed ice and blend until smooth.
Pour into a colada glass. Serve with a straw.**

Apple Daiquiri (see Daiquiri, p. 92)

2 oz. (60 ml/4 tbsp.) white rum
⅔ oz. (20 ml/1⅓ tbsp.) apple schnapps
½ oz. (15 ml/1 tbsp.) cinnamon schnapps
½ oz. (15 ml/1 tbsp.) fresh lime juice
dash gomme syrup
Shake the ingredients, then strain into a martini glass and serve.

Apple Martini (see Martini, p. 138)

2 oz. (60 ml/4 tbsp.) vodka
⅔ oz. (20 ml/1⅓ tbsp.) apple sour liqueur
⅓ oz. (10 ml/⅔ tbsp.) Cointreau
Shake the ingredients, then strain into a cocktail glass and serve.

Apple Pie (Chris Edwardes)

1 oz. (30 ml/2 tbsp.) Krupnik honey vodka
½ oz. (15 ml/1 tbsp.) apple schnapps
1 oz. (30 ml/2 tbsp.) apple purée
juice of half a lemon
½ oz. (15 ml/1 tbsp.) gomme syrup
Shake the ingredients, then pour into an old-fashioned glass and serve.

Aquamarine

1 oz. (30 ml/2 tbsp.) vodka
⅔ oz. (20 ml/1⅓ tbsp.) peach schnapps
⅓ oz. (10 ml/⅔ tbsp.) blue curaçao
⅓ oz. (10 ml/⅔ tbsp.) Cointreau
3 oz. (90 ml/6 tbsp.) apple juice
Shake the ingredients, then strain into an ice-filled old-fashioned glass and serve.

Aqueduct

3 oz. (90 ml/6 tbsp.) vodka
½ oz. (15 ml/1 tbsp.) triple sec
½ oz. (15 ml/1 tbsp.) apricot brandy
½ oz. (15 ml/1 tbsp.) fresh lime juice
Shake the ingredients, then strain into a martini glass and serve.

Aristocrat

2 oz. (60 ml/4 tbsp.) Poire William
1 oz. (30 ml/2 tbsp.) white rum
3 oz. (90 ml/6 tbsp.) pineapple juice
dash orgeat
half a pear
Blend all the ingredients, pour into a large goblet, and serve.

Aromatherapist

3 oz. (90 ml/6 tbsp.) gin
1 oz. (30 ml/2 tbsp.) sake
3 dashes Angostura bitters
Stir the ingredients in a mixing glass, then strain into a martini glass and serve.

Aster

3 oz. (90 ml/6 tbsp.) gin
dash fresh orange juice
dash fresh lemon juice

Stir the ingredients in a mixing glass, then pour into an old-fashioned glass and serve.

Astoria

2 oz. (60 ml/4 tbsp.) gin
1 oz. (30 ml/2 tbsp.) dry vermouth
dash orange bitters

Shake the ingredients, then strain into a cocktail glass and serve.

Aunt Jermina (Jemima)

1 oz. (30 ml/2 tbsp.) cognac
1 oz. (30 ml/2 tbsp.) Benedictine
1 oz. (30 ml/2 tbsp.) white crème de cacao

Pour the ingredients into a brandy glass, stir, and serve.

Aviation 2

1⅔ oz. (50 ml/1⅓ tbsp.) vodka
1 oz. (30 ml/2 tbsp.) maraschino liqueur
⅔ oz. (20 ml/1⅓ tbsp.) fresh lemon juice
maraschino cherry and a twist of lemon to garnish

Shake the ingredients, then strain into a cocktail glass. Drop the cherry in the drink, add the twist of lemon, and serve.

B-52

⅔ oz. (20 ml/1⅓ tbsp.) Tia Maria
⅔ oz. (20 ml/1⅓ tbsp.) Bailey's
⅔ oz. (20 ml/1⅓ tbsp.) Cointreau

In a shot glass, layer each of the ingredients in turn and serve.

B & B

1 oz. (30 ml/2 tbsp.) brandy
1 oz. (30 ml/2 tbsp.) Benedictine
Pour the brandy and Benedictine into a brandy glass and serve.

B & B Royale

½ oz. (15 ml/1 tbsp.) cognac
½ oz. (15 ml/1 tbsp.) Benedictine
chilled champagne
Pour the brandy and Benedictine into a champagne saucer. Fill up with champagne and serve.

Baby Fingers

2 oz. (60 ml/4 tbsp.) sloe gin
1 oz. (30 ml/2 tbsp.) gin
dash Angostura bitters
Shake the ingredients, then strain into a martini glass and serve.

Bacardi Cocktail

2 oz. (60 ml/4 tbsp.) Bacardi
1 oz. (30 ml/2 tbsp.) fresh lime juice
dash grenadine
Shake the ingredients, then strain into a martini glass and serve.

Bahia

2 oz. (60 ml/4 tbsp.) white rum
1 oz. (30 ml/2 tbsp.) coconut cream
2 oz. (60 ml/4 tbsp.) pineapple juice
1 oz. (30 ml/2 tbsp.) grapefruit juice
1 oz. (30 ml/2 tbsp.) heavy (double) cream
Blend the ingredients, pour into a large goblet, and serve.

Baked Apple

2 oz. (60 ml/4 tbsp.) calvados
1 oz. (30 ml/2 tbsp.) dark rum
4 oz. (120 ml/8 tbsp.) apple juice
dash crème de cassis
1 cinnamon stick

Pour the calvados and the dark rum into a mixing glass and stir. Strain into a highball. Add the apple juice and crème de cassis and stir. Add the cinnamon stick as a garnish and serve.

Bali Trader

2 oz. (60 ml/4 tbsp.) vodka
⅔ oz. (20 ml/1⅓ tbsp.) green banana liqueur
⅔ oz. (20 ml/1⅓ tbsp.) pineapple juice

Shake the ingredients, then strain into a cocktail glass and serve.

Ballantine's

2 oz. (60 ml/4 tbsp.) Ballantine's whisky
1 oz. (30 ml/2 tbsp.) sweet vermouth
dash crème de cassis
dash Angostura bitters

Shake the ingredients into a shaker, then strain into a martini glass and serve.

Banana Bird

2 oz. (60 ml/4 tbsp.) bourbon
1 oz. (30 ml/2 tbsp.) crème de banane
1 oz. (30 ml/2 tbsp.) heavy (double) cream
dash Cointreau

Shake the ingredients, then strain into a martini glass and serve.

Banana Daiquiri (see Daiquiri, p. 92)

1 oz. (30 ml/2 tbsp.) crème de banane
1 oz. (30 ml/2 tbsp.) white rum
1 oz. (30 ml/2 tbsp.) of fresh lime juice
½ oz. (15 ml/1 tbsp.) gomme syrup
half a banana
Blend the ingredients, then pour into a large cocktail glass and serve.

Banshee

2 oz. (60 ml/4 tbsp.) crème de banane
1 oz. (30 ml/2 tbsp.) white crème de cacao
2 oz. (60 ml/4 tbsp.) heavy (double) cream
Shake the ingredients, then strain into a goblet and serve.

Barracuda

1 oz. (30 ml/2 tbsp.) white rum
1 oz. (30 ml/2 tbsp.) Galliano
1 oz. (30 ml/2 tbsp.) pineapple juice
½ oz. (15 ml/1 tbsp.) fresh lime juice
½ oz. (15 ml/1 tbsp.) grenadine
chilled champagne
Pour all the ingredients into a highball glass, fill up with champagne, and serve.

Bastille

1 oz. (30 ml/2 tbsp.) white rum
4 blackberries
⅓ oz. (10 ml/⅔ tbsp.) crème de mure
half a slice of orange
dash gomme syrup
champagne
Muddle the berries with the gomme and crème de mure in a shaker. Add the rum. Squeeze the slice of orange over it and add ice cubes. Shake and strain into a flute. Fill with champagne. Stir and serve.

Batida

2 oz. (60 ml/4 tbsp.) cachaça
½ oz. (15 ml/1 tbsp.) gomme syrup
fresh fruit of your choice
**Blend the ingredients until chilled,
then pour into a goblet and serve.**

Bee Stinger

2 oz. (60 ml/4 tbsp.) white crème de menthe
1 oz. (30 ml/2 tbsp.) crème de cassis
**Pour the ingredients into a brandy glass.
Stir and serve.**

Bee's Kiss

Bee's Kiss

2 oz. (60 ml/4 tbsp.) white rum
½ oz. (15 ml/1 tbsp.) black coffee
½ oz. (15 ml/1 tbsp.) heavy (double) cream
**Shake the ingredients, then strain into a
cocktail glass and serve.**

Beja Flor

2 oz. (60 ml/4 tbsp.) cachaça
1 oz. (30 ml/2 tbsp.) triple sec/Cointreau
1 oz. (30 ml/2 tbsp.) crème de banane
Shake the ingredients, then strain into a cocktail glass and serve.

Belgian Coffee

1 oz. (30 ml/2 tbsp.) elixir d'anvers
6 oz. (180 ml/12 tbsp.) hot black coffee
2 tsp. raw sugar
heavy (double) cream
**Pour the elixir d'anvers and black coffee into a liqueur coffee glass,
then add the sugar. Float the cream on top and serve.**

Bella, Bella

1 oz. (30 ml/2 tbsp.) gin
⅔ oz. (20 ml/1⅓ tbsp.) Aperol
½ oz. (15 ml/1 tbsp.) limoncello
½ oz. (15 ml/1 tbsp.) mandarin liqueur
⅔ oz. (20 ml/1⅓ tbsp.) fresh orange juice
lime spiral to garnish

Shake the ingredients, then strain into a cocktail glass. Add the lime spiral and serve.

Bellini

6 oz. (180 ml/12 tbsp.) white peach purée
  (or peach nectar)
chilled champagne

Add the peach purée to a champagne flute, fill up with champagne, and serve.

Bellini (alt)

6 oz. (180 ml/12 tbsp.) fresh white peach purée
dash fresh lemon juice
dash of peach brandy
sparkling wine

Stir the peach juice and brandy in a champagne flute. Fill up with sparkling wine and serve.

Benton Old-Fashioned (Don Lee)

2 oz (60 ml/4 tbsp.) Benton's bacon fat-infused bourbon
¼ oz (8 ml/½ tbsp.) grade B maple syrup
2 dashes Angostura bitters
orange twist to garnish

Stir all ingredients over ice, then strain over ice in a rocks glass. Garnish with orange twist.

Bermuda Rose

3 oz. (90 ml/6 tbsp.) gin
⅔ oz. (20 ml/1⅓ tbsp.) apricot brandy
⅔ oz. (20 ml/1⅓ tbsp.) grenadine
Shake the ingredients, then strain into a martini glass and serve.

Berry Sweet (Makes two)

2 oz. (60 ml/4 tbsp.) cachaça
2 small limes, diced
few raspberries
few blueberries
6 strawberries, diced and hulled
1 tbsp. brown sugar
Add the sugar and the pieces of lime to the bottom of a small bowl. Muddle the lime, releasing the juices, then add berries. Muddle some more. Place a scoop of this mixture into an old-fashioned glass. Add cachaça and crushed ice and stir. Serve with a stirrer and a straw.

Between the Sheets

1 oz. (30 ml/2 tbsp.) brandy
1 oz. (30 ml/2 tbsp.) white rum
1 oz. (30 ml/2 tbsp.) Cointreau
1 oz. (30 ml/2 tbsp.) fresh lemon juice
½ oz. (15 ml/1 tbsp.) gomme syrup
Shake the ingredients, then strain into a martini glass and serve.

Big Apple

1 oz. (30 ml/2 tbsp.) apple schnapps
1 oz. (30 ml/2 tbsp.) amaretto
1 oz. (30 ml/2 tbsp.) Drambuie
1 oz. (30 ml/2 tbsp.) fresh lemon juice
Shake the ingredients, then strain into a martini glass and serve.

Bikini

2 oz. (60 ml/4 tbsp.) vodka
1 oz. (30 ml/2 tbsp.) white rum
4 oz. (120 ml/8 tbsp.) milk
½ oz. (15 ml/1 tbsp.) gomme syrup
Shake the ingredients, then strain into a highball glass and serve.

Billy Hamilton

1 oz. (30 ml/2 tbsp.) cognac
1 oz. (30 ml/2 tbsp.) crème de cacao
1 oz. (30 ml/2 tbsp.) orange curaçao
1 egg white
Shake the ingredients, then strain into a martini glass and serve.

Black and White

1 oz. (30 ml/2 tbsp.) Kahlua
1 oz. (30 ml/2 tbsp.) green crème de menthe
½ oz. (15 ml/1 tbsp.) white crème de menthe
1 oz. (30 ml/2 tbsp.) heavy (double) cream
Stir the Kahlua and green crème de menthe in an ice-filled old-fashioned glass. Mix the white crème de menthe with the cream and float on the top, then serve.

Black-Eye Martini (see Martini, p. 138)

2 oz. (60 ml/4 tbsp.) chilled dry gin
spray of Noilly Prat from an atomizer
black olive or twist of lemon to garnish
Spray a chilled martini glass with Noilly Prat, then pour in the gin. Add the black olive or lemon and serve.

Black Gold

½ oz. (15 ml/1 tbsp.) triple sec
½ oz. (15 ml/1 tbsp.) amaretto
½ oz. (15 ml/1 tbsp.) Bailey's
½ oz. (15 ml/1 tbsp.) hazelnut liqueur
6 oz. (180 ml/12 tbsp.) hot coffee
dash cinnamon schnapps
whipped cream for topping
shaved chocolate to garnish
1 cinnamon stick

Pour the triple sec, amaretto, Bailey's, and hazelnut liqueur into a liqueur coffee glass, then stir in the coffee and cinnamon schnapps. Top it with the whipped cream and sprinkle on the chocolate. Serve with a cinnamon stick as a stirrer.

Black Magic

2 oz. (60 ml/4 tbsp.) vodka
1 oz. (30 ml/2 tbsp.) Kahlua
dash lemon juice
twist of lemon to serve

Stir the ingredients in a mixing glass, then pour into an ice-filled old-fashioned glass. Serve with the lemon twist.

Black Magic (alt)

1 oz. (30 ml/2 tbsp.) vodka
⅔ oz. (20 ml/1⅓ tbsp.) Kahlua
dash fresh lemon juice
1 cup cold coffee

Pour the ingredients into an ice-filled old-fashioned glass. Stir and serve.

Black Maria

1 oz. (30 ml/2 tbsp.) vodka
1 oz. (30 ml/2 tbsp.) dark rum
4 oz. (120 ml/8 tbsp.) coffee
Shake the ingredients, then strain into an ice-filled old-fashioned glass and serve.

Black Russian

2 oz. (60 ml/4 tbsp.) vodka
2 oz. (60 ml/4 tbsp.) Kahlua
Pour the vodka, then the Kahlua into an old fashioned glass straight up or over crushed ice, then serve.

Black Sombrero

2 oz. (60 ml/4 tbsp.) Kahlua
1 oz. (30 ml/2 tbsp.) tequila
1 oz. (30 ml/2 tbsp.) vodka
Stir the Kahlua, tequila, and vodka in a mixing glass, then strain into a martini glass and serve.

Black Velvet

4 oz. (120 ml/8 tbsp.) chilled stout (or Guinness)
4 oz. (120 ml/8 tbsp.) chilled champagne
Pour the stout, then the champagne into a champagne flute and serve.

Black Widow

2 oz. (60 ml/4 tbsp.) dark rum
1 oz. (30 ml/2 tbsp.) Southern Comfort
1 oz. (30 ml/2 tbsp.) fresh lime juice
Shake the ingredients, then strain into a martini glass and serve.

Blackberry Margarita (see Margarita, p. 136)

1⅔ oz. (50 ml/3⅓ tbsp.) silver tequila
½ oz. (15 ml/1 tbsp.) blackberry liqueur
juice of half a lime
10 blackberries
2 blackberries to garnish
Pour the ingredients into a blender with crushed ice. Blend. Pour into a margarita glass. Add two blackberries on a cocktail stick set across the glass and serve with a straw.

Blanch House (Chris Edwardes)

1 oz. (30 ml/2 tbsp.) vodka
½ oz. (15 ml/1 tbsp.) crème de cassis
1 oz. (30 ml/2 tbsp.) cranberry juice
juice of half an orange
juice of half a lemon
Shake the ingredients, then strain into a martini glass and serve.

Blanche

2 oz. (60 ml/4 tbsp.) Cointreau
1 oz. (30 ml/2 tbsp.) anisette
Shake both ingredients, then strain into a martini glass and serve.

Blimey (Chris Edwardes)

dash fresh lime
1 oz. (30 ml/2 tbsp.) crème de peche
champagne to top
Squeeze a little lime juice into a champagne flute, pour on the crème de peche, and fill up with the champagne. Stir and serve.

Bloody Caesar Shooter

1 clam
1 oz. (30 ml/2 tbsp.) vodka
1 oz. (30 ml/2 tbsp.) tomato juice
2 drops Worcestershire sauce
2 drops Tabasco
½ tsp. horseradish purée
pinch celery salt

Put the clam in the bottom of a shot glass, then shake the rest of the ingredients in a shaker. Strain into the glass and serve.

Bloody Maria

2 oz. (60 ml/4 tbsp.) tequila
5 oz. (150 ml/10 tbsp.) tomato juice
juice of half a lemon
pinch celery salt
pinch black pepper
4 dashes Tabasco sauce
4 dashes Worcestershire sauce

Shake the ingredients, then strain into an ice-filled highball glass. Garnish with a celery stick and a lime wedge.

Bloody Mary (see pp. 64–65)

Blow Job

1½ oz. (45 ml/3 tbsp.) amaretto
Whipping cream

Pour the amaretto into shot glass, top with whipping cream. Drink with hands behind back in one smooth motion.

Blue Blazer

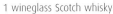

1 wineglass Scotch whisky
1 wineglass boiling water
1 tsp. sugar (to taste)
lemon twist to garnish

Warning: This cocktail requires a great degree of skill and care. Using two silver-plated mugs with handles, pour the scotch into one mug and the boiling water into the other. Ignite the whisky with a match and pour the blazing ingredients back and forth between the two mugs several times. Aim to create a long stream of liquid fire. Pour into an old-fashioned glass and add the sugar. Serve with a lemon twist.

Blue Boy

3 oz. (90 ml/6 tbsp.) dark rum
1 oz. (30 ml/2 tbsp.) sweet vermouth
dash fresh orange juice
dash orange bitters

Shake the ingredients, then strain into an old-fashioned glass and serve.

Blue Hawaiian

1 oz. (30 ml/2 tbsp.) white rum
1 oz. (30 ml/2 tbsp.) blue curaçao
3 oz. (90 ml/6 tbsp.) pineapple juice
1 oz. (30 ml/2 tbsp.) coconut cream

Blend the ingredients and pour into a large goblet and serve.

Blue Martini (see Martini, p. 138)

2 oz. (60 ml/4 tbsp.) vodka
⅓ oz. (10 ml/⅔ tbsp.) blue curaçao
⅓ oz. (10 ml/⅔ tbsp.) fresh lemon juice
8 fresh blueberries

Muddle the blueberries in the bottom of a shaker. Add the remaining ingredients. Shake, then strain into a cocktail glass and serve.

Bloody Mary

Probably the world's best-known hangover cure because of its unique life-giving ingredients!

This cocktail came to life in the 1920s in Harry's New York Bar in Paris, where a bartender, Fernand Petiot, mixed vodka with tomato juice and called it the Bloody Mary, referring to Mary Tudor.

America was introduced to the Bloody Mary after John Jacob Astor tempted Petiot to New York to work at the St. Regis Hotel. Astor insisted he rename it Red Snapper because he felt the word "bloody" was too rude for customers. Because vodka was not yet available in the U.S., Petoit used gin. However, clients liked the name Bloody Mary so the name stuck. It's one of the great restorative drinks. It gives enough alcohol to get you started, but enough flavor and liquid to build you up.

No two people can agree on what should and shouldn't go into a Bloody Mary other than vodka, tomato juice and Worcestershire sauce. And celery stalks irritate or poke you in the eye.

Canadians substitute Clamato juice for tomato, add horseradish sauce and celery salt, and call the result a Caesar.

Bloody Mary

2 oz. (60 ml/4 tbsp.) vodka
6 oz. (180 ml/8 tbsp.) tomato juice
2 dashes Worcestershire sauce
pinch black pepper
pinch of celery salt
½ oz. (15 ml/1 tbsp.) fresh lemon juice
Tabasco sauce (to taste)
Pour the vodka over ice in a highball
glass. Combine the other ingredients
in a jug, then add the mix to the vodka.
(A celery stick is optional!)

Blue Monday

1 oz. (30 ml/2 tbsp.) gin
1 oz. (30 ml/2 tbsp.) Cointreau
dash blue curaçao
club soda

**Pour the gin and the Cointreau into a
highball with ice, then fill with club soda.
Stir. Add a dash of blue curaçao. Stir and
serve with a stirrer.**

Bombay Bellini

6 oz. (180 ml/12 tbsp.) fresh white peach purée
2 oz. (60 ml/4 tbsp.) mango purée
dash fresh lemon juice
dash of peach brandy
sparkling wine

**Stir peach juice and brandy in a
champagne flute. Add the mango
purée, fill up with the sparkling wine,
stir, and serve.**

Bombay
Bellini

Bonza Monza

1 oz. (30 ml/2 tbsp.) vodka
⅔ oz. (20 ml/1⅓ tbsp.) crème de cassis
2 oz. (60 ml/4 tbsp.) grapefruit juice

**Pour the ingredients into an old-fashioned glass full of crushed ice.
Stir and serve.**

Boston Bullet

2 oz. (60 ml/4 tbsp.) chilled dry gin
spray of Noilly Prat from an atomizer
olive stuffed with an almond to garnish

**Spray a chilled martini glass with Noilly Prat then add the gin.
Add the olive and serve.**

Boston Bullet (alt)

2 oz. (60 ml/4 tbsp.) chilled vodka
spray of Noilly Prat from an atomizer
olive stuffed with an almond to garnish

**Spray a chilled martini glass with Noilly Prat then add the vodka.
Add the olive and serve.**

Brandy Alexander

1 oz. (30 ml/2 tbsp.) cognac
1 oz. (30 ml/2 tbsp.) brown crème de cacao
1 oz. (30 ml/2 tbsp.) heavy (double) cream

**Shake the ingredients, then strain into a
martini glass and serve.**

Brandy Alexander (alt)

1 oz. (30 ml/2 tbsp.) cognac
1 oz. (30 ml/2 tbsp.) brown crème de cacao
1 oz. (30 ml/2 tbsp.) heavy
   (double) cream
whipped cream
grated nutmeg to garnish

Brandy
Alexander

**Shake the first three ingredients, then strain
into a cocktail glass. Add the whipped cream
and sprinkle nutmeg to garnish.**

Brandy Cocktail

2 oz. (60 ml/4 tbsp.) cognac
1 oz. (30 ml/2 tbsp.) sweet vermouth
2 dashes Angostura bitters

**Stir the cognac, vermouth, and bitters in a mixing glass, then strain
into a martini glass and serve.**

Brandy Eggnog

2 oz. (60 ml/4 tbsp.) cognac
1 oz. (30 ml/2 tbsp.) dark rum
1 oz. (30 ml/2 tbsp.) gomme syrup
1 egg
3 oz. (90 ml/6 tbsp.) milk
grated nutmeg to garnish

Stir the cognac, rum, gomme syrup, and egg in a mixing glass, then strain into a goblet. Stir in the milk and sprinkle the grated nutmeg over the top.

Brandy Smash

2 oz. (60 ml/4 tbsp.) cognac
1 tsp. granulated sugar
6–8 fresh mint leaves

Dissolve the sugar with a dash of the cognac in the bottom of an old-fashioned glass. Add the mint and muddle. Fill with ice and stir in the remaining cognac until the glass has become frosted. Serve with a short straw.

Brave Bull

1⅓ oz. (40 ml/2⅔ tbsp.) tequila
⅔ oz. (20 ml/1⅓ tbsp.) coffee liqueur

Pour ingredients into an old-fashioned glass with ice. Stir and serve.

Breakfast Bar

2 oz. (60 ml/4 tbsp.) vodka
handful cherry tomatoes
1 fresh basil leaf
pinch ground coriander
pinch celery salt
chopped chives
pinch ground pepper

Blend the ingredients, then strain into an ice-filled highball and serve.

Breezy Nik (Chris Edwardes)

1 oz. (30 ml/2 tbsp.) vodka
½ oz. (15 ml/1 tbsp.) gin
1 oz. (30 ml/2 tbsp.) pear schnapps
juice of half a lemon
½ oz. (15 ml/1 tbsp.) blackcurrant purée
4 oz. (120 ml/8 tbsp.) cranberry juice
**Shake the ingredients, then strain
into a highball glass and serve.**

Brighton Punch

1 oz. (30 ml/2 tbsp.) bourbon
2 oz. (60 ml/4 tbsp.) orange juice
3 oz. (90 ml/6 tbsp.) brandy
¼ oz. (8 ml/½ tbsp.) Benedictine
¾ oz. (24 ml/1½ tbsp.) lemon juice
1 tsp. gomme syrup
**Shake the ingredients,
then strain into an ice-filled
highball glass and serve.**

Brighton
Punch

Brighton Rock

2 oz. (60 ml/4 tbsp.) crème de fraise
3 oz. (90 ml/6 tbsp.) cranberry juice
1 oz. (30 ml/2 tbsp.) heavy (double) cream
Shake the ingredients, then pour into a highball glass and serve.

69

Broadway Martini

2 oz. (60 ml/4 tbsp.) gin
½ oz. (15 ml/1 tbsp.) white
crème de menthe
**Shake the ingredients, then strain into a
Martini glass.**

Bronx

1 oz. (30 ml/2 tbsp.) gin
½ oz. (15 ml/1 tbsp.) sweet vermouth
½ oz. (15 ml/1 tbsp.) dry vermouth
juice of quarter of an orange
slice of orange to garnish
**Shake the ingredients, then strain into
a martini glass. Add the orange slice
and serve.**

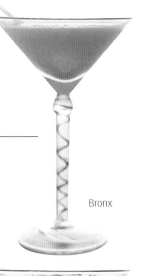

Bronx

Bronx View

1⅔ oz. (50 ml/3⅓ tbsp.) gin
1 oz. (30 ml/2 tbsp.) dry vermouth
⅓ oz. (10 ml/⅔ tbsp.) Rose's Lime Cordial
**Shake the ingredients, then strain into
a cocktail glass and serve.**

Brooklyn

1 oz. (30 ml/2 tbsp.) rye whiskey
¾ oz. (22 ml/1½ tbsp.) vermouth rosso
dash of maraschino liqueur
**Mix the ingredients in a mixing glass.
Strain into a martini glass and serve.**

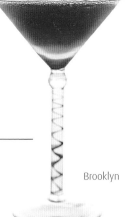

Brooklyn

Buck's Fizz

2 oz. (60 ml/4 tbsp.) fresh orange juice
chilled champagne
Pour the orange juice into a champagne flute, fill up with champagne, and serve.

Bullshot (see Bloody Mary, p. 64)

1⅔ oz. (50 ml/3⅓ tbsp.) vodka
5 oz. (150 ml/10 tbsp.) beef bouillon
dash fresh lemon juice
2 to 3 dashes Worcestershire sauce
celery salt
Tabasco sauce
ground black pepper
Shake the bouillon, lemon juice, Tabasco, and Worcestershire sauces with the vodka. Strain into an ice-filled highball. Add black pepper to taste. Serve with a stirrer.

Buster

3 oz. (90 ml/6 tbsp.) dark Puerto
Rican rum
1 oz. (30 ml/2 tbsp.) Pernod
pineapple chunks to garnish
Shake the ingredients, then pour into an old-fashioned glass. Garnish with the pineapple and serve.

Butterfly

2 oz. (60 ml/4 tbsp.) gin
1 oz. (30 ml/2 tbsp.) dry vermouth
1 oz. (30 ml/2 tbsp.) blue curaçao
1 oz. (30 ml/2 tbsp.) Poire William
Shake the ingredients, then strain into a large martini glass and serve.

Butterfly

71

Butterscotch Cocktail (Chris Stock)

¾ oz (22 ml/1½ tbsp.) Butter-washed Monkey Shoulder whisky
½ oz (15 ml/1 tbsp.) Aperol
⅛ oz (5 ml/1 tsp.) PX sherry
⅛ oz (5 ml/1 tsp.) ginger jam
2 dashes Peychaud's Bitters
orange twist to garnish
Shake all and strain into a cocktail glass.

Cactus Pear Margarita (see Margarita, p. 136)

2 oz. (60ml/4 tbsp.) tequila
⅔ oz. (20 ml/1⅓ tbsp.) Cointreau
⅓ oz. (10 ml/⅔ tbsp.) fresh lime juice
1 cactus pear, peeled and diced
lime wedge to garnish
**Muddle the pear in the bottom of a shaker. Add a scoop of ice and other
ingredients. Shake, then strain into a cocktail glass with a salted rim.
Add the lime wedge and serve.**

Cadillac Lady

1 oz. (30 ml/2 tbsp.) gin
1 oz. (30 ml/2 tbsp.) Grand Marnier
1 oz. (30 ml/2 tbsp.) fresh lemon juice
1 egg white
Shake the ingredients, then strain into a martini glass and serve.

Cadiz

1 oz. (30 ml/2 tbsp.) dry sherry
1 oz. (30 ml/2 tbsp.) crème de mure
½ oz. (15 ml/1 tbsp.) triple sec
½ oz. (15 ml/1 tbsp.) heavy (double) cream
**Shake the ingredients, then strain into an ice-filled old-fashioned
glass and serve.**

Caesar (see Bloody Mary, p. 64)

2 oz. (60 ml/4 tbsp.) Absolut Pepper vodka
5 oz. (150 ml/10 tbsp.) Clamato juice
2 dashes Worcestershire sauce
horseradish sauce
pinch white pepper
pinch celery salt
splash of fino sherry
splash of lemon juice
Tabasco sauce to taste
**Pour the vodka into an ice-filled highball glass. In a jug, combine
the other ingredients, then add to the vodka and ice. Stir and serve.**

Café de Paris

2 oz. (60 ml/4 tbsp.) gin
½ oz. (15 ml/1 tbsp.) light (single) cream
½ oz. (15 ml/1 tbsp.) anisette
1 egg white
Shake the ingredients, then strain into a martini glass and serve.

Café Normandie

1 oz. (30 ml/2 tbsp.) calvados
6 oz. (180 ml/12 tbsp.) hot black coffee
2 tsp. raw sugar
heavy (double) cream
**Pour the calvados and black coffee into a liqueur coffee glass,
then add the sugar. Float the cream on top and serve.**

Café Royale

1 oz. (30 ml/2 tbsp.) cognac
6 oz. (180 ml/12 tbsp.) hot black coffee
2 tsp. raw sugar
heavy (double) cream

**Pour the cognac and black
coffee into a liqueur coffee
glass, then add the sugar.
Float the cream on top
and serve.**

Caipirinha

1 lime
2 oz. (60 ml/4 tbsp.) cachaça
3 sugar lumps

**Cut the lime into eighths, then
muddle with the sugar in an
old-fashioned glass. Fill the glass with
crushed ice and pour in the cachaça. Stir
and serve with two straws.**

Caipirinha

Caipirovska (An interpretation of the
Caipirinha with a tart lime flavor)

2 oz. (60 ml/4 tbsp.) vodka
1 lime, diced
dash fresh lime juice
2 tsp. superfine (caster) sugar

**Muddle the diced lime and the sugar in an old-fashioned glass. Add
the vodka and the lime juice. Fill the glass with ice, stir, and serve
with two straws.**

Cajun Martini (see Martini, p. 138)

2 oz. (60 ml/4 tbsp.) chilled dry gin
spray of Noilly Prat from an atomizer
jalapeno chili to garnish
**Spray a chilled martini glass with Noilly Prat. Add the gin.
Garnish with the chili and serve.**

Cajun Martini (alt) (see Martini, p. 138)

2 oz. (60 ml/4 tbsp.) chilled vodka
spray of Noilly Prat from an atomizer
jalapeno chili to garnish
**Spray a chilled martini glass with Noilly Prat. Add the vodka.
Garnish with the chili and serve.**

Cajun Martini (Paul Prudhomme) (see Martini, p. 138)

1 fresh chili
1 bottle dry gin
1 oz. (30 ml/2 tbsp.) dry vermouth
**Slice the chili lengthwise, keeping it in one piece, and insert into a
bottle of gin. Top the bottle up with vermouth. Reseal and refrigerate
for up to sixteen hours. Strain into a clean bottle. Refrigerate until
well chilled. Serve in cocktail glasses.**

Calypso Coffee

1 oz. (30 ml/2 tbsp.) Tia Maria
6 oz. (180 ml/12 tbsp.) hot black coffee
2 tsp. raw sugar
heavy (double) cream
**Pour the Tia Maria and black coffee into a liqueur coffee glass,
then add the sugar. Float the cream on top and serve.**

Campbeltown Cocktail (Mike Aikman)

1½ oz (45 ml/3 tbsp.) Springbank 10YO whisky
½ oz (15 ml/1 tbsp.) Cherry Heering
¼ oz (8 ml/½ tbsp.) Green Chartreuse
lemon twist to garnish
Stir all ingredients over ice, then strain into a Martini glass. Garnish with lemon twist (discard).

Canadian Coffee

1 oz. (30 ml/2 tbsp.) Canadian Club
6 oz. (180 ml/12 tbsp.) hot black coffee
2 tsp. raw sugar
heavy (double) cream
Pour the Canadian Club and black coffee into a liqueur coffee glass, then add the sugar. Float the cream on top and serve.

Cape Codder

1½ oz. (45 ml/3 tbsp.) vodka
3 oz. (90 ml/6 tbsp.) cranberry juice
1 wedge of lime
Pour vodka and cranberry juice into a highball glass over ice. Stir well, add the lime, and serve.

Cargo

2 oz. (60 ml/4 tbsp.) vodka
1 oz. (30 ml/2 tbsp.) white crème de menthe
2 fresh mint leaves
Rub the rim of an old-fashioned glass with one of the mint leaves. Pour the crème de menthe and vodka into the glass and stir. Garnish with the other mint leaf and serve.

Caribbean Coffee

1 oz. (30 ml/2 tbsp.) white rum
6 oz. (180 ml/12 tbsp.) hot black coffee
2 tsp. raw sugar
heavy (double) cream

Pour the rum and black coffee into a liqueur coffee glass, then add the sugar. Float the cream on top and serve.

Caribbean Royale

½ oz. (15 ml/1 tbsp.) white rum
½ oz. (15 ml/1 tbsp.) crème de banane
chilled champagne

Pour the rum and the crème de banane into a champagne flute. Fill up with champagne, stir, and serve.

Caruso

1 oz. (30 ml/2 tbsp.) gin
¾ oz. (22 ml/1½ tbsp.) dry vermouth
¼ oz. (8 ml/½ tbsp.) green crème
   de menthe

Stir the ingredients in a mixing glass, then strain into a martini glass and serve.

Caruso

Casablanca

2 oz. (60 ml/4 tbsp.) white rum
1 oz. (30 ml/2 tbsp.) Cointreau
1 oz. (30 ml/2 tbsp.) fresh lime juice
dash orange bitters
dash Maraschino liqueur [optional]

Shake the ingredients, then strain into a martini glass and serve.

Casanova

1 oz. (30 ml/2 tbsp.) apple juice
1 oz. (30 ml/2 tbsp.) raspberry purée
champagne
raspberries to garnish

Pour the raspberry purée into a flute. Add the apple juice and stir. Fill with champagne. Stir. Drop two small raspberries into the drink.

Castro

1½ oz. (45 ml/3 tbsp.) gold rum
¾ oz. (22 ml/1½ tbsp.) calvados
1½ oz. (45 ml/3 tbsp.) orange juice
¾ oz. (22 ml/1½ tbsp.) lime juice
¾ oz. (22 ml/1½ tbsp.) Rose's
   Lime Cordial
1 tsp. gomme syrup
wedge of lime

Castro

Shake the ingredients, then strain into an ice-filled highball glass. Garnish with the lime and serve.

Celery Sour (Jason Scott)

2 oz (60 ml/4 tbsp.) Hendrick's gin
1 oz (30 ml/2 tbsp.) lemon juice
½ oz (15 ml/1 tbsp.) pineapple juice
½ oz (15 ml/1 tbsp.) sugar syrup
barspoon Bitter Truth celery bitters
1 egg white
celery shaving to garnish

Dry-shake all ingredients without ice. Shake with ice, then double-strain into a cocktail glass. Garnish with celery shaving.

Centenario

1½ oz. (45 ml/3 tbsp.) gold rum
1 oz. (30 ml/2 tbsp.) overproof white rum
¼ oz. (8 ml/½ tbsp.) Kahlua
¼ oz. (8 ml/½ tbsp.) Cointreau
dash grenadine
juice of one lime
sprig of mint to garnish
Stir the ingredients and pour over ice into a highball glass. Garnish with the mint and serve.

Ceres Joker (Ryan Chetiyawardana)

¾ oz (22 ml/1½ tbsp.) Dalmore 15YO whisky
¾ oz (22 ml/1½ tbsp.) sloe gin
¾ oz (22 ml/1½ tbsp.) lemon juice
½ oz (15 ml/1 tbsp.) sugar syrup
1 egg white
8 drops ginger bitters
Lemon-scented helium balloon and magician's string to garnish
Dry-shake all ingredients without ice. Shake with ice, then double-strain into a cocktail glass. Garnish with balloon tethered to glass. Light fuse before drinking.

Chambord Kamikaze

3 oz. (90 ml/6 tbsp.) vodka
½ oz. (15 ml/1 tbsp.) Cointreau
½ oz. (15 ml/1 tbsp.) lemon juice
½ oz. (15 ml/1 tbsp.) simple syrup
½ oz. (15 ml/1 tbsp.) Chambord
half a lime, diced
slice of lime to garnish
Place the ingredients, including the diced lime, in a shaker. Muddle violently. Strain, then pour into a cocktail glass. Garnish with a slice of lime and serve.

Champagne Cocktail

chilled champagne
1 white sugar cube
dash Angostura bitters
twist of lemon peel
wedge of orange

Place the sugar cube into a flute and add a dash of Angostura. Pour in the champagne. Add the lemon twist, garnish with the orange, and serve.

Champagne Cocktail (Classic)

1 oz. (30 ml/2 tbsp.) cognac
1 white sugar cube
4 dashes Angostura bitters
chilled champagne
maraschino cherry

In a champagne flute soak the sugar cube in the Angostura bitters. Pour on the cognac and fill up with champagne. Drop in the cherry and serve.

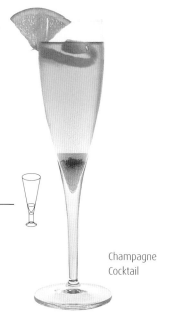

Champagne
Cocktail

Champagne Cooler

1 oz. (30 ml/2 tbsp.) Grand Marnier
½ oz. (15 ml/1 tbsp.) cognac
2 dashes Angostura bitters
chilled champagne
slice of orange to garnish

Pour the Grand Marnier, cognac, and bitters into a champagne flute. Stir. Fill up with champagne, garnish with the orange slice, and serve.

Champagne Cup

1 bottle chilled champagne
3 oz. (90 ml/6 tbsp.) Grand Marnier
3 oz. (90 ml/6 tbsp.) cognac
dash maraschino liqueur
sliced fruits in season and several fresh mint leaves to garnish
**Mix the ingredients in a large jug containing 10–15 ice cubes.
Stir in the fruit and mint, then serve in champagne flutes.**

Champagne Julep

6 fresh mint leaves
1 tsp. powdered sugar
dash cognac
chilled champagne
**Muddle the mint and sugar with the cognac in a deep
champagne saucer. Fill up with champagne and serve.**

Champers

1 oz. (30 ml/2 tbsp.) brandy
⅔ oz. (20 ml/1⅓ tbsp.) fresh orange juice
⅔ oz. (20 ml/1⅓ tbsp.) fresh lemon juice
champagne
**Shake the first three ingredients, then
strain into a champagne flute. Stir. Fill
with champagne and serve.**

Chapala

1½ oz. (45 ml/3 tbsp.) tequila
dash triple sec
¾ oz. (22 ml/1½ tbsp.) lemon juice
2 oz. (60 ml/4 tbsp.) orange juice
dash grenadine
**Stir over ice in a highball glass
and serve.**

Chapel Hill

3 oz. (90 ml/6 tbsp.) bourbon
1 oz. (30 ml/2 tbsp.) triple sec
dash fresh lemon juice
twist of orange to garnish
Shake the ingredients, then strain into a martini glass and serve with the orange twist.

Charlie Chaplin

1 oz. (30 ml/2 tbsp.) apricot brandy
1 oz. (30 ml/2 tbsp.) sloe gin
1 oz. (30 ml/2 tbsp.) fresh lemon juice
Shake the ingredients, then strain into a martini glass and serve.

Charlotte Rose (Iain Griffiths)

1¼ oz (38 ml/2½ tbsp.) pisco
½ oz (15 ml/1 tbsp.) lime
¼ oz (8 ml/½ tbsp.) Yellow Chartreuse
⅙ oz (5 ml/1/3 tbsp.) creme de violette
⅙ oz (5 ml/1/3 tbsp.) grenadine
3 dashes Peychaud's Bitters
Shake and strain into a cocktail glass.

Chartreuse Dragon

2 oz. (60 ml/4 tbsp.) vodka
2 oz. (60 ml/4 tbsp.) lychee juice
⅔ oz. (20 ml/1⅓ tbsp.) green chartreuse
⅓ oz. (10 ml/⅔ tbsp.) blue curaçao
dash fresh lime juice
lemon & lime soda
Shake the ingredients, except the lemon & lime soda. Strain into an ice-filled highball glass. Fill with lemon & lime soda, stir, and serve.

Cherry Picker

1 oz. (30 ml/2 tbsp.) gold tequila
1 oz. (30 ml/2 tbsp.) cherry brandy
juice of half a lime
1 oz. (30 ml/2 tbsp.) apple juice
twist of lime to garnish

Shake the ingredients, then strain into a cocktail glass. Add the twist of lime and serve.

Chi Chi

2 oz. (60 ml/4 tbsp.) vodka
1 oz. (30 ml/2 tbsp.) coconut cream
3 oz. (90 ml/6 tbsp.) pineapple juice

Blend all the ingredients, then pour into a large goblet and serve.

Chicago

2 oz. (60 ml/4 tbsp.) brandy
½ oz. (15 ml/1 tbsp.) triple sec
dash Angostura bitters

Shake the ingredients, then pour into a sugar-rimmed old-fashioned glass and serve.

Chime (Ryan Chetiyawardana)

2 oz (60 ml/4 tbsp.) Hibiki 12 Japanese whisky
1 oz (30 ml/2 tbsp.) fresh lemon juice
½ oz (15 ml/1 tbsp.) grenadine
2 dashes Peychaud's Bitters
¼ oz (8 ml/½ tbsp.) orange bell pepper
1 egg white
slice pepper to garnish

Muddle pepper, then add all other ingredients. Dry-shake without ice, then shake hard with ice. Double-strain into a cocktail glass and garnish with a slice of bell pepper.

Chocolate Martini (see Martini, p. 138)

2 oz. (60 ml/4 tbsp.) vodka
½ oz. (15 ml/1 tbsp.) crème de cacao
Pour ingredients into shaker filled with ice, then pour into a martini glass.

Chocolate Mint Martini (see Martini, p. 138)

2 oz. (60 ml/4 tbsp.) vodka
1 oz. (30 ml/2 tbsp.) white crème de cacao
dash white crème de menthe
**Pour ingredients into a mixing glass with ice and stir. Strain into
a martini glass and serve.**

Chocolate-Chip Mint

1 oz. (30 ml/2 tbsp.) white crème de menthe
1 oz. (30 ml/2 tbsp.) brown crème de cacao
1 oz. (30 ml/2 tbsp.) Tia Maria
1 oz. (30 ml/2 tbsp.) vodka
1 oz. (30 ml/2 tbsp.) heavy (double) cream
**Shake the ingredients, then strain into an ice-filled highball glass
and serve.**

Citrus Rum Cooler

1⅓ oz. (40 ml/2⅔ tbsp.) white rum
⅔ oz. (20 ml/1⅓ tbsp.) triple sec
1⅔ oz. (50 ml/3⅓ tbsp.) fresh orange juice
½ oz. (15 ml/1 tbsp.) fresh lime juice
few dashes gomme syrup
lemon & lime soda
**Shake the ingredients, then strain into an ice-filled highball glass. Fill
with lemon & lime soda. Serve with a straw.**

Clam Digger

1⅔ oz. (50 ml/3⅓ tbsp.) silver tequila
3 oz. (90 ml/6 tbsp.) tomato juice
3 oz. (90 ml/6 tbsp.) clam juice
2 tsp. horseradish sauce
dash Tabasco sauce
dash Worcestershire sauce
juice of one lime
lime wedge to garnish
Shake the ingredients, then strain into an ice-filled highball glass. Garnish with the lime wedge and serve.

Cliffhanger

2 oz. (60 ml/4 tbsp.) pepper vodka
1 oz. (30 ml/2 tbsp.) Cointreau
⅔ oz. (20 ml/1⅓ tbsp.) lime cordial
twist of lime to garnish
Shake the ingredients, then strain into a cocktail glass. Garnish with the lime wedge and serve.

Climax

2 oz. (60 ml/4 tbsp.) Southern Comfort
1 oz. (30 ml/2 tbsp.) Kahlua
½ oz. (15 ml/1 tbsp.) heavy (double) cream
Shake the ingredients, then strain into a martini glass and serve.

Clover Club

2 oz. (60 ml/4 tbsp.) dry gin
splash grenadine
1 oz. (30 ml/2 tbsp.) lemon juice
egg white
Shake the ingredients, then strain into a cocktail glass and serve.

Cobbler

1 tsp. powdered sugar
1 oz. (30 ml/2 tbsp.) soda water
2 oz. (60 ml/4 tbsp.) any spirit
seasonal fruit to garnish

In an old-fashioned glass, dissolve the sugar in the soda water, then fill the glass with ice. Stir in the spirit, garnish with the fruit, and serve.

Cocoloco

1 oz. (30 ml/2 tbsp.) white rum
1 oz. (30 ml/2 tbsp.) vodka
1 oz. (30 ml/2 tbsp.) tequila
1 oz. (30 ml/2 tbsp.) fresh lemon juice
1 oz. (30 ml/2 tbsp.) sweetened coconut cream

Blend the ingredients until smooth, then pour into a goblet and serve.

Coconilla Delight

1 oz. (30 ml/2 tbsp.) gold rum
1 banana, peeled
1 oz. (30 ml/2 tbsp.) coconut cream
3 oz. (90 ml/6 tbsp.) pineapple juice
3 oz. (90 ml/6 tbsp.) fresh orange juice
2 scoops vanilla ice cream

Blend the ingredients with crushed ice, then pour into a highball glass. Serve with a straw.

Coconut Groove (nonalcoholic)

3 oz. (90 ml/6 tbsp.) pineapple juice
2 oz. (60 ml/4 tbsp.) coconut cream
2 oz. (60 ml/4 tbsp.) fresh pink grapefruit juice
thin grapefruit wedge to garnish

Blend the ingredients with crushed ice. Pour into a colada glass. Add a thin grapefruit wedge on the rim and serve.

Colonel Collins

2 oz. (60 ml/4 tbsp.) bourbon
1 oz. (30 ml/2 tbsp.) lemon juice
1 tsp. superfine (caster) sugar
dash Angostura bitters (optional)
soda

Place the first three ingredients in a highball glass, half-filled with ice, and stir. Fill up with soda. Stir gently and serve.

Colonel Fizz

2 oz. (60 ml/4 tbsp.) bourbon
1 oz. (30 ml/2 tbsp.) lemon juice
1 tsp. superfine (caster) sugar
dash Angostura bitters (optional)
soda

Shake the ingredients, then strain into a highball glass, fill up with soda, and serve.

Colonel Sour (see Pisco Sour, p. 168)

2 oz. (60 ml/4 tbsp.) bourbon
¾ oz. (22 ml/1½ tbsp.) lemon juice
½ tsp. superfine (caster) sugar

Shake the ingredients, then strain into an old-fashioned glass and serve.

Continental

2 oz. (60 ml/4 tbsp.) white rum
½ oz. (15 ml/1 tbsp.) crème de menthe
dash fresh lime juice
twist of lemon to garnish

Pour the rum, crème de menthe, and lime juice into an old-fashioned glass. Stir. Garnish with the lemon twist and serve.

Cool Gold

1 oz. (30 ml/2 tbsp.) melon liqueur
1 oz. (30 ml/2 tbsp.) gold tequila
1 oz. (30 ml/2 tbsp.) cranberry juice
Shake the ingredients, then strain into a martini glass and serve.

Cool Martini (see Martini, p. 138)

2 oz. (60 ml/4 tbsp.) vodka
⅔ oz. (20 ml/1⅓ tbsp.) apple juice
½ oz. (15 ml/1 tbsp.) Cointreau
1 oz. (15 ml/1 tbsp.) fresh lemon juice
Shake the ingredients, then strain into a martini glass and serve.

Coolcumber (Chris Edwardes)

2 oz. (60 ml/4 tbsp.) cucumber vodka
chunk of cucumber
1 oz. (30 ml/2 tbsp.) grapefruit juice
juice of a lime
½ oz. (15 ml/1 tbsp.) gomme syrup
Blend the ingredients in an ice-filled container until frozen, then pour into a large goblet and serve.

Copenhagen

2 oz. (60 ml/4 tbsp.) vodka
½ oz. (15 ml/1 tbsp.) akvavit
a few slivered blanched almonds
Shake the ingredients, then strain into a cocktail glass, garnish with the almonds, and serve.

Cordless Screwdriver

1 oz. (30 ml/2 tbsp.) chilled vodka
1 orange wedge sugar
Coat the orange wedge in the sugar and pour the vodka into a shot glass. Drink the vodka, then eat the orange.

Corpse Reviver

¾ oz. (22 ml/1½ tbsp.) brandy
¾ oz. (22 ml/1½ tbsp.) calvados
¾ oz. (22 ml/1½ tbsp.) sweet vermouth
**Shake the ingredients, then strain
into a cocktail glass and serve.**

Cosmopolitan

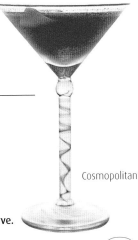

2 oz. (60 ml/4 tbsp.) vodka
1 oz. (30 ml/2 tbsp.) Cointreau
½ oz. (15 ml/1 tbsp.) lime juice
splash cranberry juice
lime twist to garnish
Cosmopolitan
**Stir the ingredients in a mixing glass, then
strain into a chilled cocktail glass with a
sugared rim. Garnish with the twist and serve.**

Cosmopolitan (alt)

1 oz. (30 ml/2 tbsp.) vodka
½ oz. (15 ml/1 tbsp.) triple sec
½ oz. (15 ml/1 tbsp.) cranberry juice
juice of 1 lime
flamed orange peel to garnish
**Shake the ingredients, then strain into a cocktail glass and serve with
the flaming garnish.**

Cuba Libre

1⅔ oz. (50 ml/3⅓ tbsp.) white rum
juice of 1 fresh lime
cola
lime wedge to garnish
**Pour the juice, then the rum into an ice-filled highball glass.
Fill with cola. Add a wedge of lime and serve with a stirrer.**

Cuban

2 oz. (60 ml/4 tbsp.) white rum
dash apricot brandy
juice of half a lime
dash gomme syrup
**Stir the rum, brandy, lime juice, and gomme syrup in a mixing glass.
Strain into a martini glass and serve.**

Cuban Cutie

2 oz. (60 ml/4 tbsp.) white rum
⅔ oz. (20 ml/1⅓ tbsp.) passion fruit juice
3 oz. (90 ml/6 tbsp.) grenadine
3 oz. (90 ml/6 tbsp.) fresh orange juice
lime wedge to garnish
**Shake the ingredients, then strain into an ice-filled highball glass.
Garnish with the lime wedge and serve.**

Cuban Island

¾ oz. (22 ml/1½ tbsp.) white rum
¾ oz. (22 ml/1½ tbsp.) vodka
¾ oz. (22 ml/1½ tbsp.) Cointreau
¾ oz. (22 ml/1½ tbsp.) lemon juice
Shake the ingredients, then strain into a cocktail glass and serve.

Czarina

2 oz. (60 ml/4 tbsp.) vodka
1 oz. (30 ml/2 tbsp.) apricot brandy
½ oz. (15 ml/1 tbsp.) dry vermouth
dash Angostura bitters
**Stir the ingredients in a mixing glass, then strain into a martini glass
and serve.**

Daiquiri (see p. 92–93)

Dandy

2 oz. (60 ml/4 tbsp.) Dubonnet
1 oz. (30 ml/2 tbsp.) bourbon
1 oz. (30 ml/2 tbsp.) Cointreau
dash Angostura bitters
Shake the ingredients, then strain into a martini glass and serve.

Dawn

1 oz. (30 ml/2 tbsp.) gin
⅔ oz. (20 ml/1⅓ tbsp.) Campari
1⅔ oz. (50 ml/3⅓ tbsp.) fresh orange juice
Shake the ingredients, then strain into an old-fashioned glass over crushed ice and serve.

Death Flip (Chris Hysted)

1 oz (30 ml/2 tbsp.) blanco tequila
½ oz (15 ml/1 tbsp.) Jägermeister
½ oz (15 ml/1 tbsp.) Yellow Chartreuse
½ oz (15 ml/1 tbsp.) sugar syrup
1 whole egg
nutmeg to garnish
Dry-shake all ingredients without ice. Shake with ice, then double-strain into a cocktail glass. Garnish with grated nutmeg.

Deauville

1 oz. (30 ml/2 tbsp.) brandy
¾ oz. (22 ml/1½ tbsp.) calvados
½ oz. (15 ml/1 tbsp.) triple sec
¾ oz. (22 ml/1½ tbsp.) fresh lemon juice
Shake the ingredients and strain into a cocktail glass, and serve.

Daiquiri

The drink, from the fashionable isle of Cuba, with a glamorous tastiness that makes it sing.

Rum's magical combination of delicate sweetness with an alcoholic kick makes it a great base for cocktails, and in the 1920s, Havana was cocktail nirvana. There, bartender Constante Ribailagua perfected a cocktail that had originally been invented in the mines in the Daiquiri mountain range in the south of the country. It was there, according to legend, that two engineers called Pagliuchi and Cox mixed together rum, lime juice, sugar, and ice.

Constante created the frozen Daiquiri, although his original is far from the mushy slush on offer today. He used crushed ice, but strained the drink rather than let the ice cause dilution in a glass.

His creation was to inspire author Ernest Hemingway—the most famous regular at el Floridita—although by the time Papa penned Islands in the Stream, ice was floating on the top.

Blenders increased the possibilities, and fresh fruit was combined with the basic recipe. Try it with bananas, mango, strawberry, raspberry, and mint.

Daiquiri

2 oz. (60 ml/4 tbsp.) white rum
juice of 1 lime
1 tsp. sugar
lemon twist to garnish
**Shake the ingredients, then
strain into a cocktail glass, add
the garnish, and serve.**

Demeanor

1 oz. (30 ml/2 tbsp.) Old Tom gin
1 oz. (30 ml/2 tbsp.) sweet vermouth
½ oz. (15 ml/1 tbsp.) Parfait Amour
Stir the ingredients in a mixing glass, strain into a martini glass and serve.

Desert Island

1 oz. (30 ml/2 tbsp.) Midori
1 oz. (30 ml/2 tbsp.) white rum
2 oz. (60 ml/4 tbsp.) pineapple juice
2 oz. (60 ml/4 tbsp.) heavy (double) cream
Shake the ingredients, apart from the cream, then strain into a deep cocktail glass. Float the cream on top and serve.

Detroit Martini (see Martini, p. 138)

2 oz. (60 ml/4 tbsp.) vodka
⅔ oz. (20 ml/1⅓ tbsp.) gomme syrup
few fresh mint leaves
Shake the ingredients, then strain into a martini glass and serve.

Devil's Advocate

2 oz. (60 ml/4 tbsp.) gin
1 oz. (30 ml/2 tbsp.) crème de framboise
2 dashes dry vermouth
Stir the gin and vermouth in a mixing glass, then strain into a cocktail glass. Add the liqueur, let it sink to the bottom, and serve.

Diamond Fizz

2 oz. (60 ml/4 tbsp.) gin
dash fresh lemon juice
1 tsp. powdered sugar
chilled champagne
Shake the gin, lemon juice, and sugar, then pour into a sugar-rimmed highball glass. Fill up with champagne and serve.

Dianna

3 oz. (90 ml/6 tbsp.) white crème de menthe
1 oz. (30 ml/2 tbsp.) cognac
**Pour the crème de menthe over crushed ice in an old-fashioned glass.
Float the cognac on top and serve.**

Dirty Martini (see Martini, p. 138)

1⅔ oz. (50 ml/3⅓ tbsp.) gin
⅔ oz. (20 ml/1⅓ tbsp.) brine from cocktail olives
⅓ oz. (10 ml/⅔ tbsp.) extra dry vermouth
olive to garnish
**Stir the ingredients in a mixing glass. Strain into a martini glass.
Add an olive on a cocktail stick and serve.**

Dock of the Bay

1 oz. (30 ml/2 tbsp.) vodka
⅔ oz. (20 ml/1⅓ tbsp.) schnapps
3 oz. (90 ml/6 tbsp.) cranberry juice
2 oz. (60 ml/4 tbsp.) pineapple juice
Shake the ingredients, the strain into an ice-filled highball glass.

Dodge

2 oz. (60 ml/4 tbsp.) gin
2 oz. (60 ml/4 tbsp.) Cointreau
dash white grape juice
Shake the ingredients, then strain into a martini glass and serve.

Dorado

1⅔ oz. (50 ml/3⅓ tbsp.) tequila
fresh juice of one lemon
2 tsp. honey
Shake the ingredients, then strain into a martini glass and serve.

Double Vision

1 oz. (30 ml/2 tbsp.) lemon vodka
1 oz. (30 ml/2 tbsp.) blackcurrant vodka
4 dashes Angostura bitters
1 oz. (30 ml/2 tbsp.) apple juice
Shake the ingredients, then strain into a martini glass and serve.

Dragon Fly

2 oz. (60 ml/4 tbsp.) vodka
⅔ oz. (20 ml/1⅓ tbsp.) melon liqueur
dash fresh lime juice
1 oz. (30 ml/2 tbsp.) apple juice
Shake the ingredients, then strain into a martini glass and serve.

Dream Juice

1 oz. (30 ml/2 tbsp.) Dubonnet
½ oz. (15 ml/1 tbsp.) triple sec
½ oz. (15 ml/1 tbsp.) fresh grapefruit juice
champagne
**Pour the ingredients, except champagne, into a mixing glass with ice.
Stir and strain into a champagne flute. Fill with champagne and serve.**

Dry Presidente

2 oz. (60 ml/4 tbsp.) white rum
1 oz. (30 ml/2 tbsp.) dry vermouth
dash Angostura bitters
olive to garnish
**Shake the ingredients, then strain into a martini glass. Garnish with
the olive and serve.**

Due Campari

¼ oz. (8 ml/½ tbsp.) Campari
¾ oz. (22 ml/1½ tbsp.) Cordiale Campari
champagne
¾ oz. (22 ml/1½ tbsp.) fresh lemon juice

Shake the lemon juice and both Camparis, then strain into a champagne flute. Fill with sparkling wine, stir, and serve.

Duke

1 egg
dash triple sec
dash maraschino liqueur
dash fresh lemon juice
dash fresh orange juice
chilled champagne

Shake the ingredients, except the champagne, then strain into a flute. Fill with champagne and serve.

Dunny

1 oz. (30 ml/2 tbsp.) Drambuie
1 oz. (30 ml/2 tbsp.) Islay malt whisky
dash fresh lime juice

Pour the Drambuie, whisky, and lime juice into an old-fashioned glass. Stir and serve.

Dutch Coffee

1 oz. (30 ml/2 tbsp.) genever
6 oz. (180 ml/12 tbsp.) hot black coffee
2 tsp. raw sugar
heavy (double) cream

Pour the genever and black coffee into a liqueur coffee glass, then add the sugar. Stir. Float the cream on top and serve.

Dynamite

½ oz. (15 ml/1 tbsp.) cognac
½ oz. (15 ml/1 tbsp.) Grand Marnier
1 oz. (30 ml/2 tbsp.) fresh orange juice
chilled champagne

Pour the cognac, Grand Marnier, and orange juice into a champagne flute. Stir. Fill up with champagne and serve.

East India

2 oz. (60 ml/4 tbsp.) cognac
½ oz. (15 ml/1 tbsp.) dark rum
dash triple sec
dash pineapple juice
dash Angostura bitters

Shake the ingredients, then strain into a martini glass and serve.

Eclipse

1 oz. (30 ml/2 tbsp.) sloe gin
1 oz. (30 ml/2 tbsp.) gin
dash grenadine
1 olive
dash fresh lemon juice

Put the olive in a martini glass, cover with the grenadine. Shake the gin and lemon, strain into the glass, not disturbing the grenadine, and serve.

Eggnog

2 oz. (60 ml/4 tbsp.) cognac
1 egg
½ oz. (15 ml/1 tbsp.) gomme syrup
dash dark rum
5 oz. (150 ml/10 tbsp.) light (single) cream
grated nutmeg to garnish

Shake the ingredients, then strain into a highball glass. Sprinkle with grated nutmeg and serve.

El Diablo

2 oz. (60 ml/4 tbsp.) silver tequila
1 oz. (30 ml/2 tbsp.) crème de cassis
juice of one lime
ginger ale
lime wedge to garnish
**Pour the ingredients into a highball with
crushed ice. Fill with ginger ale. Add the
lime wedge and serve with a straw.**

El Presidente

2 oz. (60 ml/4 tbsp.) white rum
1 oz. (30 ml/2 tbsp.) fresh lime juice
dash grenadine
dash pineapple juice
**Shake the ingredients, then strain into a
cocktail glass and serve.**

El Diablo

Eldorado

2 oz. (60 ml/4 tbsp.) gold tequila
1 oz. (30 ml/2 tbsp.) fresh lemon juice
1 tsp. honey
Shake the ingredients, then strain into a martini glass and serve.

Elixir

1 oz. (30 ml/2 tbsp.) Grand Marnier
1 oz. (30 ml/2 tbsp.) sweet vermouth
dash Punt e Mes
2 dashes Angostura bitters
Pour the ingredients into an old-fashioned glass, stir, and serve.

Epernay

1 oz. (30 ml/2 tbsp.) crème de framboise
dash Midori melon liqueur
chilled champagne

Pour the crème de framboise and melon liqueur into a champagne flute. Fill up with champagne and serve.

The Escalador (Iain Griffiths)

1½ oz (45 ml/3 tbsp.) Calle 23
Reposado tequila
¾ oz (22 ml/1½ tbsp.) Dolin dry
½ oz (15 ml/1 tbsp.) Aperol
¼ oz (8 ml/½ tbsp.) Yellow
Chartreuse
lemon twist to garnish

Stir all ingredients over ice, then strain into a Martini glass. Garnish with lemon twist.

Evans

2 oz. (60 ml/4 tbsp.) bourbon
1 oz. (30 ml/2 tbsp.) Cointreau
1 oz. (30 ml/2 tbsp.) apricot brandy

Stir the bourbon, Cointreau, and brandy in a mixing glass, then strain into an ice-filled old-fashioned glass and serve.

Evita

1 oz. (30 ml/2 tbsp.) vodka
1 oz. (30 ml/2 tbsp.) melon liqueur
2 oz. (60 ml/4 tbsp.) fresh orange juice
1 oz. (30 ml/2 tbsp.) fresh lime juice
dash gomme syrup

Shake the ingredients, then strain into an old-fashioned glass filled with ice and serve.

Filby

2 oz. (60 ml/4 tbsp.) gin
1 oz. (30 ml/2 tbsp.) Campari
1 oz. (30 ml/2 tbsp.) dry vermouth
1 oz. (30 ml/2 tbsp.) amaretto

Stir the ingredients in a mixing glass, then strain into a martini glass and serve.

Final Ward (Phil Ward)

¾ oz (22 ml/1½ tbsp.) rye whiskey
¾ oz (22 ml/1½ tbsp.) Green Chartreuse
¾ oz (22 ml/1½ tbsp.) Maraschino liqueur
¾ oz (22 ml/1½ tbsp.) lemon juice
lemon twist to garnish

Shake all ingredients, strain into a cocktail glass and garnish with lemon twist.

Fizzing Americano

1 oz. (30 ml/2 tbsp.) Campari
½ oz. (15 ml/1 tbsp.) sweet vermouth
champagne or Prosecco (Italian sparkling wine)
orange wheel to garnish

Shake the ingredients, then pour over ice in a highball glass. Fill up with champagne, add the orange, and serve.

Flirt

1 oz. (30 ml/2 tbsp.) vodka
1 oz. (15 ml/1 tbsp.) black sambuca
2 oz. (60 ml/4 tbsp.) cranberry juice

Shake the ingredients, then strain into a cocktail glass and serve.

Fizzing Americano

Floridita

1½ oz. (45 ml/3 tbsp.) white rum
½ oz. (15 ml/1 tbsp.) sweet vermouth
dash of white crème de cacao
dash of grenadine
juice of half a lime
Shake the ingredients, then strain into a cocktail glass and serve.

Floridita

Flying Dutchman

3 oz. (90 ml/6 tbsp.) Dutch gin
dash triple sec
Shake the ingredients, then strain into an ice-filled old-fashioned glass and serve.

Fortunella

1 oz. (30 ml/2 tbsp.) Ketel One vodka
¾ oz. (22 ml/1½ tbsp.) Bombay Sapphire gin
¾ oz. (22 ml/1½ tbsp.) Caravella
splash Cointreau
splash Campari
1 tsp. candied kumquat nectar
twist of lemon to garnish
twist of kumquat to garnish
Coat the shaker with the Cointreau and Campari, and then discard the excess. Shake the rest of the ingredients, then strain into a cocktail glass and serve with the garnish.

Fragile Baby

1 oz. (30 ml/2 tbsp.) frangelico
2 oz. (60 ml/4 tbsp.) Bailey's
2 tsp. raw sugar
1 oz. (30 ml/2 tbsp.) heavy (double) cream
Pour the frangelico, Bailey's, and sugar into a liqueur coffee glass. Float the cream on top, then serve.

Fraises Royale

2 strawberries
1 oz. (30 ml/2 tbsp.) crème de fraise
chilled champagne
**Blend the strawberries with the liqueur, then pour into a champagne
flute. Fill with champagne and serve.**

French 125

1 oz. (30 ml/2 tbsp.) cognac
½ oz. (15 ml/1 tbsp.) fresh lime juice
chilled champagne
twist of lime to garnish
**Mix the cognac and lime juice in a champagne flute. Fill with
champagne, garnish, and serve.**

French 75

¾ oz. (22 ml/1½ tbsp.) gin
¼ oz. (8 ml/½ tbsp.) fresh lemon juice
dash gomme syrup
dash grenadine
champagne
**Shake the first four ingredients, then
strain into a champagne flute, fill with
champagne, and serve.**

French 75 (alt)

1½ oz. (45 ml/3 tbsp.) gin
1½ oz. (45 ml/3 tbsp.) fresh lemon juice
chilled champagne
twist of lemon to garnish
**Mix the gin and lemon juice in a
champagne flute. Fill with champagne, garnish, and serve.**

French 75

French 76

¾ oz. (22 ml/1½ tbsp.) vodka
¼ oz. (8 ml/½ tbsp.) lime juice
dash gomme syrup
dash grenadine
champagne

Shake the first four ingredients, then strain into a champagne flute, fill with champagne, and serve.

French Kiss

1 oz. (30 ml/2 tbsp.) vodka
1 oz. (30 ml/2 tbsp.) crème de mure
½ oz. (15 ml/1 tbsp.) white crème de cacao
1 oz. (30 ml/2 tbsp.) heavy (double) cream

Shake the ingredients, then strain into a martini glass and serve.

French Kiss 2

⅔ oz. (20 ml/1⅓ tbsp.) raspberry purée
1 oz. (30 ml/2 tbsp.) ginger beer
dash apricot brandy
champagne
1 raspberry to garnish

Pour the raspberry purée, apricot brandy, and ginger beer into a champagne flute. Stir. Fill with champagne. Drop a raspberry in the drink and serve.

French Martini (see Martini, p. 138)

2 oz. (60 ml/4 tbsp.) vodka
dash Chambord
dash pineapple juice

Shake the ingredients, then strain into a martini glass and serve.

French Sherbet

1 oz. (30 ml/2 tbsp.) cognac
½ oz. (15 ml/1 tbsp.) kirsch
lemon sherbet
chilled champagne
**Stir the spirits with the sherbet in a deep champagne saucer.
Fill up with champagne and serve.**

French Whore

1 oz. (30 ml/2 tbsp.) cognac
1 oz. (30 ml/2 tbsp.) Tia Maria
Mix the cognac and Tia Maria in an old-fashioned glass and serve.

Frostbite

1 oz. (30 ml/2 tbsp.) silver tequila
1 oz. (30 ml/2 tbsp.) white crème de menthe
1 oz. (30 ml/2 tbsp.) heavy (double) cream
Shake the ingredients, then strain into a martini glass and serve.

Frozen Apple

2 oz. (60 ml/4 tbsp.) calvados
1 oz. (30 ml/2 tbsp.) fresh lime juice
dash gomme syrup
1 egg white
**Blend the ingredients with crushed ice until frozen, then pour
into a goblet and serve.**

Frozen Daiquiri (see Daiquiri, p. 92)

2 oz. white rum
juice of 1 lime
1 tsp. sugar
**Blend the ingredients with crushed ice until frozen, then pour
into a cocktail glass.**

Frozen Margarita (see Margarita, p. 136)

2 oz. (60 ml/4 tbsp.) tequila
1oz. (30 ml/ 2 tbsp) Cointreau
juice of half a lime
juice of half a lemon
Blend the ingredients with crushed ice until frozen, then pour into a margarita glass. You can add any fruit to turn this drink into a frozen margarita.

Fuzzy Navel

1½ oz. (45 ml/3 tbsp.) peach schnapps
orange juice to taste
Pour peach schnapps into an ice-filled Collins glass. Fill with orange juice and stir to combine.

Gaelic Coffee

1 oz. (30 ml/2 tbsp.) Scotch whisky
6 oz. (180 ml/12 tbsp.) hot black coffee
2 tsp. raw sugar
heavy (double) cream
Pour the whisky and black coffee into a liqueur coffee glass, then add the sugar. Float the cream on top and serve.

Gastown (Geoff Robinson)

1½ oz (45 ml/3 tbsp.) mezcal
¼ oz (8 ml/½ tbsp.) Fernet Branca
¼ oz (8 ml/½ tbsp.) Cynar
⅛ oz (5 ml/1 tsp.) maple syrup
2 dashes Angostura bitters
1 dash Decanter Bitters
Stir all and strain into a cocktail glass.

The Gatsby (Andrea Montague)

1½ oz (45 ml/3 tbsp.) Plymouth Gin
½ oz (15 ml/1 tbsp.) Kamm and Sons ginseng spirit
½ oz (15 ml/1 tbsp.) nettle cordial
3 dashes Regan's Orange Bitters
Stir and strain into a cocktail glass. Garnish with lemon twist.

German Coffee

1 oz. (30 ml/2 tbsp.) kirsch
6 oz. (180 ml/12 tbsp.) hot black coffee
2 tsp. raw sugar
heavy (double) cream
Pour the kirsch and black coffee into a liqueur coffee glass, then add the sugar. Float the cream on top and serve.

Giada

1 oz. (30 ml/2 tbsp.) vodka
½ oz. (15 ml/1 tbsp.) Campari
½ oz. (15 ml/1 tbsp.) Galliano
dash pineapple juice
Shake the ingredients, then strain into a cocktail glass and serve.

Gimlet

Gimlet

2 oz. (60 ml/4 tbsp.) gin or vodka
1 oz. (30 ml/2 tbsp.) lime cordial
wedge of lime to garnish
Pour the spirit and lime cordial over ice cubes in an cocktail glass and serve.

Gin Alexander

1 oz. (30 ml/2 tbsp.) gin
1 oz. (30 ml/2 tbsp.) brown crème de cacao
1 oz. (30 ml/2 tbsp.) heavy (double) cream
**Shake the ingredients, then strain
into a martini glass and serve.**

Gin Basil Smash (Jorg Meyer)

3 oz (90 ml/6 tbsp.) Hendrick's gin
1 oz (30 ml/2 tbsp.) lemon juice
⅔ oz (20 ml/1⅓ tbsp.) sugar syrup
1 bunch basil
basil leaf to garnish
**Add all ingredients to a shaker,
then muddle basil into liquid.
Shake hard, double-strain over ice
in a rocks glass, and garnish with
basil leaf.**

Ginger Jest

1 oz. (30 ml/2 tbsp.) bourbon
1 oz. (30 ml/2 tbsp.) pineapple juice
2 to 3 slices fresh ginger
champagne
**Muddle the ginger in a shaker. Add the bourbon, pineapple juice,
and ice cubes. Shake and strain into a champagne flute. Fill with
champagne, stir, and serve.**

Gloom Raiser

2 oz. (60 ml/4 tbsp.) gin
1 oz. (30 ml/2 tbsp.) vermouth
2 dashes grenadine
2 dashes absinthe or Pernod
Shake the ingredients, then strain into a cocktail glass and serve.

Goddess

1 oz. (30 ml/2 tbsp.) Pernod
1 oz. (30 ml/2 tbsp.) amaretto
Shake the Pernod and amaretto, then strain into a martini glass and serve.

Godfather

2 oz. (60 ml/4 tbsp.) Scotch whisky
1 oz. (30 ml/2 tbsp.) amaretto
Pour the scotch and amaretto into an old-fashioned glass and serve.

Godmother

2 oz. (60 ml/4 tbsp.) vodka
1 oz. (30 ml/2 tbsp.) amaretto
Pour the vodka and amaretto into an old-fashioned glass and serve.

Golden Apple (Chris Edwardes)

1 oz. (30 ml/2 tbsp.) Mount Gay rum
½ oz. (15 ml/1 tbsp.) apple schnapps
1 oz. (30 ml/2 tbsp.) apple purée
juice of 1 lime
½ oz. (15 ml/1 tbsp.) gomme syrup
Shake the ingredients, then strain into a martini glass and serve.

Golden Cadillac

1 oz. (30 ml/2 tbsp.) crème de cacao
1 oz. (30 ml/2 tbsp.) Galliano
1 oz. (30 ml/2 tbsp.) heavy (double) cream
Shake the ingredients, then strain into a martini glass and serve.

Golden Margarita (see Margarita, p. 136)

2 oz. (60 ml/4 tbsp.) gold tequila
1 oz. (30 ml/2 tbsp.) Grand Marnier
juice of 1 lime
lime wedge to garnish
Shake the ingredients, then strain into a margarita glass with a salted rim. Add the lime wedge and serve.

Good Fellow

1 oz. (30 ml/2 tbsp.) cognac
1 oz. (30 ml/2 tbsp.) Benedictine
2 dashes Angostura bitters
½ oz. (15 ml/1 tbsp.) gomme syrup
Shake the ingredients, then strain into a martini glass and serve.

Goose Bumps

1 oz. (30 ml/2 tbsp.) vodka
1 oz. (30 ml/2 tbsp.) red cherry purée
dash cherry liqueur
champagne
Pour the vodka, cherry purée, and cherry liqueur into a champagne flute. Stir, then fill with champagne. Stir and serve.

Grand Mimosa

2 oz. (60 ml/4 tbsp.) Grand Marnier
1 oz. (30 ml/2 tbsp.) fresh orange juice
chilled champagne
Pour the Grand Marnier and orange juice into a champagne flute, stir, then fill with champagne and serve.

Grapefruit Daiquiri (see Daiquiri, p. 92)

2 oz. (60 ml/4 tbsp.) white rum
1 oz. (30 ml/2 tbsp.) fresh grapefruit juice
dash gomme syrup
Shake the ingredients, then strain into a cocktail glass and serve.

Green Beast (Charles Vexenat)

1 oz (30 ml/2 tbsp.) Pernod Absinthe
1 oz (30 ml/2 tbsp.) lime juice
4 oz (120 ml/8 tbsp.) water
1 oz (30 ml/2 tbsp.) sugar syrup
Cucumber to garnish
Build in a highball glass over ice. Garnish with slices of cucumber.

Green Dinosaur

⅔ oz. (20 ml/1⅓ tbsp.) vodka
⅔ oz. (20 ml/1⅓ tbsp.) gold tequila
⅔ oz. (20 ml/1⅓ tbsp.) light rum
⅔ oz. (20 ml/1⅓ tbsp.) gin
⅔ oz. (20 ml/1⅓ tbsp.) triple sec
1 oz. (30 ml/2 tbsp.) fresh lime juice
dash gomme syrup
dash melon liqueur
Shake the ingredients, except the melon liqueur, and strain into an ice-filled highball. Float the melon liqueur over the top and serve.

Green Point (Mickey McIlroy)

2 oz (60 ml/4 tbsp.) Rittenhouse bonded rye
1 oz (30 ml/2 tbsp.) Punt e Mes
⅛ oz (5 ml/1 tsp.) Yellow Chartreuse
1 dash Angostura bitters
Stir all and strain into a cocktail glass.

111

Gumdrop

2 oz. (60 ml/4 tbsp.) Scotch whisky
1 oz. (30 ml/2 tbsp.) Galliano
Pour the scotch and Galliano into an old-fashioned glass, stir, and serve.

H. G. Wells

2 oz. (60 ml/4 tbsp.) bourbon
1 oz. (30 ml/2 tbsp.) dry vermouth
½ oz. (15 ml/1 tbsp.) Pernod
2 dashes Angostura bitters
Stir the ingredients in a mixing glass, then strain into an ice-filled old-fashioned glass and serve.

Hair of the Dog

2 oz. (60 ml/4 tbsp.) Scotch whisky
1 oz. (30 ml/2 tbsp.) honey
1 oz. (30 ml/2 tbsp.) heavy (double) cream
Shake the ingredients, then strain into a martini glass and serve.

Hair Raiser

2 oz. (60 ml/4 tbsp.) 100 proof vodka
1½ oz. (45 ml/3 tbsp.) rye whiskey
½ oz. (15 ml/1 tbsp.) fresh lemon juice
Shake the ingredients, then strain into a martini glass and serve.

Half and Half

2 oz. (60 ml/4 tbsp.) dry vermouth
2 oz. (60 ml/4 tbsp.) sweet vermouth
twist of lemon to garnish
Pour the vermouths into an old-fashioned glass, stir, then garnish with the lemon twist and serve.

Happy Birthday

1 oz. (30 ml/2 tbsp.) Cointreau
1 oz. (30 ml/2 tbsp.) blue curaçao
½ oz. (15 ml/1 tbsp.) Galliano
½ oz. (15 ml/1 tbsp.) white rum
Stir the ingredients in a mixing glass, then strain into a martini glass and serve.

Happy Youth

2 oz. (60 ml/4 tbsp.) cherry brandy
1 oz. (30 ml/2 tbsp.) fresh orange juice
1 sugar cube
chilled champagne
cherry to garnish
Pour the cherry brandy and orange juice over the sugar cube in a flute. Fill with champagne. Garnish with the cherry and serve.

Harmony

2 oz. (60 ml/4 tbsp.) cognac
½ oz. (15 ml/1 tbsp.) crème de fraises
2 dashes orange bitters
dash maraschino liqueur
Stir the ingredients in an old-fashioned glass and serve.

Harper Cranberry

2 oz. (60 ml/4 tbsp.) I. W. Harper bourbon
3 oz. (90 ml/6 tbsp.) cranberry juice
Stir the ingredients in a mixing glass, then strain into an ice-filled highball glass.

Harper
Cranberry

Harry's Cocktail

2 oz. (60 ml/4 tbsp.) gin
1 oz. (30 ml/2 tbsp.) sweet vermouth
dash pastis
1 sprig of mint
Shake the ingredients, then strain into a martini glass and serve.

Harvey Wallbanger

2 oz. (60 ml/4 tbsp.) vodka
5 oz. (150 ml/10 tbsp.) fresh orange juice
1 oz. (30 ml/2 tbsp.) Galliano
slice of orange
Pour the vodka and orange juice into an ice-filled highball and stir. Float the Galliano on top. Garnish with the orange and serve with a stirrer.

Harvey Wallbanger

Hemingway

1 oz. (30 ml/2 tbsp.) Pernod
chilled champagne
Pour the Pernod into a champagne flute, then fill with champagne and serve.

Holy Trinity (Ryan Chetiyawardana)

2 oz (60 ml/4 tbsp.) No 3 gin
¼ oz (8 ml/½ tbsp.) Petit Chablis
knifepoint dried wormwood
radish to garnish
Stir all ingredients over ice, then strain into a Martini glass. Garnish with radish.

Honeymoon Paradise

1 oz. (30 ml/2 tbsp.) blue curaçao
1 oz. (30 ml/2 tbsp.) Cointreau
1 oz. (30 ml/2 tbsp.) fresh lemon juice
chilled champagne
Pour the blue curaçao and Cointreau into a high-ball glass. Fill with champagne and serve.

Horse's Neck

2 oz. (60 ml/4 tbsp.) bourbon
2 dashes Angostura bitters
ginger ale
twist of lemon
Coat a highball glass with bitters. Add ice and the bourbon. Stir, then fill with ginger ale and the lemon twist. Stir briefly and serve.

Horse's Neck

Hot Brandy Alexander

1 oz. (30 ml/2 tbsp.) brandy
1 oz. (30 ml/2 tbsp.) brown crème
    de cacao
4 oz. (120 ml/8 tbsp.) steamed milk
whipped cream
chocolate shavings to garnish
Pour the brandy, crème de cacao, and milk into a heatproof glass. Top with the whipped cream and chocolate shavings, then serve.

Hot Brandy Flip

2 oz. (60 ml/4 tbsp.) cognac
½ oz. (15 ml/1 tbsp.) gomme syrup
1 egg yolk
4 oz. (120 ml/8 tbsp.) hot milk
grated nutmeg to decorate
Mix the cognac, gomme syrup, and egg yolk in a highball glass. Stir in the hot milk and sprinkle with the nutmeg.

Hot Eggnog

1 oz. (30 ml/2 tbsp.) dark rum
1 oz. (30 ml/2 tbsp.) cognac
1 oz. (30 ml/2 tbsp.) gomme syrup
1 egg
6 oz. (180 ml/12 tbsp.) hot milk
grated nutmeg to garnish

Shake the rum, cognac, gomme syrup, and egg, then strain into a highball glass. Stir in the hot milk, sprinkle with the nutmeg, and serve.

Hot Pants

2 oz. (60 ml/4 tbsp.) tequila
1 oz. (30 ml/2 tbsp.) peppermint schnapps
½ oz. (15 ml/1 tbsp.) grapefruit juice

Shake the ingredients, then pour into a salt-rimmed old-fashioned glass and serve.

Hot Toddy

1 lemon wheel
6 cloves
1 oz. (30 ml/2 tbsp.) Scotch whisky
1 oz. (30 ml/2 tbsp.) fresh lemon juice
1 tsp. brown sugar
dash orgeat syrup
1 cinnamon stick
boiling water

Stud the lemon wheel with the cloves and put in a heatproof goblet. Add the rest of the ingredients, then fill up with boiling water. Stir with the cinnamon stick and serve.

Hot Buttered Rum

1 tsp. brown sugar
boiling water
1 tsp. butter
2 oz. (60 ml/4 tbsp.) dark rum
grated nutmeg to garnish

Put the brown sugar in a heatproof glass and fill to two-thirds full with boiling water. Stir in the butter and rum, then sprinkle with the nutmeg and serve.

Hurricane

1 oz. (30 ml/2 tbsp.) white rum
1 oz. (30 ml/2 tbsp.) dark rum
⅔ oz. (20 ml/1⅓ tbsp.) triple sec
juice of 1 lime
⅔ oz. (20 ml/1⅓ tbsp.) gomme syrup
⅓ oz (10 ml/⅔ tbsp.) grenadine
3 oz. (90 ml/6 tbsp.) fresh orange juice
3 oz. (90 ml/6 tbsp.) pineapple juice

Shake the ingredients, then strain into an ice-filled highball glass and serve.

Hurricane (alt)

1 oz. (30 ml/2 tbsp.) dark rum
1 oz. (30 ml/2 tbsp.) white rum
½ oz. (15 ml/1 tbsp.) grenadine
2 dashes fresh lime juice

Shake the ingredients, then strain into a martini glass and serve.

IBF

½ oz. (15 ml/1 tbsp.) cognac
½ oz. (15 ml/1 tbsp.) orange curaçao
½ oz. (15 ml/1 tbsp.) Madeira
chilled champagne

Pour the cognac, curaçao, and Madeira into a champagne flute. Fill with champagne and serve.

Iceberg

2 oz. (60 ml/4 tbsp.) vodka
dash Pernod

Stir the vodka and Pernod in a mixing glass, then pour into an ice-filled old-fashioned glass and serve.

Imagine!

2 oz. (60 ml/4 tbsp.) vodka
2 oz. (60 ml/4 tbsp.) clear apple juice
pulp of one passion fruit
ginger ale

Scoop out the passion fruit pulp and put it into a shaker with crushed ice. Add the vodka and apple juice. Shake. Strain into an ice-filled highball glass. Fill with ginger ale, stir, and serve.

Imperial

1 oz. (30 ml/2 tbsp.) gin
1 oz. (30 ml/2 tbsp.) dry vermouth
dash maraschino liqueur
dash Angostura bitters

Shake the ingredients, then strain into a martini glass and serve.

Indian Summer

2 oz. (60 ml/4 tbsp.) apple schnapps
6 oz. (180 ml/12 tbsp.) hot apple cider
1 tsp. ground cinnamon to garnish
Pour the schnapps and cider into an old-fashioned glass rimmed with ground cinnamon, stir, and serve.

Irish Coffee

1 oz. (30 ml/2 tbsp.) Irish whiskey
6 oz. (180 ml/12 tbsp.) hot black coffee
2 tsp. raw sugar
heavy (double) cream
Pour the whiskey and black coffee into a liqueur coffee glass, then add the sugar. Float the cream on top and serve.

Irish Nut

1 oz. (30 ml/2 tbsp.) Irish whiskey
1 oz. (30 ml/2 tbsp.) Bailey's
1 oz. (30 ml/2 tbsp.) frangelico
Pour the ingredients into an old-fashioned glass, stir, and serve.

Iron Lady

1 oz. (30 ml/2 tbsp.) noix de coco
1 oz. (30 ml/2 tbsp.) white crème de cacao
1 oz. (30 ml/2 tbsp.) crème de cassis
2 oz. (60 ml/4 tbsp.) heavy (double) cream
Shake the ingredients, then strain into a highball glass and serve.

Italian Coffee

1 oz. (30 ml/2 tbsp.) Strega
6 oz. (180 ml/12 tbsp.) hot black coffee
2 tsp. raw sugar
heavy (double) cream

Pour the Strega and black coffee into a liqueur coffee glass, then add the sugar. Float the cream on top and serve.

Itza Paramount

1 oz. (30 ml/2 tbsp.) gin
1 oz. (30 ml/2 tbsp.) Drambuie
1 oz. (30 ml/2 tbsp.) Cointreau

Stir the gin, Drambuie, and Cointreau in a mixing glass, then strain into a martini glass and serve.

Jack Rabbit

2 oz. (60 ml/4 tbsp.) applejack or calvados
dash fresh lemon juice
dash fresh orange juice
dash gomme syrup

Shake the ingredients, then strain into a martini glass and serve.

Jack Zeller

1 oz. (30 ml/2 tbsp.) Old Tom gin
1 oz. (30 ml/2 tbsp.) Dubonnet

Stir the gin and Dubonnet in a mixing glass, then strain into a martini glass and serve.

Jacuzzi

1 oz. (30 ml/2 tbsp.) gin
⅔ oz. (20 ml/1⅓ tbsp.) peach schnapps
1 oz. (30 ml/2 tbsp.) fresh orange juice
champagne
Shake the ingredients, except the champagne, and strain into a champagne flute. Fill with champagne. Stir and serve.

Jade Lady

1 oz. (30 ml/2 tbsp.) gin
1 oz. (30 ml/2 tbsp.) blue curaçao
1 oz. (30 ml/2 tbsp.) advocaat
1⅓ oz. (40 ml/2⅔ tbsp.) fresh orange juice
Shake the ingredients, then strain into a cocktail glass and serve.

James Bond

1 oz. (30 ml/2 tbsp.) vodka
1 sugar cube
3 dashes Angostura bitters
chilled champagne
Place the sugar cube in a champagne flute and soak in the bitters, then pour on the vodka. Fill with champagne and serve.

Japanese Garden (Hidetsugu Ueno)

1½ oz (45 ml/3 tbsp.) Hakushu 12YO whisky
¾ oz (22 ml/1½ tbsp.) Midori
½ oz (15 ml/1 tbsp.) Hermes Green Tea liqueur
Stir and strain over ice in a rocks glass.

James
Bond

121

Jocose Julep

2½ oz. (75 ml/5 tbsp.) bourbon
½ oz. (15 ml/1 tbsp.) green crème de menthe
1 oz. (30 ml/2 tbsp.) gomme syrup
1 oz. (30 ml/2 tbsp.) fresh lime juice
8–10 fresh mint leaves
sprig of mint to garnish
**Blend the ingredients until frozen, then pour into a large goblet.
Garnish with the mint and serve.**

Joe Collins

2 oz. (60 ml/4 tbsp.) vodka
1 oz. (30 ml/2 tbsp.) lemon juice
1 tsp. superfine (caster) sugar
dash Angostura (optional)
soda
**Place the first three ingredients in a highball glass half-filled with ice
and stir. Fill up with soda. Stir gently and serve.**

Joe Fizz

2 oz. (60 ml/4 tbsp.) vodka
1 oz. (30 ml/2 tbsp.) lemon juice
1 tsp. superfine (caster) sugar
dash Angostura (optional)
soda
**Shake the ingredients, then strain into a highball glass, fill up with
soda, stir, and serve.**

Joe Sour (see Pisco Sour, p. 168)

2 oz. (60 ml/4 tbsp.) vodka
¾ oz. (22 ml/1½ tbsp.) lemon juice
½ tsp. superfine (caster) sugar
Shake the ingredients, then strain into a cocktail glass and serve.

Jumping Jelly Bean

1 oz. (30 ml/2 tbsp.) tequila
1 oz. (30 ml/2 tbsp.) Grand Marnier
1 oz. (30 ml/2 tbsp.) fresh lemon juice
chilled champagne
Shake the tequila, Grand Marnier, and lemon juice, then strain into a martini glass. Fill with champagne and serve.

Juniper Royale

1 oz. (30 ml/2 tbsp.) gin
½ oz. (15 ml/1 tbsp.) fresh orange juice
½ oz. (15 ml/1 tbsp.) cranberry juice
dash grenadine
champagne
Shake the ingredients, except the champagne, then strain into a champagne flute. Fill with champagne. Stir and serve.

Kahlua Cocktail

1 oz. (30 ml/2 tbsp.) Kahlua
1 oz. (30 ml/2 tbsp.) brandy
Pour the Kahlua and brandy into an old-fashioned glass, stir, and serve.

Kaiser

1 oz. (30 ml/2 tbsp.) gin
1 oz. (30 ml/2 tbsp.) Kummel
½ oz. (15 ml/1 tbsp.) dry vermouth
Stir the ingredients, then strain into a martini glass and serve.

Kamikaze

1 oz. (30 ml/2 tbsp.) vodka
1 oz. (30 ml/2 tbsp.) fresh lime juice
1 oz. (30 ml/2 tbsp.) triple sec
Shake the ingredients, then strain into a shot glass and serve.

Kentucky Sunset

2 oz. (60 ml/4 tbsp.) bourbon
½ oz. (15 ml/1 tbsp.) Strega
½ oz. (15 ml/1 tbsp.) anisette
twist of lemon to garnish
Stir the ingredients in a mixing glass, then strain into a martini glass.
Serve garnished with the lemon twist.

Kir Royale

½ oz. (15 ml/1 tbsp.) crème de cassis
champagne
Pour the crème de cassis in a champagne flute, then fill with
champagne and serve.

Kiwi

2 oz. (60 ml/4 tbsp.) gin
½ oz. (15 ml/1 tbsp.) triple sec
1 oz. (30 ml/2 tbsp.) kiwifruit purée
dash gomme syrup
Shake the ingredients, then strain into an old-fashioned glass with
crushed ice and serve.

Knee-breaker

1 oz. (30 ml/2 tbsp.) Cointreau
1 oz. (30 ml/2 tbsp.) Parfait Amour
½ oz. (15 ml/1 tbsp.) cherry brandy
½ oz. (15 ml/1 tbsp.) frangelico
dash grenadine
Shake the ingredients, then strain into a martini glass and serve.

Knickerbocker

2 oz. (60 ml/4 tbsp.) gin
1 oz. (30 ml/2 tbsp.) dry vermouth
2 dashes sweet vermouth
twist of lemon to garnish

Stir the ingredients in a mixing glass, then strain into a martini glass and serve with the lemon twist.

Knickerbocker Knocker!

2 oz. (60 ml/4 tbsp.) white rum
½ oz. (15 ml/1 tbsp.) crème de framboise
½ oz. (15 ml/1 tbsp.) orange curaçao
dash fresh lemon juice
pineapple wedge to garnish

Shake the ingredients, then strain into a cocktail glass. Add the wedge of pineapple and serve.

Knickerbocker Special

2 oz. (60 ml/4 tbsp.) white rum
½ oz. (15 ml/1 tbsp.) triple sec
dash fresh orange juice
dash fresh lemon juice
dash raspberry syrup

Shake the ingredients, then strain into a martini glass and serve.

Kurrant Affair

1 oz. (30 ml/2 tbsp.) blackcurrant vodka
1 oz. (30 ml/2 tbsp.) lemon vodka
4 oz. (120 ml/8 tbsp.) apple juice

Shake the ingredients, then strain into an ice-filled highball glass and serve.

L'Amour

2 oz. (60 ml/4 tbsp.) gin
dash cherry brandy
dash grenadine
dash fresh lemon juice
2 sprigs mint

Shake the ingredients, including the mint. Strain into a cocktail glass and serve.

La Bomba

1 oz. (30 ml/2 tbsp.) gold tequila
⅔ oz. (20 ml/1⅓ tbsp.) Cointreau
⅔ oz. (20 ml/1⅓ tbsp.) pineapple juice
⅔ oz. (20 ml/1⅓ tbsp.) fresh orange juice
2 dashes grenadine

Shake the ingredients, then strain into a cocktail glass with a salted rim. Add the grenadine and serve.

La Conga

2 oz. (60 ml/4 tbsp.) silver tequila
2 tsp. pineapple juice
3 dashes Angostura bitters
club soda
lemon slice to garnish

Pour the ingredients, except the soda, into an ice-filled old-fashioned glass. Stir. Fill with soda. Stir. Add the lemon slice and serve.

La Dolce Vita

1 oz. (30 ml/2 tbsp.) vodka
5 seedless grapes
1 tsp. honey
dry sparkling wine (prosecco)

Muddle the grapes in a shaker. Add the vodka and honey and shake. Strain into a champagne flute. Fill with prosecco and serve.

La Floridita

2 oz. (60 ml/4 tbsp.) Havana white rum
dash maraschino liqueur
juice of 1 lime
dash gomme syrup
lime wedge to garnish

Shake the ingredients with crushed ice, then strain into a cocktail glass filled with dry crushed ice. Add a lime wedge and serve with a straw.

Lady Finger

1 oz. (30 ml/2 tbsp.) gin
1 oz. (30 ml/2 tbsp.) cherry brandy
1 oz. (30 ml/2 tbsp.) kirsch

Shake the ingredients, then strain into a martini glass and serve.

Laser Beam

1 oz. (30 ml/2 tbsp.) tequila
1 oz. (30 ml/2 tbsp.) Jack Daniels
1 oz. (30 ml/2 tbsp.) amaretto
½ oz. (15 ml/1 tbsp.) triple sec

Shake the ingredients, then strain into an old-fashioned glass and serve.

Last Gentleman Standing (Metinee Kongsrivilai)

1½ oz (45 ml/3 tbsp.) Speyside malt
½ oz (15 ml/1 tbsp.) Noval Tawny Port
¼ oz (8 ml/½ tbsp.) Green Chartreuse
⅛ oz (5 ml/1 tsp.) morello cherry-infused Maraschino
orange zest and cherry to garnish

Stir and strain into a cocktail glass. Garnish with orange twist (discard) and a cherry.

Legend

1 oz. (30 ml/2 tbsp.) Midori
1 oz. (30 ml/2 tbsp.) Kahlua
1 oz. (30 ml/2 tbsp.) frangelico
Pour the ingredients into an old-fashioned glass, stir, and serve.

Lemon Drop

1 lemon wedge
1 tsp. sugar
1 oz. (30 ml/2 tbsp.) vodka
Dip the lemon wedge in the sugar and pour the vodka into a shot glass.
Drink the vodka first, then suck the lemon.

Liberty Bell

2 oz. (60 ml/4 tbsp.) bourbon
1 oz. (30 ml/2 tbsp.) peach schnapps
dash apricot brandy
dash Campari
Stir the ingredients in a mixing glass, then strain into a martini glass
and serve.

Lime Life-Saver (nonalcoholic) (Serves 2)

2 fresh limes
6 medium carrots
knob of ginger
2 fresh apples
Cut the limes in half and juice. Juice the carrots. Peel the ginger and juice.
Juice the apples. Stir, then pour equally into two tumblers and serve.

Limey

1 oz. (30 ml/2 tbsp.) lemon vodka
1 oz. (30 ml/2 tbsp.) orange liqueur
1 oz. (30 ml/2 tbsp.) fresh lime juice
Shake the ingredients, then strain into a cocktail glass and serve.

Limp Dick

1 oz. (30 ml/2 tbsp.) Southern Comfort
1 oz. (30 ml/2 tbsp.) Grand Marnier
½ oz. (15 ml/1 tbsp.) amaretto
½ oz. (15 ml/1 tbsp.) white crème de menthe
Stir the ingredients in a glass, then strain into a cocktail glass and serve.

London Cocktail

2 oz. (60 ml/4 tbsp.) London dry gin
dash maraschino liqueur
2 dashes orange bitters
dash gomme syrup
Shake the ingredients, then strain into a cocktail glass and serve.

London Special

2 dashes Angostura bitters
1 twist of orange
chilled champagne
Put the bitters and twist into a flute. Fill with champagne and serve.

Long Island Iced Tea

½ oz. (15 ml/1 tbsp.) light rum
½ oz. (15 ml/1 tbsp.) vodka
½ oz. (15 ml/1 tbsp.) gin
½ oz. (15 ml/1 tbsp.) tequila
½ oz. (15 ml/1 tbsp.) triple sec
juice of 1 lime
cola
Squeeze the lime into a highball, then add ice cubes and the spirits. Stir and fill up with cola. Serve with straws.

Long Island
Iced Tea

129

Luxury

3 oz. (90 ml/6 tbsp.) cognac
chilled champagne
3 dashes Angostura bitters
Pour the cognac and bitters into a champagne flute, stir, fill with champagne. Stir gently, then serve.

Lychee Martini (see Martini, p. 138)

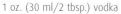

1 oz. (30 ml/2 tbsp.) vodka
⅓ oz. (10 ml/⅔ tbsp.) lychee liqueur
⅓ oz. (10 ml/⅔ tbsp.) crème de banane
1 oz. (30 ml/2 tbsp.) pineapple juice
Shake the ingredients, then strain into a martini glass and serve.

Made in Cuba (Tom Walker)

2 oz (60 ml/4 tbsp.) Bacardi Superior
1 oz (30 ml/2 tbsp.) lime juice
½ oz (15 ml/1 tbsp.) sugar syrup
handful mint leaves
3 slices cucumber
absinthe rinse
soda
cucumber to garnish
Shake ingredients, double-strain into absinthe-rinsed cocktail glass and top with a splash of soda. Garnish with cucumber slice.

Madras

1½ oz. (45 ml/3 tbsp.) vodka
4 oz. (120 ml/8 tbsp.) cranberry juice
1 oz. (30 ml/2 tbsp.) orange juice
1 wedge of lime
Pour the liquid ingredients into a highball glass over ice. Add the lime wedge and serve.

Madroska

2 oz. (60 ml/4 tbsp.) vodka
3 oz. (90 ml/6 tbsp.) apple juice
2 oz. (60 ml/4 tbsp.) cranberry juice
1 oz. (30 ml/2 tbsp.) fresh orange juice
Pour the ingredients into an ice-filled highball, stir and serve.

Mai Tai No. 1

1 oz. (30 ml/2 tbsp.) white rum
½ oz. (15 ml/1 tbsp.) Cointreau
¼ oz. (8 ml/½ tbsp.) Rose's Lime Cordial
1½ oz. (45 ml/3 tbsp.) orange juice
1½ oz. (45 ml/3 tbsp.) unsweetened
   pineapple juice
splash grenadine
½ oz. (15 ml/1 tbsp.) gold rum
wedge of pineapple to garnish
Shake the ingredients, strain into a high-ball half-filled with ice. Add the grena-dine and gold rum. Garnish and serve.

Mai Tai
No. 1

Mai Tai No. 2

2 oz. (60 ml/4 tbsp.) gold rum
1 oz. (30 ml/2 tbsp.) curaçao
1½ oz. (45 ml/3 tbsp.) Rose's Lime Cordial
½ oz. (15 ml/1 tbsp.) orgeat syrup
1 tsp. gomme syrup
splash grenadine
½ oz. (15 ml/1 tbsp.) overproof rum
wedge of pineapple
wedge of lime to garnish
Shake the ingredients, then strain into a highball glass half-filled with ice. Add the grenadine and overproof rum. Stir. Garnish with the pineapple and lime wedges and serve.

Maiden's Prayer

1 oz. (30 ml/2 tbsp.) gin
½ oz. (15 ml/1 tbsp.) Cointreau
juice of half an orange
juice of half a lemon
Shake the ingredients, then strain into a cocktail glass and serve.

Maiden's Wish

1 oz. (30 ml/2 tbsp.) gin
1 oz. (30 ml/2 tbsp.) Kina Lillet
1 oz. (30 ml/2 tbsp.) calvados
Stir the ingredients in a mixing glass, then strain into a martini glass and serve.

Main Chance

1 oz. (30 ml/2 tbsp.) gin
1 oz. (30 ml/2 tbsp.) triple sec
1 oz. (30 ml/2 tbsp.) fresh grapefruit juice
twist of lime to garnish
Shake the ingredients, then strain into a cocktail glass. Add the twist and serve.

Major Bailey

2 oz. (60 ml/4 tbsp.) gin
dash fresh lime juice
dash fresh lemon juice
1 tsp. granulated sugar
8–10 fresh mint leaves
Muddle the lime, juices, sugar, and mint in an old-fashioned glass. Add ice and stir in the gin until the glass is frosted. Serve.

Mandarine Martini
(see Martini, p. 138)

1½ oz. (45 ml/3 tbsp.) gin
½ oz. (15 ml/1 tbsp.) vodka
splash Mandarine Napoleon
dash Cointreau
twist of mandarin to garnish
**Pour the liqueurs in the shaker. Coat and
discard surplus. Shake the spirits. Strain into
a martini glass. Add the twist and serve.**

Mandarine
Martini

Mango Masher (nonalcoholic)

half a ripe mango
fresh juice of one orange
fresh juice of one lime
handful fresh raspberries
ice cubes
**Take the seeds out of the mango and scoop out the flesh. Cut the citrus
fruit in half and juice them. Put it all in the blender with ice cubes.
Blend until smooth. Pour into a large tumbler and serve.**

Manhattan (see pp. 134–35)

Manhattan (dry) (see Manhattan, pp. 134-35)

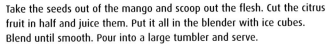

2oz. (60 ml/ 4 tbsp) Bourbon or Rye
1 oz. (30 ml/2 tbsp.) dry vermouth
dash Angostura bitters
twist of lemon to garnish
**Half-fill a mixing glass with ice cubes and add the ingredients. Stir, then
strain into a martini glass. Garnish with the lemon and serve.**

Manhattan

When it comes to classic aperitifs with a powerful taste, we'll take Manhattan, thanks all the same.

While its name is a clear indication of where this classic whiskey cocktail was created, no-one knows who invented the Manhattan. The idea that it was Winston Churchill's mother has been debunked. What is apparent is that it predates the Dry Martini. At its heart beats the essential ingredients of nineteenth-century cocktails: sweet vermouth and bitters.

There is almost as much debate over Manhattans as there is over dry Martinis, but while the cocktail has undoubtedly become drier over the years, it should not be a dry drink. The magnificence of the Manhattan lies in the way the bitters and sweetness join in an unlikely alliance to round off the whiskey's more abrasive edges. The original recipe was probably made with rye whiskey—a style which is re-establishing itself—but bourbon is commonly used. The light style of Canadian whisky has to be carefully balanced.

But which brand? That's a matter of personal preference. Speaking personally, I'd choose Wild Turkey when I need a weighty belt of liquor after a tough day, or Maker's Mark for sophisticated sipping.

Manhattan

2 oz. rye whiskey
1 oz. sweet vermouth
3 dashes Angostura
drop of maraschino juice
maraschino cherry
Stir the ingredients in a mixing glass, then strain into cocktail glass. Drop the cherry in the glass and serve.

Margarita

This was the first tequila cocktail and there is no other with its ability to stimulate the appetite.

The Margarita has been rather overlooked in the brave new world of the postmodern cocktail. This is partly because it was abused by unfeeling and uncaring bartenders during the 1970s and 1980s, who turned it from a lip-smacking aperitif that cleared your head and made your eyes gleam, into a glorified slush puppy.

The cocktail had a refined history before the madmen with their blenders got hold of it. Legend recounts that it was invented by Margaret Sames, an American socialite of the 1940s, who used to serve it at parties in Acapulco. A similar drink was already popular in Mexico before Margaret's husband graciously attached her name to it.

The first Margarita was a mix of tequila, Cointreau, and lime juice. The best Margaritas still follow this basic recipe. Just like Daiquiris, though, as soon as the blenders began to be wielded with reckless abandon, so fruit began to be whizzed into the mix. Strawberry is a common variant, although the best I ever tasted was a blueberry one. Experiment, but don't use too much ice in the blender!

Margarita

2 oz. (60 ml/4 tbsp.) gold tequila
1 oz. (30 ml/2 tbsp.) Cointreau or
    triple sec
juice of half a lime
juice of half a lemon
**Shake the ingredients, then strain
into a salt-rimmed margarita glass
and serve.**

Martini (Dry)

James Bond is entirely responsible for the myth that a Martini should be shaken, not stirred.

Gin is the original cocktail spirit and in the late nineteenth century gave the world its most famous cocktail—the dry Martini. It may have started life as a dry version of the Martinez, which itself was a variation of the Gin Cocktail. Both were sweet drinks. It could even, as suggested by Anistatia Miller and Jared Brown, have taken its name from Martini Dry Vermouth.

The Martini began as an equal mix between gin and vermouth; now the ratio is anywhere from 4:1 to 25:1. The aim is to get a drink that has the illusion of purity, but has complexity. Why is mixing one so difficult? Because simplicity is difficult thing to achieve. Atomizer sprays, vermouth-flavored ice cubes, vermouth-soaked olives—all have been used to try to reach perfection.

All the ingredients must be chilled—from glasses to gin. Only use the best-quality gin. Be single minded. You are the only person who can make the perfect example.

Martini (Dry)

3 oz. (90 ml/6 tbsp.) chilled dry gin
1 tsp. Noilly Prat
olive or twist of lemon to garnish
There is no more dangerous recipe to write than this—and aficionados should be prepared to be annoyed.

Place the vermouth in shaker with ice. Shake and strain away the excess. Add the gin. Stir and strain into a pre-chilled cocktail glass. Add the lemon twist. Serve. You can vary the amount of vermouth to taste, but the principle remains the same.

Manhattan (Perfect) (see Manhattan, p. 134)

2oz. (60 ml/2 tbsp) Bourbon or Rye
½ oz. (15 ml/1 tbsp) dry vermouth
½ oz. (15 ml/1 tbsp) sweet vermouth
dash Angostura bitters
Half-fill a mixing glass with ice cubes and add the ingredients. Stir, then strain into a martini glass. Garnish with the cherry and serve.

Manhattan (Sweet) (see Manhattan, p. 134)

2 oz. (60 ml/4 tbsp.) bourbon or rye
1 oz. (30 ml/2 tbsp.) sweet vermouth
dash Angostura bitters
maraschino cherry to garnish
Half-fill a mixing glass with ice cubes and pour in all the ingredients. Stir, then strain into a martini glass. Garnish with the cherry and serve.

Margarita (see pp. 136–37)

Martini (Dry) (see pp. 138–39)

Martini Melon (see Martini, pp. 138-39)

1⅔ oz. (50 ml/3⅓ tbsp.) vodka
a quarter of a slice of watermelon
dash fresh lemon juice
Muddle the melon in a shaker. Add ice and the vodka. Shake and strain into a cocktail glass and serve.

Martini Thyme

3 oz. (90 ml/6 tbsp.) gin
¾ oz. (22 ml/1½ tbsp.) Green Chartreuse
1 sprig of thyme to garnish
Stir the gin and Chartreuse in a mixing glass. Strain into a martini glass, garnish with the thyme, and serve.

Mary Pickford

1½ oz. (45 ml/3 tbsp.) white rum
dash maraschino liqueur
1½ oz. (45 ml/3 tbsp.)
unsweetened
    pineapple juice dash
grenadinelime twist to garnish
**Shake the ingredients, then strain
into a cocktail glass. Add the twist and serve.**

Mary
Pickford

Matador

2 oz. (60 ml/4 tbsp.) gold tequila
⅔ oz. (20 ml/1⅓ tbsp.) triple sec
juice of 1 lime
5 oz. (150 ml/10 tbsp.) pineapple juice
lime wedge to garnish
**Shake the ingredients, then strain into
an ice-filled highball glass, garnish with a
lime wedge, and serve.**

Matador (alt)

2 oz. (60 ml/4 tbsp.) tequila
¼ oz. (8 ml/½ tbsp.) Cointreau
juice of half a lime
1 tsp. gomme syrup
1 chunk pineapple
**Shake the ingredients with crushed ice,
then strain into a highball glass with a
sugared rim and serve.**

Matador

141

Mayas Daiquiri (David Cordoba)

2 oz (60 ml/4 tbsp.) Bacardi 8YO
¾ oz (22 ml/1½ tbsp.) lime juice
¼ oz (8 ml/½ tbsp.) agave nectar
¼ avocado
pineapple leaf to garnish
Muddle avocado, add all ingredients, shake and double-strain into a cocktail glass. Garnish with pineapple leaf.

Melonball

2 oz. (60 ml/4 tbsp.) Midori melon liqueur
1 oz. (30 ml/2 tbsp.) vodka
pineapple juice
Half-fill a tall glass with ice. Pour in the Midori and vodka. Fill the glass with pineapple juice. Orange juice may also be used.

Melon Margarita (see Margarita, pp. 136-37)

1 oz. (30 ml/2 tbsp.) tequila
⅓ oz. (10 ml/⅔ tbsp.) Cointreau
⅓ oz. (10 ml/⅔ tbsp.) melon liqueur
juice of half a lime
few slices yellow melon, diced
Blend the ingredients. Add crushed ice. Blend, then pour into a margarita glass. Add a straw and serve.

Metropolitan

2 oz. (60 ml/4 tbsp.) blackcurrant vodka
⅔ oz. (20 ml/1⅓ tbsp.) Cointreau
1 oz. (30 ml/2 tbsp.) cranberry juice
dash fresh lime juice
Shake the ingredients, then strain into a cocktail glass and serve.

Metropolitan (alt)

2 oz. (60 ml/4 tbsp.) Absolut Kurant
½ oz. (15 ml/1 tbsp.) Rose's Lime Cordial
½ oz. (15 ml/1 tbsp.) lime juice
1 oz. (30 ml/2 tbsp.) cranberry juice
lime wedge to garnish
Shake the ingredients, then strain into a cocktail glass, garnish with the wedge of lime, and serve.

Mexican Coffee

1 oz. (30 ml/2 tbsp.) Kahlua
6 oz. (180 ml/12 tbsp.) hot black coffee
2 tsp. raw sugar
heavy (double) cream
Pour the Kahlua and black coffee into a liqueur coffee glass, then add the sugar. Float the cream on top and serve.

Mexican Hat

1 oz. (30 ml/2 tbsp.) tequila
1 oz. (30 ml/2 tbsp.) crème de cassis
1 oz. (30 ml/2 tbsp.) champagne
Fill a highball glass three-quarters full with crushed ice, then pour on the tequila, crème de cassis, and lastly, the champagne. Stir carefully and serve.

Mexican Madras

1 oz. (30 ml/2 tbsp.) gold tequila
3 oz. (90 ml/6 tbsp.) cranberry juice
⅔ oz. (20 ml/1⅓ tbsp.) fresh orange juice
dash fresh lime juice
slice of orange to garnish
Shake the ingredients, then strain into an old-fashioned glass filled with ice cubes. Garnish with the slice of orange and serve.

Mexican Mule

2 oz. (60 ml/4 tbsp.) gold tequila
juice of 1 lime
1 tsp. gomme syrup
ginger ale
Shake the ingredients, then strain into an ice-filled highball. Fill up with ginger ale and serve.

Mexican Runner

1 oz. (30 ml/2 tbsp.) gold tequila
1 oz. (30 ml/2 tbsp.) rum
⅔ oz. (20 ml/1⅓ tbsp.) banana syrup
⅔ oz. (20 ml/1⅓ tbsp.) blackberry syrup
juice of 1 lime
6 strawberries
Blend the ingredients with crushed ice. Pour into a tumbler and serve.

Mexicana

1½ oz. (45 ml/3 tbsp.) tequila
1½ oz. (45 ml/3 tbsp.) unsweetened pineapple juice
¼ oz. (8 ml/½ tbsp.) fresh lime juice
dash grenadine
Shake the ingredients, then strain into an ice-filled highball glass. Serve with straws.

Mexicana

Mickey

1 oz. (30 ml/2 tbsp.) dark rum
½ oz. (15 ml/1 tbsp.) Cointreau
½ oz. (15 ml/1 tbsp.) bourbon
dash grenadine
Shake the ingredients, then strain into a martini glass and serve.

Midnight Snowstorm

1 oz. (30 ml/2 tbsp.) white crème de menthe
7 oz. (200 ml/14 tbsp.) hot chocolate
1 oz. (30 ml/2 tbsp.) heavy (double) cream
**Pour the crème de menthe and hot chocolate into a highball glass.
Float the cream on top and serve.**

Mikado

1 oz. (30 ml/2 tbsp.) cognac
½ oz. (15 ml/1 tbsp.) Cointreau
½ oz. (15 ml/1 tbsp.) crème de Noyaux
dash grenadine
**Stir the ingredients, then strain into an ice-filled old-fashioned glass
and serve.**

Mimosa

2 oz. (60 ml/4 tbsp.) fresh orange juice
2 dashes Grand Marnier
champagne
**Fill a champagne flute to a quarter-full with orange juice. Add the Grand
Marnier. Stir. Fill with champagne, stir carefully, and serve.**

Mint Daiquiri (see Daiquiri, p. 92)

2 oz. white rum
½ oz. Cointreau
handful of mint leaves
juice of half a lime
1 tsp. superfine (caster) sugar
**Blend the ingredients with crushed ice, then strain into a cocktail glass
and serve.**

Mint Julep No. 1 (see pp. 146–47)

Mint Julep No. 1

"A dram of spirituous liquor that has mint in it, taken by Virginians of a morning."

If Manhattans spark debate, then Mint Juleps can incite war. To crush or not to crush the mint, the quality of the ice, the receptacle, which bourbon to use. All you need are fresh mint, ice, gomme syrup, and bourbon.

If you are one of those Julepians who doesn't believe in bruising the leaves, try gently squeezing the leaves instead or bruise them gently with a muddler in the bottom of the glass. How much mint to use for garnish? Six sprigs are about right. Gary Regan, in his Book of Bourbon, advises cutting the mint at the last minute and allowing some flavor to bleed from the stems into the drink.

A Mint Julep cools you down and freshens you up, making the world a beautiful place. The danger is over-indulgence. Too many, and what should be a soothing Southern experience is turned into something bitter and twisted. The genteel air slips, revealing the decaying, distorted gothic madness that fuels Tennessee Williams, William Faulkner, and the songs of Nick Cave. Then again, some people like that.

Mint Julep No. 1

3 oz. (90 ml/6 tbsp.) bourbon
1 oz. (30 ml/2 tbsp.) simple syrup
3 cups finely crushed ice
6 sprigs of mint

Fill a highball glass two-thirds full with crushed ice. Add the bourbon and syrup. Stir. Pack the glass with more ice so it domes over the top. Garnish with the mint and insert straws. Let stand until a thin layer forms on the glass, then serve.

Mint Julep No. 2 (see Mint Julep, p. 146)

3 oz. (90 ml/6 tbsp.) bourbon
1 oz. (30 ml/2 tbsp.) simple syrup
handful of mint leaves
3 cups freshly finely crushed ice

Cover the mint leaves with bourbon for 15 minutes. Take the leaves out and put in a muslin cloth, then wring over the bourbon. Put the fresh bourbon and the syrup in another bowl. Add the mint "stock" to taste. Fill a glass with crushed ice so it domes over the top. Add the bourbon/mint/syrup mixture. Add straws and a sprig of mint as a garnish, then serve.

Mint Julep
No. 2

Mint Julep (alt)

1 oz. (30 ml/2 tbsp.) peach brandy
1 oz. (30 ml/2 tbsp.) brandy
12 sprigs of fresh mint
1 tsp. granulated sugar
chunk of pineapple

Put the mint in an old-fashioned glass with the sugar and brandies. Fill the glass with crushed ice and rub the pineapple around the rim.

Misty

1 oz. (30 ml/2 tbsp.) vodka
1 oz. (30 ml/2 tbsp.) Cointreau
1 oz. (30 ml/2 tbsp.) apricot brandy
dash crème de banane

Stir the ingredients in a mixing glass, then strain into a martini glass and serve.

Mofuco

2 oz. (60 ml/4 tbsp.) white rum
dash Angostura bitters
½ oz. (15 ml/1 tbsp.)
   gomme syrup
1 egg
1 slice lemon peel
Shake the ingredients, then strain into a martini glass and serve.

Mojito

2 oz. (60 ml/4 tbsp.) white rum
1 tsp. gomme syrup
half a lime
fresh mint leaves
soda water
sprig of mint
In a highball glass, muddle the mint leaves and syrup. Squeeze lime juice into the glass and add the lime half. Add the rum, ice, and stir. Add soda water, stir briefly, garnish with the mint, and serve.

Mojito

Molotov Cocktail

3 oz. (90 ml/6 tbsp.) Finlandia vodka
½ oz. (15 ml/1 tbsp.) Black Bush
½ oz. (15 ml/1 tbsp.) Irish Mist
Shake the ingredients, then strain into a cocktail glass and serve.

Molotov
Cocktail

Monkey Gland

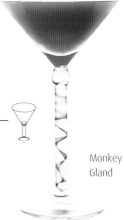

2 oz. (60 ml/4 tbsp.) gin
1 oz. (30 ml/2 tbsp.) Benedictine
1 oz. (30 ml/2 tbsp.) grenadine
2 oz. (60 ml/4 tbsp.) fresh orange juice
**Shake the ingredients, then strain into a
martini glass and serve.**

Monkey Gland (alt)

2 oz. (60 ml/4 tbsp.) gin
2 oz. (60 ml/4 tbsp.) fresh orange juice
dash absinthe or Pernod
dash grenadine
**Shake the ingredients, then strain into a
cocktail glass and serve.**

Monkey
Gland

Monte Carlo Highball

2 oz. (60 ml/4 tbsp.) gin
½ oz. (15 ml/1 tbsp.) white crème de menthe
1 oz. (30 ml/2 tbsp.) fresh lemon juice
champagne
**Shake the gin, crème de menthe, and lemon juice, then strain into a
highball glass. Fill up with the champagne and serve.**

Monte Cristo

1 oz. (30 ml/2 tbsp.) Kahlua
1 oz. (30 ml/2 tbsp.) Grand Marnier
6 oz. (180 ml/12 tbsp.) hot black coffee
1 oz. (30 ml/2 tbsp.) heavy (double) cream
**Pour the Kahlua, Grand Marnier, and coffee into a heatproof mug. Float
the cream on top and serve.**

Moscow Mule (see pp. 152–53)

Mother's Milk

1 oz. (30 ml/2 tbsp.) vodka
½ oz. (15 ml/1 tbsp.) gin
½ oz. (15 ml/1 tbsp.) Tia Maria
½ oz. (15 ml/1 tbsp.) orgeat syrup
4 oz. (120 ml/8 tbsp.) milk
Shake the ingredients, then pour into an old-fashioned glass and serve.

Mudslide

2 oz. (60 ml/4 tbsp.) vodka
2 oz. (60 ml/4 tbsp.) Kahlua
2 oz. (60 ml/4 tbsp.) Bailey's Irish cream
Mix with crushed ice in a shaker. Serve in a chilled highball glass.

Mulled Wine

1 bottle claret
4 oz. (120 ml/8 tbsp.) port
rind of 1 lemon
rind of 1 orange
4 tbsp. sugar
10 cloves
2 whole cinnamon sticks
4 oz. (120 ml/8 tbsp.) boiling water
Heat the wine and port with all the other ingredients in a saucepan for a minimum of 15 minutes. Pour individual servings into heatproof glasses. Serve hot.

Moscow Mule

No two words conjure up a more amusing idea
than a plodding mule and an effervescent beer.

Back in the 1940s when America hadn't woken up to vodka, John
Martin of the drinks import company, Heublein, met in New York
with Jack Morgan, the owner of the Cock 'n' Bull restaurant in
Hollywood, California. Morgan had landed himself with a surplus
of ginger beer, which was proving difficult to shift.

Martin wanted to get rid of the equally slow-moving Smirnoff
vodka, for which he'd put his reputation on the line. Morgan and
Martin put their heads and their products together, added a splash
of lime juice, and created the Moscow Mule.

They then ordered 500 copper mugs engraved with a kicking mule
and marketed it to cocktail bars. On the backpack of the mule,
Smirnoff vodka's sales tripled between 1947 and 1950, and then
doubled again the year after. America would never be the same
again. And it's still alive and kickin' as a popular drink, despite the
canned and bottled varieties on offer.

Moscow Mule

2 oz. (60 ml/4 tbsp.) vodka
ginger beer
squeeze lime juice
wedge of lime to garnish
Pour the vodka over ice in a highball glass. Add the other ingredients. Stir, add the garnish, and serve.

Multiple Orgasm

1 oz. (30 ml/2 tbsp.) gold tequila
²⁄₃ oz. (20 ml/1⅓ tbsp.) amaretto
²⁄₃ oz. (20 ml/1⅓ tbsp.) coffee liqueur
²⁄₃ oz. (20 ml/1⅓ tbsp.) Irish cream liqueur
1 oz. (30 ml/2 tbsp.) heavy
   (double) cream
2 oz. (60 ml/4 tbsp.) milk
**Shake the ingredients, except the
tequila, strain into an ice-filled highball
glass. Float the tequila on top and serve.**

Naked Lady

1 oz. (30 ml/2 tbsp.) white rum
1 oz. (30 ml/2 tbsp.) apricot brandy
1 oz. (30 ml/2 tbsp.) fresh lemon juice
dash grenadine
1 egg white
**Shake the ingredients, then strain
into a martini glass and serve.**

Naked
Lady

Naked Lady (alt)

1½ oz. (45 ml/3 tbsp.) white rum
1½ oz. (45 ml/3 tbsp.) sweet vermouth
4 dashes apricot brandy
2 dashes grenadine
4 dashes lemon & lime juice
Shake the ingredients, then strain into a martini glass and serve.

Naked Martini (see Martini, p. 138)

2 oz. (60 ml/4 tbsp.) dry gin (at room temperature)
1 olive infused with vermouth
**Pour the gin directly into a martini glass, then add the olive.
Stir and serve.**

Napoleon

2 oz. (60 ml/4 tbsp.) gin
2 dashes orange curaçao
2 dashes Dubonnet
Stir all the ingredients, then strain into a martini glass and serve.

Negroni

1 oz. (30 ml/2 tbsp.) Campari
1 oz. (30 ml/2 tbsp.) sweet vermouth
slice of orange to garnish
splash of soda water (optional)
**Over ice, pour the Campari and sweet
vermouth into an old-fashioned
glass and stir. Add the soda, garnish
with the orange slice, and serve
with straws.**

Negroni
(alt)

Negroni (alt)

1½ oz. (45 ml/3 tbsp.) gin
1½ oz. (45 ml/3 tbsp.) Campari
1½ oz. (45 ml/3 tbsp.) sweet vermouth
soda water (optional)
slice of orange to garnish
**Shake the ingredients, then pour over
ice in a highball glass. Fill with soda,
add the garnish, and serve.**

Neopolitan

2 oz. (60 ml/4 tbsp.) Cointreau
1 oz. (30 ml/2 tbsp.) Grand Marnier
1 oz. (30 ml/2 tbsp.) white rum
Shake the ingredients, then strain into a martini glass and serve.

Nevada

2 oz. (60 ml/4 tbsp.) white rum
1 oz. (30 ml/2 tbsp.) grapefruit juice
juice of 1 lime

Shake the ingredients, then strain into a martini glass and serve.

New England Iced Tea

1 oz. (30 ml/2 tbsp.) vodka
1 oz. (30 ml/2 tbsp.) triple sec
1 oz. (30 ml/2 tbsp.) gold tequila
1 oz. (30 ml/2 tbsp.) light rum
1 oz. (30 ml/2 tbsp.) gin
1 oz. (30 ml/2 tbsp.) fresh lime juice
1 oz. (30 ml/2 tbsp.) gomme syrup
cranberry juice

Shake the ingredients, except the cranberry juice. Strain into an ice-filled highball glass. Fill up with cranberry juice and stir. Serve.

New Orleans Gin Fizz

2 oz. (60 ml/4 tbsp.) gin
1 oz. (30 ml/2 tbsp.) Cointreau
½ oz. (15 ml/1 tbsp.) kirsch
wedge of lemon
2 oz. (60 ml/4 tbsp.) light (single) cream
orange flower water
soda water

Coat the rim of a tall glass with sugar and half-fill it with ice. Add all the liquid ingredients except for the orange flower water which can be used either to coat the glass or as a float on top of the cocktail. Garnish with the lemon wedge.

Nineteen

2 oz. (60 ml/4 tbsp.) dry vermouth
½ oz. (15 ml/1 tbsp.) kirsch
½ oz. (15 ml/1 tbsp.) gin
2 dashes Angostura bitters
½ oz. (15 ml/1 tbsp.) gomme syrup
Shake the ingredients, then strain into a martini glass and serve.

North Pole

2 oz. (60 ml/4 tbsp.) gin
1 oz. (30 ml/2 tbsp.) maraschino liqueur
1 oz. (30 ml/2 tbsp.) fresh lemon juice
1 egg white
½ oz. (15 ml/1 tbsp.) heavy (double) cream
Shake the ingredients, except the cream, then strain into a martini glass. Float the cream on top and serve.

Nth Degree (Nate Dumas)

1 oz (30 ml/2 tbsp.) aged rhum agricole
1 oz (30 ml/2 tbsp.) bonded applejack
½ oz (15 ml/1 tbsp.) Green Chartreuse
¼ oz (8 ml/½ tbsp.) Demerara sugar syrup
2 dashes Whiskey Barrel Bitters
lemon and orange peel to garnish
Stir over ice, then strain into an ice-filled rocks glass. Garnish with lemon and orange twist.

Nuptial

2 oz. (60 ml/4 tbsp.) gin
1 oz. (30 ml/2 tbsp.) kirsch
dash Cointreau
dash fresh lemon juice
Shake the ingredients, then strain into a martini glass and serve.

Old-Fashioned

3 oz. (90 ml/6 tbsp.) bourbon
3 dashes Angostura bitters
1 sugar cube
ice cubes
slice of orange
maraschino cherry to garnish

**Put the bitters, sugar cube, and a dash of
the bourbon into an old-fashioned glass and
muddle. Add two ice cubes and 2 tablespoons
of the bourbon and stir. Squeeze some of the
juice from the orange slice into the glass,
then add two more ice cubes and 2 more
tablespoons of the bourbon and stir again.
Finally, add two more ice cubes and the
remaining bourbon. Garnish with the orange
slice and the cherry.**

Old- Fashioned

Old Vermouth

1 oz. (30 ml/2 tbsp.) Old Tom gin
1 oz. (30 ml/2 tbsp.) dry vermouth
½ oz. (15 ml/1 tbsp.) sweet vermouth
2 dashes Angostura bitters
slice of lemon to garnish
**Pour the ingredients into an old-fashioned glass and stir. Garnish with
the lemon slice and serve.**

Olympia

2 oz. (60 ml/4 tbsp.) white rum
½ oz. (15 ml/1 tbsp.) Cherry Heering
juice of 1 lime
Shake the ingredients, then strain into a martini glass and serve.

On a Wave

1 oz. (30 ml/2 tbsp.) gin
1 oz. (30 ml/2 tbsp.) light rum
⅔ oz. (20 ml/1⅓ tbsp.) blue curaçao
3 oz. (90 ml/6 tbsp.) pineapple juice
1 oz. (30 ml/2 tbsp.) fresh lime juice
2 dashes gomme syrup
pineapple wedge to garnish
Shake the ingredients, then strain into a colada glass filled with crushed ice. Garnish with a pineapple wedge and serve.

On the Beach (nonalcoholic)

¼ of a ripe yellow melon, diced
8 raspberries
3 oz. (90 ml/6 tbsp.) fresh orange juice
juice of half a lime
dash grenadine
lemon & lime soda
Blend ingredients for a few seconds, then add a scoop of ice. Blend. Pour into a tumbler and fill with lemon & lime soda. Stir and serve with a straw.

Onion Breath

2 oz. (60 ml/4 tbsp.) vodka
½ oz. (15 ml/1 tbsp.) vinegar from cocktail onions
1 drop Worcestershire sauce
½ oz. (15 ml/1 tbsp.) lemon juice
2 cocktail onions to garnish
Shake the ingredients, then strain into a martini glass. Garnish with the onions and serve.

Opal

1⅔ oz. (50 ml/3⅓ tbsp.) gin
⅔ oz. (20 ml/1⅓ tbsp.) Cointreau
1 oz. (30 ml/2 tbsp.) fresh orange juice
twist of orange to garnish
Shake the ingredients and strain into a cocktail glass. Add the twist of orange and serve.

Orange Blossom

2 oz. (60 ml/4 tbsp.) vodka
2 oz. (60 ml/4 tbsp.) orange juice
dash orange flower water
Shake the ingredients, then strain into a cocktail glass and serve.

Orange Blossom Special

1⅔ oz. (50 ml/3⅓ tbsp.) gin
⅔ oz. (20 ml/1⅓ tbsp.) Cointreau
⅔ oz. (20 ml/1⅓ tbsp.) lychee liqueur
⅓ oz. (10 ml/⅔ tbsp.) fresh lemon juice
Shake the ingredients, then strain into a cocktail glass and serve.

Orange Cadillac

1 oz. (30 ml/2 tbsp.) white crème de cacao
1 oz. (30 ml/2 tbsp.) Galliano
½ oz. (15 ml/1 tbsp.) Cointreau
½ oz. (15 ml/1 tbsp.) fresh orange juice
1 oz. (30 ml/2 tbsp.) heavy (double) cream
Shake the ingredients, then strain into a martini glass and serve.

Orange Caipirovska

2 oz. (60 ml/4 tbsp.) orange vodka
⅔ oz. (20 ml/1⅓ tbsp.) fresh lemon juice
half an orange, diced
**Muddle the orange and sugar in an old-fashioned glass. Add the
remaining ingredients. Fill with crushed ice and serve.**

Orchid

2 oz. (60 ml/4 tbsp.) Seager gin
1 oz. (30 ml/2 tbsp.) crème de noyeaux
1 oz. (30 ml/2 tbsp.) lemon juice
½ oz. (15 ml/1 tbsp.) forbidden fruit liqueur
½ oz. (15 ml/1 tbsp.) crème yvette
**Frost the rim of a Cocktail glass with sugar. Shake all the
ingredients and strain into the glass.**

Oriental

2 oz. (45 ml/3 tbsp.) gin
⅔ oz. (20 ml/1⅓ tbsp.) limoncello
1 oz. (30 ml/2 tbsp.) passion fruit purée
dash passion fruit syrup
twist of lemon to garnish
**Shake the ingredients, then strain into a
cocktail glass. Add a twist of lemon and serve.**

Original Martinez (see Martini, p. 138)

2 oz. (60 ml/4 tbsp.) Old Tom gin
½ oz. (15 ml/1 tbsp.) sweet vermouth
2 dashes maraschino liqueur
dash orange (or lemon) bitters
**Shake the ingredients, then strain into a
martini glass and serve.**

Original
Martinez

161

Oye Mi Canto (Alex Kratena)

2 oz (60 ml/4 tbsp.) Martini Rosato
1 oz (30 ml/2 tbsp.) Tapatio blanco infused with sweet tamarind
⅛ oz (5 ml/1 tsp.) Mezcal Chichicapa
1 dash orange and mandarin bitters
jasmine flower and apple blossom to garnish
Stir, then strain into a cocktail glass with one ice cube. Garnish with flowers.

Pacific Gold

1 oz. (30 ml/2 tbsp.) crème de banane
1 oz. (30 ml/2 tbsp.) Cointreau
½ oz. (15 ml/1 tbsp.) Grand Marnier
2 dashes kummel
Stir the ingredients in a mixing glass, then strain into a martini glass and serve.

Painkiller

2 oz. (60 ml/4 tbsp.) white rum
4 oz. (120 ml/8 tbsp.) pineapple juice
1 oz. (30 ml/2 tbsp.) fresh orange juice
1 oz. (30 ml/2 tbsp.) coconut cream
Shake the ingredients, then strain into an ice-filled highball glass and serve.

Pan-Am

1 oz. (30 ml/2 tbsp.) bourbon
1 oz. (30 ml/2 tbsp.) mescal
dash Angostura bitters
dash gomme syrup
Pour the ingredients into an old-fashioned glass, stir, and serve.

Parked Car

1 oz. (30 ml/2 tbsp.) Campari
1 oz. (30 ml/2 tbsp.) tequila
½ oz. (15 ml/1 tbsp.) Cointreau
1 egg white
Shake the ingredients, then strain into a martini glass and serve.

Parson's Nose

2 oz. (60 ml/4 tbsp.) vodka
½ oz. (15 ml/1 tbsp.) amaretto
½ oz. (15 ml/1 tbsp.) crème de peche
dash Angostura bitters
Stir the ingredients in a mixing glass, then strain into a martini glass and serve.

Passion (Chris Edwardes)

1 oz. (30 ml/2 tbsp.) eight-year-old Bacardi
½ oz. (15 ml/1 tbsp.) crème de peche
juice of 1 lime
½ oz. (15 ml/1 tbsp.) gomme syrup
1 oz. (30 ml/2 tbsp.) passion fruit purée
champagne
Shake the ingredients, except the champagne, then strain into an ice-filled highball glass. Fill with champagne and serve.

Passion Batida

1⅔ oz. (50 ml/3⅓ tbsp.) cachaça
1 oz. (30 ml/2 tbsp.) passion fruit purée
⅓ oz. (10 ml/⅔ tbsp.) gomme syrup
lime wedge to garnish
Pour the ingredients into an ice-filled old-fashioned glass. Stir and garnish with a lime wedge.

Peach Cocktail

2 oz. (60 ml/4 tbsp.) crème de peche
1 oz. (30 ml/2 tbsp.) dry vermouth
dash grenadine
Shake the ingredients, then strain into a martini glass and serve.

Peach Margarita (see Margarita, p. 136)

1 oz. (30 ml/2 tbsp.) silver tequila
½ oz. (15 ml/1 tbsp.) Cointreau
½ oz. (15 ml/1 tbsp.) peach schnapps
juice of half a lime
1 peach, peeled and diced
Blend the peach pieces, then add the other ingredients. Blend. Pour into a margarita glass and serve.

Pear Daiquiri (see Daiquiri, p. 92)

1 oz. (30 ml/2 tbsp.) white rum
⅓ oz. (10 ml/⅔ tbsp.) pear schnapps
1 oz. (30 ml/2 tbsp.) fresh pear purée
1 oz. (30 ml/2 tbsp.) fresh lime juice
dash gomme syrup
Blend the ingredients with crushed ice. Pour into a large cocktail glass and serve.

Penicillin (Sam Ross)

2 oz (60 ml/4 tbsp.) blended Scotch
¾ oz (22 ml/1½ tbsp.) lemon juice
⅛ oz (5 ml/1 tsp.) honey syrup
½ oz (15 ml/1 tbsp.) sweetened ginger juice
¼ oz (8 ml/½ tbsp.) Islay Scotch float
candied ginger to garnish
Shake all except float, then strain over ice in a rocks glass. Garnish with candied ginger.

Pearl Harbor

1 oz. (30 ml/2 tbsp.) vodka
⅔ oz. (20 ml/1 tbsp.) melon liqueur
1 oz. (30 ml/2 tbsp.) pineapple juice
Shake the ingredients, then strain into a cocktail glass and serve.

Pernod Cocktail

2 oz. (60 ml/4 tbsp.) Pernod
2 oz. (60 ml/4 tbsp.) iced water
2 dashes Angostura bitters
Pour the Pernod, water, and the bitters into an old-fashioned glass and serve.

Pierre Collins

2 oz. (60 ml/4 tbsp.) cognac
1 oz. (30 ml/2 tbsp.) lemon juice
1 tsp. superfine (caster) sugar
dash Angostura bitters (optional)
soda
Place the first three ingredients in a highball glass half-filled with ice and stir to mix. Fill up with soda. Stir gently and serve.

Pierre Fizz

2 oz. (60 ml/4 tbsp.) cognac
1 oz. (30 ml/2 tbsp.) lemon juice
1 tsp. superfine (caster) sugar
dash Angostura bitters (optional)
soda
Shake the ingredients, then strain into a highball glass, fill up with soda, and serve.

Pimm's Royal

1 oz. (30 ml/2 tbsp.) Pimm's
5 oz. (150 ml/10 tbsp.) champagne

**Pour the Pimm's and champagne into a
champagne flute, stir, then serve.**

Pina Colada

2 oz. (60 ml/4 tbsp.) white rum
1 oz. (30 ml/2 tbsp.) sweetened
   coconut cream
2 oz. (60 ml/4 tbsp.) pineapple juice
4 chunks fresh pineapple
pinch of salt

**Blend the ingredients until smooth,
then pour into a colada glass and
serve with straws.**

Pina
Colada

Pine Smoothie (nonalcoholic)

quarter of a large fresh pineapple
juice of one orange
2 handfuls raspberries
ice cubes

**Peel the pineapple and dice the flesh. Blend with the orange juice
and berries. Add the ice cubes last. Blend and pour into a tumbler
and serve.**

Pineapple Upside-Down Cake

½ oz. (15 ml/1 tbsp.) Bailey's
½ oz. (15 ml/1 tbsp.) vodka
½ oz. (15 ml/1 tbsp.) butterscotch schnapps
½ oz. (15 ml/1 tbsp.) pineapple juice

**Stir the ingredients in a mixing glass, then strain into a shot glass
and serve.**

Pink Awakening (nonalcoholic) (Makes 2 glasses)

2 large handfuls raspberries
ripe banana
fresh juice of one pink grapefruit

Rinse the raspberries and place in a blender. Add the peeled banana and grapefruit juice. Blend, pour into a tumbler, and serve.

Pink Caddie-O

1 oz. (30 ml/2 tbsp.) gold tequila
⅔ oz. (20 ml/1⅓ tbsp.) Grand Marnier
1 oz. (30 ml/2 tbsp.) cranberry juice
fresh juice of 1 lime

Shake the ingredients, then strain into a cocktail glass and serve.

Pink Cadillac

1 oz. (30 ml/2 tbsp.) crème de cacao
½ oz. (15 ml/1 tbsp.) Galliano
½ oz. (15 ml/1 tbsp.) grenadine
1 oz. (30 ml/2 tbsp.) heavy (double) cream
dash fresh orange juice

Shake the ingredients, then strain into a martini glass and serve.

Pink Fetish

1 oz. (30 ml/2 tbsp.) vodka
1 oz. (30 ml/2 tbsp.) peach schnapps
2 oz. (60 ml/4 tbsp.) cranberry juice
2 oz. (60 ml/4 tbsp.) fresh orange juice
lime wedge to garnish

Shake the ingredients, then strain into an ice-filled old-fashioned glass. Add a lime wedge and serve.

Pisco Sour

One or two lead to three or four and you might end up behaving like the Pisco Kid!

Sours are one of the great workhorses of the cocktail bar. Any spirit can be combined with lemon juice and sugar to make a mouth-puckering drink. The Pisco Sour is exceptional, and it is the national drink of Chile and Peru, sipped as a cooling drink during the hot South American summers.

It's easy to drink, thanks to the aromatic, apparently benign influence of the Pisco. So, you have another—and another. All of a sudden, this gentle drink turns around and belts you on the back of the neck, distorting your vision. You might feel an overwhelming urge to dance like a crazy fool. Be warned, once Pisco madness is unleashed it is difficult to keep under control.

Use a top brand, and go for the top designation of Gran Pisco. This is the driest and most flavorsome—and flavor is the whole point of the exercise. Most arguments revolve around whether to use egg whites or not. Pisco Sour experts prefer to keep them away. Bitters are also used by some, although they can be a touch abrasive. If you must, try to find and use orange or Peychaud bitters rather than Angostura bitters.

Pisco Sour

2 oz. (60 ml/4 tbsp.) Gran Pisco
1 oz. (30 ml/2 tbsp.) lemon juice
1 tsp. superfine (caster) sugar
egg white (optional)
bitters (optional)
Shake the ingredients well, particularly if you are using an egg white, then strain into an old-fashioned glass and serve.

Pink Gin

4 oz. (120 ml/8 tbsp.) gin
2 dashes Angostura bitters
**Coat a chilled cocktail glass with the
Angostura bitters. Discard the excess,
fill up with the gin, and serve.**

Pink Lady

1 oz. (30 ml/2 tbsp.) gin
2 dashes grenadine
one egg white
juice of half a lemon
**Shake the ingredients, then strain
into a martini glass and serve.**

Pink Gin

Pink Rose

2 oz. (60 ml/4 tbsp.) gin
½ oz. (15 ml/1 tbsp.) light (single) cream
½ oz. (15 ml/1 tbsp.) fresh orange juice
2 dashes grenadine
one egg white
Shake the ingredients, then strain into a martini glass and serve.

Pisco Sour (see pp. 168–69)

Planter's

2 oz. (60 ml/4 tbsp.) dark rum
juice of 1 lime
½ oz. (15 ml/1 tbsp.) gomme syrup
Shake the ingredients, then strain into a martini glass and serve.

Poinsettia

1 oz. (30 ml/2 tbsp.) Cointreau
chilled champagne
twist of orange to garnish
**Pour the Cointreau and champagne into a champagne flute.
Stir, add the garnish, and serve.**

Polish Martini (see Martini, p. 138)

1½ oz. (45 ml/3 tbsp.) Wyborowa vodka
½ oz. (15 ml/1 tbsp.) Krupnik vodka
dash apple juice
Shake the ingredients, then strain into a martini glass and serve.

Prado

1 oz. (30 ml/2 tbsp.) tequila
2 tsp. maraschino liqueur
juice of 1 lime
2 dashes grenadine
1 tsp. egg white powder
maraschino cherry and slice of lime to garnish
**Shake the ingredients, then strain into an ice-filled old-fashioned glass.
Add the maraschino cherry and slice of lime and serve.**

Prairie Oyster (nonalcoholic)

1 tsp. olive oil
3 dashes Worcestershire sauce
1 egg yolk
salt
black pepper
1 oz. (30 ml/2 tbsp.) tomato ketchup
dash white wine vinegar
**Rinse a wine glass with the olive oil and discard the oil. Add the tomato
ketchup and egg yolk. Season with Worcestershire sauce, wine vinegar,
and salt and pepper. Serve with a small glass of iced water on the side.**

President

2 oz. (60 ml/4 tbsp.) dark rum
dash grenadine
juice of half a ruby orange
dash lemon juice
**Shake the ingredients, then strain into a
martini glass and serve.**

Presidente

2 oz. (60 ml/4 tbsp.) white rum
¼ oz. (8 ml/½ tbsp.) Cointreau
¾ oz. (22 ml/1½ tbsp.) dry vermouth
¼ oz. (8 ml/½ tbsp.) sweet vermouth
dash grenadine
dash lime juice
**Shake the ingredients, then strain into
a cocktail glass and serve.**

Presidente

Prince of Wales

¾ oz. (22 ml/1½ tbsp.) brandy
¼ oz. (8 ml/½ tbsp.) Benedictine
champagne
dash of Angostura bitters
1 sugar cube
slice of orange to garnish
cherry to garnish
**Place the sugar cube in a highball glass and soak it with the Angostura.
Add the ice, brandy, and fruit. Stir, then add the champagne. Finally,
add the Benedictine, garnish, and serve.**

Purple Hooter

1 oz. (30 ml/2 tbsp.) citrus vodka
½ oz. (15 ml/1 tbsp.) triple sec
½ oz. (15 ml/1 tbsp.) Chambord
Shake the ingredients, then strain into a shot glass and serve.

Pussy Foot

2 oz. (60 ml/4 tbsp.) white rum
1 oz. (30 ml/2 tbsp.) fresh lime juice
1 oz. (30 ml/2 tbsp.) fresh orange juice
1 oz. (30 ml/2 tbsp.) pineapple juice
2 dashes grenadine
1 oz. (30 ml/2 tbsp.) heavy (double) cream
Shake the ingredients, then strain into a highball glass and serve.

Queen Elizabeth

2 oz. (60 ml/4 tbsp.) gin
1 oz. (30 ml/2 tbsp.) dry vermouth
½ oz. (15 ml/1 tbsp.) Benedictine
Stir the gin, vermouth, and Benedictine in a mixing glass, then strain into a martini glass and serve.

Quiet Rage

1⅔ oz. (50 ml/3⅓ tbsp.) vodka
2 oz. (60 ml/4 tbsp.) guava juice
2 oz. (60 ml/4 tbsp.) pineapple juice
4 fresh lychees
1 oz. (30 ml/2 tbsp.) coconut cream
dash grenadine
Blend the ingredients with crushed ice. Pour into a highball glass and serve.

Raja

1 oz. (30 ml/2 tbsp.) cognac
1 oz. (30 ml/2 tbsp.) champagne
Stir the cognac and champagne in a mixing glass, then strain into a martini glass and serve.

Rapscallion (Adeline Shepherd and Craig Harper)

2¼ oz (68 ml/4½ tbsp.) Talisker 10YO whisky
¾ oz (22 ml/1½ tbsp.) PX sherry
Absinthe rinse
lemon twist to garnish
Stir and strain into absinthe-rinsed cocktail glass. Garnish with lemon twist (discard).

Raspberry Collins

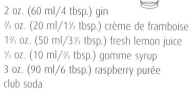

2 oz. (60 ml/4 tbsp.) gin
⅔ oz. (20 ml/1⅓ tbsp.) crème de framboise
1⅔ oz. (50 ml/3⅓ tbsp.) fresh lemon juice
⅓ oz. (10 ml/⅔ tbsp.) gomme syrup
3 oz. (90 ml/6 tbsp.) raspberry purée
club soda
3 raspberries to garnish
Shake the ingredients, except the soda. Strain into a highball. Fill with soda. Add the raspberries on a cocktail stick and serve.

Raspberry Mint Daiquiri (see Daiquiri, p. 92)

1⅔ oz. (50 ml/3⅓ tbsp.) white rum
handful fresh raspberries
6 mint leaves
Shake the ingredients, then strain into a large cocktail glass.

Raspberry Martini (see Martini, p. 138)

2 oz. (60 ml/4 tbsp.) vodka
1 oz. (30 ml/2 tbsp.) crème de framboise
10 raspberries

Muddle the raspberries in a shaker. Add the vodka and crème de framboise. Shake, then strain into a martini glass and serve.

Raspberry Sip

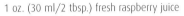

1 oz. (30 ml/2 tbsp.) fresh raspberry juice
½ oz. (15 ml/1 tbsp.) Cointreau
½ oz. (15 ml/1 tbsp.) crème de banane
champagne

Shake the ingredients, except the champagne, then strain the mixture into a champagne flute. Fill with champagne, stir, and serve.

Red Russian

1 oz. (30 ml/2 tbsp.) vodka
1 oz. (30 ml/2 tbsp.) white crème de cacao
2 dashes grenadine

Shake the ingredients, then strain into an ice-filled old-fashioned glass and serve.

Ritz Fizz

dash amaretto
dash blue curaçao
dash fresh lemon juice
chilled champagne

Pour the first three ingredients into a champagne flute, stir, then fill with champagne and serve.

Road Runner

1 oz. (30 ml/2 tbsp.) vodka
⅔ oz. (20 ml/1⅓ tbsp.) amaretto
⅔ oz. (20 ml/1⅓ tbsp.) coconut cream
Shake the ingredients, then strain into a martini glass and serve.

Rob Roy

2 oz. (60 ml/4 tbsp.) Scotch whisky
1 oz. (30 ml/2 tbsp.) sweet vermouth
dash Angostura bitters
Stir the scotch, vermouth, and bitters in a mixing glass, then strain into a martini glass and serve.

Rob Roy Perfect

2 oz. (60 ml/4 tbsp.) Scotch whisky
½ oz. (15 ml/1 tbsp.) sweet vermouth
½ oz. (15 ml/1 tbsp.) dry vermouth
dash Angostura bitters
Stir the ingredients in a mixing glass, then strain into a cocktail glass and serve.

Ronaldo

1 oz. (30 ml/2 tbsp.) cachaça
1 oz. (30 ml/2 tbsp.) gold rum
½ oz. (15 ml/1 tbsp.) crème de banane
½ oz. (15 ml/1 tbsp.) unsweetened pineapple juice
dash lime juice
lime wedge to garnish
Shake the ingredients, then strain into a highball glass half-filled with ice. Garnish with the lime wedge and serve.

Rosalita

¾ oz. (22 ml/1½ tbsp.) tequila
¼ oz. (8 ml/½ tbsp.) dry vermouth
¼ oz. (8 ml/½ tbsp.) sweet vermouth
¼ oz. (8 ml/½ tbsp.) Campari
Shake the ingredients, then strain into a cocktail glass and serve.

Royal Blush

1 oz. (30 ml/2 tbsp.) vodka
1 oz. (30 ml/2 tbsp.) crème de framboise
1 oz. (30 ml/2 tbsp.) heavy (double) cream
2 dashes grenadine
Shake the ingredients, then strain into a martini glass and serve.

Rude Cosmopolitan

2 oz. (60 ml/4 tbsp.) gold tequila
⅔ oz. (20 ml/1⅓ tbsp.) triple sec
1 oz. (30 ml/2 tbsp.) cranberry juice
juice of half a lime
twist of orange to garnish
Shake the ingredients, then strain into a cocktail glass. Add the orange twist and serve.

Rum 'n' Coke Float (Ryan Chetiyawardana)

1½ oz (45 ml/3 tbsp.) aged rum
⅗ oz (18 ml/1⅕ tbsp.) Coca-Cola syrup
1 whole egg
lime twist to garnish
Dry-shake all ingredients without ice. Shake with ice, then double-strain into a contour glass. Garnish with lime twist.

Rum Punch

Rum punches are equally open to interpretation. On every island in the Caribbean, every bar will have its own variation, but all will be mixing sour, sweet, strong, and weak components. Sourness is given by lime juice and bitters, sweetness from fruit juices, syrup, and grenadine. Rum is the sole alcohol and most recipes dilute the punch with either water or ice. The end result is a gentle, soothing drink, not some confected mess. In Jamaica, Wray & Nephew dilutes lime, grenadine/syrup, and overproof rum with water, and adds dashes of bitters and nutmeg. In Haiti, they combine orange and passion fruit juice for sweetness and use crushed ice to dilute.

Rum Shrub

2 oz. (60 ml/4 tbsp.) dark rum
1 oz. (30 ml/2 tbsp.) shrub (fruit and herb syrup)
1 oz. (30 ml/2 tbsp.) soda
Fill wine goblet two-thirds with ice. Add the rum, shrub, and soda. Stir lightly and serve.

Russian Bear

1 oz. (30 ml/2 tbsp.) vodka
1½ oz. (45 ml/3 tbsp.) light (single) cream
¼ oz. (8 ml/½ tbsp.) crème de cacao
1 tsp. sugar
Shake the ingredients, then strain into a champagne flute or a cocktail glass and serve.

Russian
Bear

Russian Cocktail

1 oz. (30 ml/2 tbsp.) vodka
1 oz. (30 ml/2 tbsp.) gin
1 oz. (30 ml/2 tbsp.) white crème de cacao
**Shake the ingredients, then strain
into a martini glass and serve.**

Russian Coffee

1 oz. (30 ml/2 tbsp.) vodka
6 oz. (180 ml/12 tbsp.) hot black
coffee
2 tsp. raw sugar
heavy (double) cream
**Pour the vodka and black coffee into a
liqueur coffee glass, then add the sugar.
Float the cream on top and serve.**

Rusty Nail

Rusty Nail

2 oz. (60 ml/4 tbsp.) Scotch whisky
1 oz. (30 ml/2 tbsp.) Drambuie
**Pour the scotch and Drambuie
into an old-fashioned glass and
serve with a stirrer.**

Salty Dog

2 oz. (60 ml/4 tbsp.) vodka
2 oz. (60 ml/4 tbsp.) grapefruit juice
**Shake the vodka with the grapefruit juice,
then strain into a champagne
flute or a martini glass and serve.**

Salty Dog

Sangrita
(nonalcoholic) (Serves 10)

35 oz. (1 L/4½ cups) tomato juice
16 oz. (450 ml/2 cups) orange juice
5 tsp. honey
3 oz. (90 ml/6 tbsp.) lime juice
pinch salt and black pepper
1 chili, finely chopped
¼ oz. white onion, finely chopped
10 to 20 dashes Worcestershire sauce

Pour the ingredients into a bowl. Stir well. Place in the refrigerator to chill for two hours. Take out, then strain into a large glass jug. Serve in individual wine glasses.

Sazerac

2½ oz. (75 ml/5 tbsp.) bourbon
2 tsp. absinthe or Pernod
½ tsp. gomme syrup
3 dashes Peychaud's bitters
twist of lemon to garnish

Pour the absinthe/Pernod into a highball glass, coat, and discard the excess. Shake the other ingredients and pour over ice into the glass, then serve.

Scandinavian Coffee

1 oz. (30 ml/2 tbsp.) akvavit
6 oz. (180 ml/12 tbsp.) hot black coffee
2 tsp. raw sugar
heavy (double) cream

Pour the akvavit and black coffee into a liqueur coffee glass, then add the sugar. Float the cream on top and serve.

Scarborough Fair

2 oz. (60 ml/4 tbsp.) Plymouth gin
¼ oz. (8 ml/½ tbsp.) Chambery
sprig of thyme
sprig of rosemary
sprig of flat leaf parsley
2 fresh sage leaves
Muddle the sage, parsley, and Chambery in a shaker. Add the gin. Shake, then strain into a cocktail glass. Garnish with rosemary and thyme leaves and serve.

Screwdriver

2 oz. (60 ml/4 tbsp.) vodka
5 oz. (145 ml/10 tbsp.) fresh orange juice
Pour the vodka into an ice-filled highball glass. Add the orange juice, stir, and serve with a stirrer.

Sea Breeze

2 oz. (60 ml/4 tbsp.) vodka
3 oz. (90 ml/6 tbsp.) cranberry juice
2 oz. (60 ml/4 tbsp.) grapefruit juice
Pour the ingredients into an ice-filled highball glass. Stir, then serve with a stirrer and straws.

Sea Breeze

Second Secret (Paul Graham)

1 oz (30 ml/2 tbsp.) rye
1 oz (30 ml/2 tbsp.) bonded applejack
1 oz (30 ml/2 tbsp.) lemon juice
½ oz (15 ml/1 tbsp.) grenadine
lemon twist to garnish
Shake and double-strain into a cocktail glass. Garnish with lemon twist.

Sidecar

A classic with a minimalist beauty, perhaps the spiritual father of the Pisco Sour and the Daiquiri.

There are plenty of theories when it comes to naming the person who first made this cocktail. What's beyond doubt is that it is a Parisian creation, but trying to find out who was the first to put cognac, Cointreau, and lemon juice together ends up with you following clues that only lead you up some blind alley in an obscure arrondissement. It is generally thought it was created for a military chap in Paris during the First World War, who used to arrive at Harry's New York Bar, located in a small side street off a main boulevard, in a chauffeur-driven motorcycle sidecar.

It qualifies as a classic for the simple reason that it's a cocktail that has a minimalist beauty—it is, after all, a sour and as such a relative of the Pisco Sour, the Whisky Sour and the Margarita. The important element is to get the correct balance between the mouth-puckering acidity of fresh lemon juice (lime won't do, which is why a Sidecar isn't just a Daiquiri made with brandy) and the clean, sweet, orange richness of triple sec. If these sweet and sour elements are in balance, they provide the ideal frame for the fruity richness and kick of the Cognac.

Sidecar

1 oz. (30 ml/2 tbsp.) brandy
⅔ oz. (20 ml/1⅓ tbsp.) Cointreau
⅔ oz. (20 ml/1⅓ tbsp.) fresh lemon juice
**Shake the ingredients, then strain into
a cocktail glass and serve.**

Seelbach Cocktail

1 oz. (30 ml/2 tbsp.) Old Forester bourbon
½ oz. (15 ml/1 tbsp.) Cointreau
7 dashes Angostura bitters
7 dashes Peychaud orange bitters
5 oz. (120 ml/10 tbsp.) champagne
twist of orange to garnish

**Pour the bourbon, Cointreau, and both
bitters into a champagne flute and stir.
Add the champagne, stir, garnish with
the twist of orange, and serve.**

September Morn

2 oz. (60 ml/4 tbsp.) white rum
splash grenadine
1 oz. (30 ml/2 tbsp.) lemon juice
1 egg white

**Shake the ingredients for about 30 seconds,
then strain into a cocktail glass and serve.**

September
Morn

Sex on the Beach

½ oz. (15 ml/1 tbsp.) chambord
½ oz. (15 ml/1 tbsp.) midori
½ oz. (15 ml/1 tbsp.) vodka
1 oz. (30 ml/2 tbsp.) pineapple juice
cranberry juice

**Stir the ingredients in a mixing glass, then
strain into a shot glass. Fill up with the
cranberry juice and serve.**

Shirley Temple (nonalcoholic)

7 oz. (200 ml/14 tbsp.) ginger ale
1 oz. (30 ml/2 tbsp.) grenadine syrup
Lemon slice to garnish
Cherry to garnish
Build a pile of ice in a highball glass. Add ginger ale over the ice and sprinkle with grenadine syrup. Garnish with a lemon slice and a cherry.

Short Fuse

2 oz. (60 ml/4 tbsp.) gold tequila
⅔ oz. (20 ml/1⅓ tbsp.) apricot brandy
2 tsp. juice of maraschino cherries
juice of 1 lime
3 oz. (90 ml/6 tbsp.) grapefruit juice
lime wedge to garnish
Shake the ingredients, then strain into an ice-filled highball glass. Add the lime wedge and serve.

Showtime

1 oz. (30 ml/2 tbsp.) gin
⅔ oz. (20 ml/1⅓ tbsp.) lychee liqueur
⅔ oz. (20 ml/1⅓ tbsp.) pineapple liqueur
⅔ oz. (20 ml/1⅓ tbsp.) fresh peach purée
peach slice to garnish
Shake the ingredients, strain into a cocktail glass, add peach slice, and serve.

Sidecar (see pp. 182–83)

Sidecar (alt) (see pp. 182–83)

1½ oz. (45 ml/3 tbsp.) cognac
¾ oz. (22 ml/1½ tbsp.) Cointreau
¾ oz. (22 ml/1½ tbsp.) lemon juice
twist of lemon to garnish
Sugar the rim of a cocktail glass. Shake the ingredients, then strain into the glass, garnish with the twist of lemon, and serve.

Singapore Sling

The writers Somerset Maugham and Joseph Conrad were fans of this legendary, exotic cocktail.

Bartenders are naturally inquisitive people, always playing around with ingredients, seeing just what happens when another ingredient is added to a classic cocktail base. It was therefore inevitable that one of the oldest "simple" cocktails, the Gin Sling, would serve as the base for a range of outlandish experiments.

The Gin Sling itself is Tom highball and takes its name from the German schlingen (to swallow). Slings evolved into the highball family but the name lives on in the Singapore Sling, which was allegedly created in 1915 by Ngiam Tong Boon, the bartender of that enduring symbol of British colonialism, Singapore's Raffles Hotel.

Some gin experts disagree, claiming it dates from earlier. Certainly records show that there was a drink called a Straits Sling in existence before the Raffles recipe, which was a variant on the sling theme with Benedictine, but what we now know as the Singapore Sling appears to have its origins in the Raffles' bar.

Singapore Sling

2 oz. (60 ml/4 tbsp.) Beefeater gin
2 oz. (60 ml/4 tbsp.) fresh lime juice
½ oz. (15 ml/1 tbsp.) Cointreau
½ oz. (15 ml/1 tbsp.) Peter Heering
2 tsp. sugar
dash of Angostura bitters
slice of lemon to garnish
red maraschino cherry to garnish
Pour the gin, lime juice, and bitters over crushed ice in a highball glass. Add the sugar and stir. Then add the Cointreau and Peter Heering, fill up with soda, and serve.

Sidney

2 oz. (60 ml/4 tbsp.) rye or bourbon
½ oz. (15 ml/1 tbsp.) dry vermouth
1 splash yellow Chartreuse
dash orange bitters
twist of lemon to garnish

Stir the ingredients in a mixing glass, then strain into a cocktail glass. Add the lemon twist and serve.

Silk Stocking

1 oz. (30 ml/2 tbsp.) tequila
1 oz. (30 ml/2 tbsp.) white crème de cacao
1 oz. (30 ml/2 tbsp.) heavy (double) cream
dash grenadine

Shake the ingredients, then strain into a martini glass and serve.

Silver Bronx

2 oz. (60 ml/4 tbsp.) dry gin
1 oz. (30 ml/2 tbsp.) sweet vermouth
1 oz. (30 ml/2 tbsp.) fresh orange juice
half an egg white

Shake the ingredients, then strain into a champagne flute or a cocktail glass and serve.

Silver Bullet

2 oz. (60 ml/4 tbsp.) vodka
1 oz. (30 ml/2 tbsp.) kummel

Pour the ingredients into an old-fashioned glass, stir, and serve.

Silver
Bronx

Singapore Sling (see pp. 186–87)

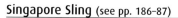

Silver Streak

2 oz. (60 ml/4 tbsp.) gin
1 oz. (30 ml/2 tbsp.) kummel
Pour the ingredients into an old-fashioned glass, stir, and serve.

Singapore Gin Sling (see Singapore Sling pp. 186–87)

2 oz. (60 ml/4 tbsp.) gin
½ oz. (15 ml/1 tbsp.) Cointreau
1½ oz. (45 ml/3 tbsp.) fresh lime juice
1 tsp. superfine (caster) sugar
1 tsp. gomme syrup
soda water
¾ oz. (22 ml/1½ tbsp.) Cherry Heering
lime wedge to garnish
Shake the first five ingredients, then strain into a highball glass. Fill up with soda and float the Cherry Heering over the top. Garnish with the lime and serve.

Slow Seducer

½ oz. (15 ml/1 tbsp.) crème de framboise
½ oz. (15 ml/1 tbsp.) Cointreau
1 oz. (30 ml/2 tbsp.) pink grapefruit juice
champagne
Shake the ingredients, except the champagne, then strain into a champagne flute. Fill with champagne, stir, and serve.

Slowly Does It

1 oz. (30 ml/2 tbsp.) tequila
⅔ oz. (20 ml/1⅓ tbsp.) dark rum
2 dashes Tia Maria
1 oz. (30 ml/2 tbsp.) coconut cream
half a banana
2 oz. (60 ml/4 tbsp.) pineapple juice
Blend the ingredients, except the dark rum, with crushed ice. Pour into a tumbler. Float the dark rum on top and serve with a straw.

Smoky Martini (see Martini, p. 138)

2 oz. (60 ml/4 tbsp.) gin
¼ oz. (8 ml/½ tbsp.) Scotch whisky
½ tsp. dry vermouth
Shake the ingredients, then strain into a cocktail glass and serve.

Snow Bunny

1 oz. (30 ml/2 tbsp.) triple sec
6 oz. (180 ml/12 tbsp.) hot chocolate
1 cinnamon stick to garnish
**Pour the triple sec into a heatproof glass and fill with the hot chocolate.
Garnish with the cinnamon stick and serve.**

Soixante-Neuf

1 oz. (30 ml/2 tbsp.) gin
1 oz. (30 ml/2 tbsp.) fresh lemon juice
chilled champagne
twist of lemon to garnish
**Shake the gin and lemon juice, then strain into a champagne flute.
Fill with champagne, add the twist, and serve.**

South of the Border

South of
the Border

1 oz. (30 ml/2 tbsp.) tequila
¾ oz. (22 ml/1½ tbsp.) Kahlua
half a lime
**Squeeze the lime over ice in an old-
fashioned glass. Stir, then add the
spirits. Stir and serve.**

Southern Bull

1 oz. (30 ml/2 tbsp.) Kahlua
1 oz. (30 ml/2 tbsp.) Southern Comfort
1 oz. (30 ml/2 tbsp.) tequila
Shake the ingredients, then strain into a martini glass and serve.

Spanish Fly

2 oz. (60 ml/4 tbsp.) mescal
1 oz. (30 ml/2 tbsp.) Grand Marnier
1 tsp. instant coffee to garnish
**Pour the mescal and Grand Marnier into an old-fashioned glass.
Sprinkle with the coffee and serve.**

Spice Whirl

1 oz. (30 ml/2 tbsp.) spiced rum
⅔ oz. (20 ml/1⅓ tbsp.) triple sec
1 oz. (30 ml/2 tbsp.) fresh orange juice
1 oz. (30 ml/2 tbsp.) papaya juice
⅔ oz. (20 ml/1⅓ tbsp.) fresh lime juice
**Shake the ingredients, then strain into an ice-filled highball.
Serve with a straw.**

Star

1 oz. (30 ml/2 tbsp.) dry gin
1 oz. (30 ml/2 tbsp.) calvados
dash Noilly Prat
dash dry vermouth
dash grapefruit juice
**Stir the ingredients in a mixing glass, then strain
into a cocktail glass and serve.**

Stinger

2 oz. (60 ml/4 tbsp.) brandy
1 oz. (30 ml/2 tbsp.) white crème de menthe
**Pour the brandy and crème de menthe into a brandy
glass, stir, and serve. Alternatively, shake the
ingredients, then strain into a martini or old-
fashioned glass.**

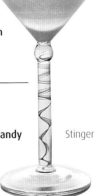

Stinger

Straits Sling (see Singapore Sling, pp. 186–87)

2 oz. (60 ml/4 tbsp.) Beefeater gin
2 oz. (60 ml/4 tbsp.) fresh lime juice
½ oz. (15 ml/1 tbsp.) Benedictine
½ oz. (15 ml/1 tbsp.) Peter Heering
2 tsp. sugar
dash of Angostura Bitters
**Pour the gin, lime juice, and bitters
over crushed ice in a highball glass.
Add the sugar and stir. Then add
the Benedictine and Peter Heering,
fill up with soda, and serve.**

Strawberry Cream Tea

1 oz. (30 ml/2 tbsp.) Kahlua
1 oz. (30 ml/2 tbsp.) Bailey's
1 oz. (30 ml/2 tbsp.) fraise
1 oz. (30 ml/2 tbsp.) vodka
1 oz. (30 ml/2 tbsp.) lassi (Indian
   yogurt drink)
strawberry to garnish
**Blend the ingredients, then pour into an
ice-filled highball glass. Serve with a
strawberry on the rim. Lassi gives this
cocktail a lighter, cleaner flavor.**

Strawberry
Cream Tea

Strawberry Daiquiri

½ oz. (15 ml/1 tbsp.) strawberry schnapps
1 oz. (30 ml/2 tbsp.) light rum
1 oz. (30 ml/2 tbsp.) lime juice
1 oz. (30 ml/2 tbsp.) powdered sugar
1 oz. (25 g) strawberries, pulped
Shake all ingredients with ice, strain into a cocktail glass, and serve.

Superior

2 oz. (60 ml/4 tbsp.) white rum
1 oz. (30 ml/2 tbsp.) sweet vermouth
1 oz. (30 ml/2 tbsp.) fresh lemon juice
2 fresh apricots
slice of orange to garnish
Blend the ingredients until frozen, then pour into a large goblet. Garnish with the orange slice and serve.

Swamp Water

1 oz. (30 ml/2 tbsp.) green crème de menthe
1 oz. (30 ml/2 tbsp.) Bailey's
1 oz. (30 ml/2 tbsp.) cherry brandy
Pour the ingredients into an ice-filled brandy glass, stir, and serve.

Swan Song

1 oz. (30 ml/2 tbsp.) midori
½ oz. (15 ml/1 tbsp.) Cointreau
½ oz. (15 ml/1 tbsp.) frangelico
grated chocolate to garnish
Shake the ingredients, then strain into a cocktail glass. Sprinkle with the chocolate and serve.

Sydney Sling (see Singapore Sling, pp. 186–87)

2 oz. (60 ml/4 tbsp.) white rum
⅔ oz. (20 ml/1⅓ tbsp.) lemon juice
⅔ oz. (20 ml/1⅓ tbsp.) cherry brandy
2 oz. (60 ml/4 tbsp.) guava juice
2 oz. (60 ml/4 tbsp.) pineapple juice
few dashes peach schnapps
half a ripe banana
Blend the ingredients, then add two scoops of crushed ice and blend again. Pour into a tumbler and serve with a straw.

Tabu

2 oz. (60 ml/4 tbsp.) rum
1 oz. (30 ml/2 tbsp.) gomme syrup
1 oz. (30 ml/2 tbsp.) cranberry juice
½ oz. (15 ml/1 tbsp.) fresh lemon juice
3 oz. (90 ml/6 tbsp.) pineapple juice
Blend the ingredients until smooth, then pour into a large goblet and serve.

Tail Spin Cocktail

1 oz. (30 ml/2 tbsp.) gin
1 oz. (30 ml/2 tbsp.) sweet vermouth
1 oz. (30 ml/2 tbsp.) green chartreuse
dash Angostura bitters
Shake the ingredients, then strain into a martini glass and serve.

Tapika

3½ oz. (105 ml/7 tbsp.) Chinaco Plata tequila
½ oz. (15 ml/1 tbsp.) Cointreau
½ oz. (15 ml/1 tbsp.) prickly pear cactus syrup
1 oz. (30 ml/2 tbsp.) lime juice
lime slice to garnish
Coat a cocktail glass with Cointreau, moistening the rim, and discard. Sprinkle the rim with salt. Shake the tequila, prickly pear syrup, and lime juice, then strain into the glass. Garnish with the lime and serve.

Tequila Canyon

2 oz. (60 ml/4 tbsp.) tequila
dash triple sec
4 oz. (120 ml/8 tbsp.) cranberry juice
⅓ oz. (10 ml/⅔ tbsp.) pineapple juice
⅓ oz. (10 ml/⅔ tbsp.) fresh orange juice
Pour the first three ingredients into an ice-filled highball glass. Stir, then add the pineapple and orange juices. Stir, then serve with a stirrer.

Tequila Manhattan (see Manhattan, p. 136)

2 oz. (60 ml/4 tbsp.) tequila
1 oz. (30 ml/2 tbsp.) sweet vermouth
dash fresh lime juice
slice of orange to garnish
**Shake the ingredients, then strain into an ice-filled old-fashioned glass.
Garnish with the slice of orange and serve.**

Tequila Mockingbird

2 oz. (60 ml/4 tbsp.) tequila
1 oz. (30 ml/2 tbsp.) green crème de menthe
1 oz. (30 ml/2 tbsp.) fresh lime juice
Shake the ingredients, then strain into a cocktail glass and serve.

Tequila Mockingbird (alt)

1 oz. (30 ml/2 tbsp.) tequila
⅓ oz. (10 ml/⅔ tbsp.) green crème de menthe
dash fresh lime juice
lime wedge to garnish
**Pour the ingredients into an old-fashioned
glass with crushed ice.
Stir, garnish with the lime, and serve
with a straw.**

Tequila Sunrise

2 oz. (60 ml/4 tbsp.) tequila
4 oz. (120 ml/8 tbsp.) fresh orange juice
2 dashes grenadine
orange spiral to garnish
**Pour the tequila and orange juice into
an ice-filled highball glass. Stir, then
slowly add the grenadine. Add the
garnish and serve with straws.**

Tequila
Sunrise

Tequila Sunset

2 oz. (60 ml/4 tbsp.) tequila
1 oz. (30 ml/2 tbsp.) fresh lemon juice
1 tsp. honey
lemon spiral to garnish

Shake the ingredients, then strain into a cocktail glass. Garnish with a spiral of lemon and serve.

Tequini

¾ oz. (22 ml/1½ tbsp.) tequila
¾ oz. (22 ml/1½ tbsp.) vodka
¾ oz. (22 ml/1½ tbsp.) Noilly Prat
dash Angostura bitters
lemon twist to garnish

Shake the ingredients, then strain into a cocktail glass, add the garnish, and serve.

Three Storms Flip
(Ryan Chetiyawardana

1½ oz (45 ml/3 tbsp.) aged rum
¾ oz (22 ml/1½ tbsp.) Velvet Falernum
⅛ oz (5 ml/1 tsp.) Lagavulin whisky
1 whole egg
pinch salt and pepper
2 dashes Regan's Orange Bitters
nutmeg to garnish

Dry-shake all ingredients without ice. Shake with ice, then double-strain into a cocktail glass. Garnish with grated nutmeg.

Thumbs Up (Mickey McIlroy)

½ oz (15 ml/1 tbsp.) gin
½ oz (15 ml/1 tbsp.) Maraschino
½ oz (15 ml/1 tbsp.) Yellow Chartreuse
½ oz (15 ml/1 tbsp.) lime juice
½ oz (15 ml/1 tbsp.) Aperol
Shake all and strain into a cocktail glass.

Thunder and Lightning

2 oz. (60 ml/4 tbsp.) cognac
1 oz. (30 ml/2 tbsp.) Cointreau
1 egg yolk
4 drops Tabasco sauce
Shake the ingredients, then strain into a cocktail glass and serve.

Tijuana Taxi

1 oz. (30 ml/2 tbsp.) gold tequila
½ oz. (15 ml/1 tbsp.) blue curaçao
½ oz. (15 ml/1 tbsp.) tropical fruit schnapps
club soda
Pour the tequila, curaçao, and schnapps into an ice-filled highball glass. Fill with soda, stir, and serve.

Tipperary

1 oz. (60 ml/4 tbsp.) Irish whiskey
¾ oz. (22 ml/1½ tbsp.) dry vermouth
¼ oz. (8 ml/½ tbsp.) green Chartreuse
Shake the ingredients, then strain into a cocktail glass and serve.

Tokyo Collins (Geoffrey Robinson)

1 oz (30 ml/2 tbsp.) gin
1 oz (30 ml/2 tbsp.) Yuzu sake
1 oz (30 ml/2 tbsp.) grapefruit juice
½ oz (15 ml/1 tbsp.) lemon
½ oz (15 ml/1 tbsp.) sugar syrup
soda
grapefruit slice and cherry to garnish
Build over ice in a highball glass, then stir. Top with soda and garnish with grapefruit slice and cherry.

Tom and Jerry

1 egg
1 oz. (30 ml/2 tbsp.) cognac
1 tsp. superfine (caster) sugar
2 oz. (60 ml/4 tbsp.) dark rum
4 oz. (120 ml/8 tbsp.) hot milk
Separate the egg yolk from the white and thoroughly beat both independently. Stir the beaten egg yolk and white together, then add the sugar and 1 tbsp. of the rum to preserve the mixture. Put 1 tbsp. of the mixture in a heatproof mug, then add the rest of the rum and stir in the hot milk to almost fill the mug. Add the cognac and serve.

Tom Collins

2 oz. (60 ml/4 tbsp.) gin
1 oz. (30 ml/2 tbsp.) fresh lemon juice
1 tsp. superfine (caster) sugar
dash Angostura bitters (optional)
soda
Place the first three ingredients in an ice-filled highball glass, then stir to mix. Fill up with soda. Stir gently and serve.

Tom Fizz

2 oz. (60 ml/4 tbsp.) gin
1 oz. (30 ml/2 tbsp.) lemon juice
1 tsp. superfine (caster) sugar
dash Angostura bitters (optional)
soda
Shake the ingredients, strain into a highball glass, top with soda, serve.

Tom Sour (see Pisco Sour, p. 168)

2 oz. (60 ml/4 tbsp.) gin
¾ oz. (22 ml/1½ tbsp.) fresh lemon juice
½ tsp. superfine (caster) sugar
Shake the ingredients, then strain into a cocktail glass and serve.

Tomahawk

1 oz. (30 ml/2 tbsp.) tequila
1 oz. (30 ml/2 tbsp.) triple sec/Cointreau
2 oz. (60 ml/4 tbsp.) cranberry juice
2 oz. (60 ml/4 tbsp.) pineapple juice
Shake the ingredients, then strain into an ice-filled highball glass and serve.

Top Knotch

1 oz. (30 ml/2 tbsp.) sloe gin
1 oz. (30 ml/2 tbsp.) dry vermouth
½ oz. (15 ml/1 tbsp.) crème de framboise
maraschino cherry to garnish
Pour the ingredients into an old-fashioned glass, then stir. Garnish with the cherry and serve.

Traffic Light

1 oz. (30 ml/2 tbsp.) crème de noix
1 oz. (30 ml/2 tbsp.) Galliano
1 oz. (30 ml/2 tbsp.) Midori
In a shot glass, layer each of the ingredients in turn and serve.

Triple Sunrise

1 oz. (30 ml/2 tbsp.) tequila
⅔ oz. (20 ml/1⅓ tbsp.) triple sec
⅔ oz. (20 ml/1⅓ tbsp.) fresh lime juice
half a fresh mango, diced
dash grenadine

Blend the ingredients. Add crushed ice. Blend, then pour into a tumbler and serve.

Tropical Storm

2 oz. (60 ml/4 tbsp.) golden rum
1 oz. (30 ml/2 tbsp.) vodka
1 oz. (30 ml/2 tbsp.) fresh orange juice
½ oz. (15 ml/1 tbsp.) fresh lime juice
½ oz. (15 ml/1 tbsp.) pineapple juice
dash grenadine
dash Angostura bitters

Blend the ingredients until smooth, then pour into an ice-filled highball glass and serve.

Tropical

2 oz. (60 ml/4 tbsp.) Jamaican rum
1 slice pineapple
1 tsp. granulated sugar
juice of 1 lime
dash grenadine

Sprinkle a slice of pineapple with the sugar. Crush with a muddler in the shaker base, then add the rum, lime juice, grenadine, and some crushed ice. Shake long and vigorously, then strain into a cocktail glass and serve.

Tropicana (nonalcoholic)

1 oz. (30 ml/2 tbsp.) coconut milk
2 oz. (60 ml/4 tbsp.) pineapple juice
2 oz. (60 ml/4 tbsp.) mango juice
1 banana
Blend the ingredients. Add crushed ice. Blend, then pour into a tumbler.
Serve with a straw.

Tulip

1 oz. (30 ml/2 tbsp.) calvados
1 oz. (30 ml/2 tbsp.) sweet vermouth
½ oz. (15 ml/1 tbsp.) apricot brandy
2 dashes fresh lemon juice
½ oz. (15 ml/1 tbsp.) gomme syrup
Shake the ingredients, strain into a cocktail glass, and serve.

Typhoon

1 oz. (30 ml/2 tbsp.) gin
dash anisette
½ oz. (15 ml/1 tbsp.) fresh lime juice
chilled champagne
Shake the gin, anisette, and lime juice, then strain into an ice-filled
highball glass. Fill up with champagne and serve.

Union Jack

2 oz. (60 ml/4 tbsp.) gin
1 oz. (30 ml/2 tbsp.) sloe gin
2 dashes grenadine
Shake the gins and the grenadine, then strain into a cocktail glass
and serve.

Valencia Royale

1 oz. (30 ml/2 tbsp.) apricot brandy
½ oz. (15 ml/1 tbsp.) fresh orange juice
chilled champagne
Pour the brandy and orange juice into a champagne flute. Fill up with champagne and serve.

Vampire

1 oz. (30 ml/2 tbsp.) gin
1 oz. (30 ml/2 tbsp.) dry vermouth
2 dashes fresh lime juice
Shake the ingredients, then strain into a martini glass and serve.

Vampiro

2 oz. (60 ml/4 tbsp.) tequila
3 oz. (90 ml/6 tbsp.) tomato juice
1 oz. (30 ml/2 tbsp.) fresh orange juice
1 tsp. honey
⅓ oz. (10 ml/⅔ tbsp.) fresh lime juice
half onion slice, finely chopped
few thin slices fresh red chili
few drops Worcestershire sauce
lime wedge to garnish
Shake the ingredients, then strain into an ice-filled highball glass. Garnish with the lime wedge and serve.

Velvet Hammer

2 oz. (60 ml/4 tbsp.) vodka
1 oz. (30 ml/2 tbsp.) white crème de cacao
1 oz. (30 ml/2 tbsp.) heavy (double) cream
Shake the ingredients, then strain into a cocktail glass and serve.

Venus

2 oz. (60 ml/4 tbsp.) gin
1 oz. (30 ml/2 tbsp.) Cointreau
dash gomme syrup
dash Peychaud's bitters
6 raspberries
3 raspberries to garnish

Shake the ingredients, then strain into a cocktail glass. Add three raspberries on a cocktail stick across the glass and serve.

Very Chanilla (Chris Edwardes)

1 oz. (30 ml/2 tbsp.) vanilla vodka
½ oz. (15 ml/1 tbsp.) cherry schnapps
1 oz. (30 ml/2 tbsp.) cherry purée
juice of 1 lime
½ oz. (15 ml/1 tbsp.) gomme syrup
4 griottine cherries

Shake the ingredients, then pour into an old-fashioned glass and serve.

Very
Chanilla

Vesper (Vespa)

3 oz. (90 ml/6 tbsp.) Gordon's Gin
1 oz. (30 ml/2 tbsp.) Moskovskaya vodka
½ oz. (15 ml/1 tbsp.) Lillet Blanc
twist of lemon to garnish

Shake the gin, vodka, and Lillet Blanc, then strain into a martini glass, add the lemon twist, and serve.

VIP

1 oz. (30 ml/2 tbsp.) Cointreau
1 oz. (30 ml/2 tbsp.) bourbon
1 oz. (30 ml/2 tbsp.) dry vermouth
slice of orange to garnish

Pour the ingredients into an old-fashioned glass and stir, then garnish with the orange slice and serve.

Virgin Lea (nonalcoholic)

4 oz. (120 ml/8 tbsp.) tomato juice
2 oz. (60 ml/4 tbsp.) passion fruit juice
half yellow pepper, sliced
1 tsp. honey
1 to 2 dashes Worcestershire sauce

Place the pepper slices in a blender and add juices. Blend on low. Add the honey, Worcestershire sauce, and ice cubes. Blend on high. Pour through a strainer into an ice-filled highball glass and serve.

Virgin Mary (nonalcoholic)

5 oz. (150 ml/10 tbsp.) tomato juice
1 oz. (30 ml/2 tbsp.) fresh lemon juice
1 to 2 dashes Worcestershire sauce
1 to 2 dashes Tabasco sauce
salt
black pepper
1 stick celery

Pour the tomato juice into an ice-filled highball. Season to taste with spices. Stir. Add the celery stick as a stirrer and serve.

Virgin's Answer

1 oz. (30 ml/2 tbsp.) white rum
1 oz. (30 ml/2 tbsp.) brown crème de cacao
1 oz. (30 ml/2 tbsp.) crème de banane
1 oz. (30 ml/2 tbsp.) fresh lemon juice
1 oz. (30 ml/2 tbsp.) fresh orange juice
half of a banana

Blend the ingredients until smooth, then pour into a large goblet and serve.

Viva La Donna!

2 oz. (60 ml/4 tbsp.) tequila
2 oz. (60 ml/4 tbsp.) passion fruit juice
2 oz. (60 ml/4 tbsp.) fresh orange juice
⅔ oz. (20 ml/1⅓ tbsp.) fresh lime juice
Shake the ingredients, then strain into an ice-filled highball glass.

Vodka Martini (see Martini, p. 138)

2 oz. (60 ml/4 tbsp.) chilled vodka
spray of Noilly Prat from an atomizer
olive or twist of lemon to garnish
Spray a chilled martini glass with Noilly Prat.
Add the vodka, the olive or lemon and serve.

Vodkatini

3 oz. (90 ml/6 tbsp.) vodka
2 drops dry vermouth
lemon twist to garnish
Pour the vodka into a frozen martini glass.
Splash the vermouth on top of the vodka.
Add the twist of lemon and serve.

Vodka
Martini

Vulga

2 oz. (60 ml/4 tbsp.) vodka
½ oz. (15 ml/1 tbsp.) fresh orange juice
½ oz. (15 ml/1 tbsp.) fresh lime juice
2 dashes grenadine
dash orange bitters
Shake the ingredients, then strain into a martini glass and serve.

Wally

1 oz. (30 ml/2 tbsp.) cognac
1 oz. (30 ml/2 tbsp.) Benedictine
2 dashes fresh lemon juice
chilled champagne

**Pour the cognac, Benedictine, and lemon juice into a champagne flute.
Fill with champagne and serve.**

Ward Eight Cocktail

2 oz. (60 ml/4 tbsp) Bourbon
1 oz. (30ml/2 tbsp) Fresh lemon juice
½ oz. (15ml/1 tbsp) Gomme
Dash grenadine

**Shake the ingredients, then strain into an ice-filled old-fashioned glass
and serve.**

Watermelon Smash

1⅔ oz. (50 ml/3⅓ tbsp.) tequila
⅔ oz. (20 ml/1⅓ tbsp.) Limoncello
dash basil syrup
quarter of a slice of watermelon
ginger beer

**Shake the ingredients, except the ginger beer, then strain into an
ice-filled highball glass. Fill with ginger beer and serve.**

Where the Buffalo Roam

2 oz. (60 ml/4 tbsp.) Wyborowa vodka
½ oz. (15 ml/1 tbsp.) Zubrowka bison grass vodka
dash Chambery
ice cubes
blade of bison grass

**Coat a shaker with Chambery and discard the excess. Add the ice, both
vodkas, and shake, then strain into a cocktail glass. Garnish with the
blade of grass and serve.**

Whisky Sour (see Pisco Sour, p. 168)

2 oz. (60 ml/4 tbsp.) whisky
1 oz. (30 ml/2 tbsp.) fresh lemon juice
½ oz. (15 ml/1 tbsp.) gomme syrup
Shake the whiskey, lemon juice, and syrup, then pour into an old-fashioned glass and serve.

Whisky Mac

1 oz. (30 ml/2 tbsp.) Scotch whisky
1 oz. (30 ml/2 tbsp.) Stones Ginger Wine
Pour the scotch and ginger wine into an old-fashioned glass and serve.

White Baby

2 oz. (60 ml/4 tbsp.) gin
1 oz. (30 ml/2 tbsp.) fresh lime juice
½ oz. (15 ml/1 tbsp.) Cointreau
Shake the ingredients, then strain into a cocktail glass and serve.

White Bull

1 oz. (30 ml/2 tbsp.) tequila
1 oz. (30 ml/2 tbsp.) coffee liqueur
⅔ oz. (20 ml/1⅓ tbsp.) heavy (double) cream
⅔ oz. (20 ml/1⅓ tbsp.) milk
Shake the ingredients, then strain into a cocktail glass and serve.

White Lady

2 oz. (60 ml/4 tbsp.) gin
1 oz. (30 ml/2 tbsp.) Cointreau
1 oz. (30 ml/2 tbsp.) fresh lemon juice
1 tsp. superfine (caster) sugar
1 egg white
Shake the ingredients, then strain into a martini glass and serve.

White Negroni (Wayne Collins)

2 oz (60 ml/4 tbsp.) Plymouth Gin
1 oz (30 ml/2 tbsp.) Lillet Blanc
¾ oz (22 ml/1½ tbsp.) Suze
orange twist to garnish
Stir over ice, then strain into an ice-filled rocks glass. Garnish with orange twist.

White Russian

1 oz. (30 ml/2 tbsp.) vodka
1 oz. (30 ml/2 tbsp.) Kahlua
1 oz. (30 ml/2 tbsp.) heavy (double) cream
Shake the ingredients, then strain into a martini glass and serve. Alternatively, layer the ingredients in an ice-filled old-fashioned glass.

Why Not?

1 oz. (30 ml/2 tbsp.) gin
1 oz. (30 ml/2 tbsp.) apricot brandy
½ oz. (15 ml/1 tbsp.) dry vermouth
dash fresh lemon juice
Shake the ingredients, then strain into a martini glass and serve.

Windowlene

1 oz. (30 ml/2 tbsp.) blue curaçao
½ oz. (15 ml/1 tbsp.) white rum
½ oz. (15 ml/1 tbsp.) gin
½ oz. (15 ml/1 tbsp.) vodka
4 oz. (120 ml/8 tbsp.) chilled champagne
spiral of lemon rind to garnish
Pour the ingredients into a highball glass and stir. Add the lemon rind spiral and serve.

Woo Woo

1 oz. (30 ml/2 tbsp.) vodka
1 oz. (30 ml/2 tbsp.) peach schnapps
3 oz. (90 ml/6 tbsp.) cranberry juice
Shake the ingredients, then pour into an old-fashioned glass and serve.

Woodstock

1 oz. (30 ml/2 tbsp.) gin
1 oz. (30 ml/2 tbsp.) lemon juice
1 tsp. of maple syrup
dash Angostura bitters
Shake the ingredients, then strain into a martini glass and serve.

Woolworth (John Deragon)

2 oz (60 ml/4 tbsp.) Compass Box Asyla whisky
1 oz (30 ml/2 tbsp.) manzanilla sherry
½ oz (15 ml/1 tbsp.) Benedictine
2 dashes orange bitters
lemon twist to garnish
Stir all and strain into a cocktail glass.

Yellow Bird

2 oz. (60 ml/4 tbsp.) white rum
1 oz. (30 ml/2 tbsp.) Cointreau
1 oz. (30 ml/2 tbsp.) Galliano
2 oz. (60 ml/4 tbsp.) fresh orange juice
Shake the ingredients, then strain into a highball glass and serve.

Yellow
Bird

Yellow Fever

2 oz. (60 ml/4 tbsp.) vodka
⅔ oz. (20 ml/1⅓ tbsp.) Galliano
⅔ oz. (20 ml/1⅓ tbsp.) fresh lime juice
1 oz. (30 ml/2 tbsp.) pineapple juice
**Shake the ingredients, then strain into
a cocktail glass and serve.**

Yellow Monkey

Yellow
Fever

1 oz. (30 ml/2 tbsp.) Galliano
1 oz. (30 ml/2 tbsp.) white crème de cacao
1 oz. (30 ml/2 tbsp.) crème de banane
1 oz. (30 ml/2 tbsp.) white rum
1 oz. (30 ml/2 tbsp.) heavy (double) cream
Shake the ingredients, then strain into a martini glass and serve.

Yellow Rattler

1 oz. (30 ml/2 tbsp.) gin
½ oz. (15 ml/1 tbsp.) sweet vermouth
½ oz. (15 ml/1 tbsp.) dry vermouth
½ oz. (15 ml/1 tbsp.) orange juice
1 cocktail onion
**Shake all ingredients (except cocktail onion) with ice and strain into a
cocktail glass. Add the cocktail onion and serve.**

Yolanda

½ oz. (15 ml/1 tbsp.) brandy
½ oz. (15 ml/1 tbsp.) gin
½ oz. (15 ml/1 tbsp.) anisette
1 oz. (30 ml/2 tbsp.) sweet vermouth
dash grenadine
twist of orange to garnish
**Shake the ingredients together, then strain into a martini glass and
serve with the orange twist.**

Zanzibar

2 oz. (60 ml/4 tbsp.) dry vermouth
½ oz. (15 ml/1 tbsp.) gin
2 dashes fresh lemon juice
2 dashes gomme syrup
twist of lemon to garnish

Shake the ingredients, then strain into a martini glass, add the twist of lemon, and serve.

Za-za

2 oz. (60 ml/4 tbsp.) gin
2 oz. (60 ml/4 tbsp.) Dubonnet
twist of lemon to garnish

Stir the ingredients in a mixing glass, then strain into a martini glass, add the twist of lemon, and serve.

Zombie

¾ oz. (22 ml/1½ tbsp.) gold rum
2 oz. (60 ml/4 tbsp.) dark rum
¾ oz. (22 ml/1½ tbsp.) overproof rum
¾ oz. (22 ml/1½ tbsp.) Cherry Heering
1¼ oz. (38 ml/2½ tbsp.) fresh lime juice
dash grenadine
¾ oz. (22 ml/1½ tbsp.) fresh orange juice

Shake the ingredients, then strain into a highball glass half-filled with ice. Add two straws and serve.

Zombie

What's Your Poison?

The earliest distillers worked with the ingredients that were given to hand – grapes, sugar cane, barley or agave – but in time these spirits took on a human element, became rooted in the physical environment and more abstract national identity.

The greatest spirits have always drawn their character from this melding of the environmental and cultural landscape. The very greatest of their kind inspire a flood of memories and associations.

Whisky

"Love makes the world go round? Not at all. Whisky makes it go round twice as fast."

Compton Mackenzie, *Whisky Galore*

Whisky is, on one hand, a simple distilled mash of cereals, yeast and water and, on the other, a highly complex drink which shifts its shape depending on a host of different factors. You can have single malt whisky from Scotland, and within that a mass of different styles depending on still shape, wood type and even whether some burning carbonised heather has been added. Scotland produces grain whisky, too, and, in combination with malt, it gives the whisky the world is most familiar with: blended Scotch.

America has provided its own spin on proceedings with corn-accented bourbon, aged in sweet, flavoursome, white oak casks. Canada has a softer, gentler take on the whisky template while Japan, too, has created its own distinct personality. Far from being a commodity, whisky is a multi-faceted spirit and the choice of great whiskies has never been as wide as it is now.

Malt Whisky

Malt whisky is produced from three ingredients: malted barley, water and yeast. The barley is germinated, dried, mixed with hot water, fermented and then distilled in pot stills. The clear spirit is then aged in used oak casks for a minimum of three years.

Still life: The magical transformation of "beer" to spirit

Every distillery in Scotland follows this recipe, yet every malt whisky differs, sometimes substantially, from the next. This variety in style between the one hundred and five distilleries currently producing in Scotland is one element in malt's allure and part of its enigmatic magic. The fact is that every aspect of production is subtly different in each distillery. The same process may be taking place but each site has its own methods.

Malting involves fooling the barley into growth. As it grows, enzymes are activated, breaking down proteins and readying starch to be changed into fermentable sugars. This germination is stopped by drying the malt in a kiln. Traditionally the fire would have been lit with peat whose perfumed smoke is then permanently locked within the barley. In general these days, peating is very light with many malts being completely unpeated. The most heavily peated malts are from the islands, especially Islay.

The malted barley is then ground and passed into the mash tun. As hot water is added, the conversion from starch to sugar takes place. The sweet liquid is drained off, cooled and pumped to a fermenter where yeast is added. Fermentation takes a minimum of forty-five hours leaving a strong beige coloured beer of around 8% ABV. If the ferment is kept at under 48 hours the new spirit will have a nutty, spicy character. Longer periods of fermentation produce more complex flavours.

Now comes the final transformation which takes place in two copper pot stills. The first distillation gives a spirit known as low wines (around 21% ABV) which is collected, pumped into the second still and redistilled. This is when the stillman wants to separate the heart of the distillation from the foreshots which appear at the start and the feints which come across at the end.

From tiny acorns: Glen Grant whisky maturing in oak barrels

The size, shape and manner in which the stills are run is the major contributor to each distillery's signature character. In principle (and this holds for all spirits), the taller the still the lighter the resulting spirit, the smaller they are the heavier the new make will be. This is because the copper in the still removes 'heavy' flavours. Only the lightest, most fragrant and lightly fruity alcohols can easily climb the height of a tall necked still. The speed of the distillation is also important. The slower, the better is the rule. It allows the different flavour compounds (or congeners) to be released gently. A slow distillation will also encourage a process known as reflux in which alcohol vapours rise up the still but rather than carrying over the neck, condense on the sides and fall back into the boiling liquid. This increases the complexity of the end spirit.

Even the way in which the spirit is condensed has an impact on flavour. Distilleries using worm tubs tend to produce a meaty character, while those using condensers make a lighter style. This is just a guide though, there is always at least one exception which disproves the rule! Glenfiddich, for example, has tiny stills yet makes a light spirit, Royal Lochnagar uses worms yet makes a non-meaty style.

It is estimated that up to seventy percent of a whisky's flavour comes from the interaction between the spirit and the cask. Scotch is mostly aged in previously used casks which fall into two broad types, ex-Bourbon barrels made from American white oak and sherry butts made from European oak. These two species give significantly different results. European oak is rich in colour and tannins and imparts sweet, clove-like, resinous notes to the whisky. American oak is rich in vanillins and provides flavours of spice, coconut and chocolate. When you consider that the flavour profile will change each time the cask is refilled you can begin to see how distillers can create a complex range of flavours.

Islay and Jura

There's much debate as to how much influence location can have in dictating the flavour of a whisky and while "regionality" is a handy way of explaining the spirit, the idea that a whisky gets its character from its surroundings is overly simplistic. A "regional" style emerged via the distillers in the 19th century who crafted whiskies which appealed to blenders, but it would be wrong to suggest that whisky has "terroir". While some malts matured by the sea can show a briny character, water has minimal impact on flavour and the fact that heather grows around a distillery won't make its spirit heathery.

You could say that Islay malts share some similar flavours, but to say they were all the same would be wrong. This is a whisky-making island – maybe even the first place where whisky was made in Scotland – and this heritage and the island's geographical peculiarities have contributed to its highly individual style. What sets Islay apart is its peat. Because the island has been regularly submerged its peat contains layers of marine vegetation. When burned, it gives off a seaweedy, tarry, iodine note not found in mainland peat.

Not all of Islay's malts are peated. Bunnahabhain on the far northeast coast and Bruichladdich are both virtually unpeated in their main expressions, though both also make heavily peated variants, while Caol Ila reverses the approach by being heavily peated for most of the year but also making an unpeated version. The malt made on the neighbouring island of Jura has no peat at all. Bowmore is medium peated; the mighty Kildalton malts of the south coast: Ardbeg, Lagavulin and Laphroaig have peat belching from every orifice; while Caol Ila confounds every theory by being medium-peated part of the year and unpeated for the rest. You can certainly find a beachy note in most of Islay's malts – conceivably from the casks breathing in sea air, but they are not all stylistically the same. Ileachs are masterly whisky makers and there is an Islay malt for every occasion.

Tasting notes

Ardbeg Islay's most heavily peated malt, and also one of its most complex. Sooty smoke galore as well as marmalade, lime, malt and subtle spice.

Bowmore A medium-peated malt from Islay's capital. Bowmore's signature is a lightly floral note mixed with cereal, mango, orange peel and briny smoke.

Bunnahabhain A light, highly attractive malt with a signature gingery note.

Bruichladdich The restless experimenters of Islay produce three styles: fresh, floral, lightly fruity Bruichladdich; medium-peated and smoky Port Charlotte; and the tarry Octomore.

Caol Ila Although peated to the same level as Lagavulin, Caol Ila is lighter in character, mixing grass, juniper, a seashell brininess and an oily texture.

Jura Islay's near neighbour makes an unpeated malt, fresh and heathery at 10 years, slightly frutier at 16 but at its best at 21 or older.

Kilchoman Islay's smallest and newest distillery. Smoky with notes of scallop, seaweed and a mix of sweet vanilla and clove on the palate.

Lagavulin Perfumed and elegant: cigar smoke, lapsang souchong tea, heather, beach bonfires. The 16-year-old is a classic.

Laphroaig Full-on peated malt: tarry, medicinal, with pipe smoke and iodine. Go for the 10-year-old or Quarter Cask.

Campbeltown and the Lowlands

Whisky-making just doesn't fit with our impressions of the Lowlands yet this area produces the bulk of Scotland's whisky – grain whisky that is. Malt distilleries are harder to find. There are currently five in operation. There's little peat here, so traditionally Lowland whiskies rarely had any smoky notes. Ninetenth-century distillers also made whisky on a large scale to satisfy a large urban population and the big Lowland stills made a lighter style of spirit. Add in the fashion for triple distillation and you have the template for Lowland whisky.

A light style does not mean an insipid taste. Far from it. Glenkinchie and the triple-distilled Auchentoshan are delicate, flavoursome aperitif malts, while Bladnoch has a wonderful floral complexity.

Ailsa Bay is part of the Grant's distillery complex in Girvan and produces a wide range of styles (both peated and unpeated) for the firms blends. Dadtmill in Fife is a tiny farm distillery whose whiskies are showing considerable promise.

Campbeltown too offers slim pickings for the malt aficionado, compared to when it was at its whisky-making height at the turn of the twentieth century when the town had 21 distilleries. The firm has also rebuilt the neighbouring Glengyle distillery where it makes the Kilkerran brand. In recent years the town's other distillery, Glen Scotia, has also started up production once more. The town—and the whisky industry—owes the Mitchell and Wright families a huge debt.

There are various theories as to why Campbeltown collapsed so spectacularly. Maybe the heavy, oily smoky style simply fell from favour, perhaps distillers began making their whisky too quickly. It's ironic that the one distillery to still fly the flag, Springbank, was considered in the early 20th century to be making an atypical Campbeltown style!

Tasting notes

Auchentoshan Delicate and ultra fresh at 12-year-old. Very clean, dry – a good lunchtime dram. The 21-year-old has more weight.

Bladnoch The 8-year-old has a fresh, almost minty nose with a hint of caramelized orange and flowers. A delicate, slightly sweet start, before drying out a little mid-palate.

Glenkinchie The 10-year-old has a fresh, almost citric nose with grassy aromas. Crisp, clean and smooth on the palate. The **amontillado finish** is rounded with a little malt loaf and some nut. Soft, sweet, grassy palate and a long, sweet finish with a nutty drive.

Rosebank Appears light initially, but there's a deceptive richness behind. Dry on the palate, but balanced elegant fruit. Some wood on the finish. This distillery is no longer operational.

Springbank A distinctive briny note along with an oily rich palate, coupled with a huge range of complex fruits and a hint of smoke. One of the great whiskies. Anything from this distillery is worth trying

South of the Great Glen

The Highlands is an enormous region with relatively few distilleries for its size. There are clusters in Perthshire and northern Aberdeenshire, as well as the splendidly remote Dalwhinnie (the point where three old drove roads meet) but very few on the fertile east coast, and fewer still on the west. Why, if blenders created the modern Scotch industry we know today are there so few plants close to major barley-growing regions and old blending centres such as Perth?

The fact is that Speyside distillers had a head start on their southern cousins. When small-scale distilling was banned in the Highlands it was the farmers in the remote parts of Speyside who kept making their hooch – it was the best way they could make a living from their poor quality barley. It wasn't as necessary for farmers in the south to take up this life of crime. Many did take out licences after the change of law in 1824 which ushered in larger-scale whisky-making, but of the host of Highland distilleries which started up at that point only twenty remain, among them one which could be the oldest distillery in Scotland, Glen Garioch. Ardmore is a massive distillery, built to supply fillings for the Teacher's blend, while neighbour Glendronach is also built on a grand scale. The west coast, isolated in the days of the nineteenth century whisky boom, has only two plants and both of these, Oban and Ben Nevis, are railheads with fast connections to the central belt. Even today it takes a long time to travel from east to west in Scotland and once Speyside was up and running the writing was on the wall for any commercial distilling in the west.

Edradour: Scotland's smallest distillery has retained its farmyard air

Tasting notes

Dalwhinnie A honeyed character with the occasional touch of heather.

Edradour Owned by independent bottler Signatory Vintage, makes a robust fruity style of spirit best suited to ex-sherry casks, as well as a heavily peated variant, Ballechin.

Glengoyne Unpeated with a clover-like juiciness. The 12-year-old is a lunchtime malt, but the 17- and 21-year-old are both superb. Full of character.

Oban The 10-year-old has a clean, tingly fruity nose of dried herbs and sea breezes. Gentle but with a refreshing quality.

Royal Lochnagar Tiny distillery making a complex spirit which can cope well with European oak, giving the grassy character an extra, chewy weight. Worth seeking out.

Speyside

Speyside is shaped like a rough wedge stretching from the outskirts of Forres in the west, to Buckie in the east and south to Kingussie, with the greatest concentration of distilleries around the towns of Elgin, Keith, Rothes and the region's capital Dufftown. The landscape encompasses high moorland, coastal plains, sand dunes, mountains and rivers and this diverse geography is reflected in a far wider range of flavours and styles than many people think. Speyside can also lay claim to be the spiritual birthplace of the modern Scotch industry, the region (Glenlivet specifically) where the new style licences were taken out in 1824, allowing commercial production in the Highlands, many of those founding fathers: The Glenlivet, Cardhu, Glenfarclas are still with us.

It was the combination of a long period of illicit distilling followed by the arrival of the railways which first attracted blenders to Speyside. Entrepreneurial Victorian distillers, landowers, businessmen, gentlemen farmers, all saw the success of many of the original plants and decided to try their hand. Soon the area had become Scotland's pre-eminent whisky-making region. Speyside is an example of old-style, self-sufficient distilling grown on a grand scale. The distilleries tend to be large, they still use barley grown and malted nearby, while there is an infrastructure of cooperages, coppersmiths and haulage firms supporting the industry. The big names in single malt are all here: Macallan, Glenlivet, Glenfiddich, Glen Grant, Aberlour as well as some lesser known but equally great malts: Mortlach, Balvenie, Glenrothes, Glen Elgin, Benrinnes. Now, if there was such a thing as a single regional style or some connection between location and flavour then Dufftown should provide proof, after all Wm Grant has three plants (Glenfiddich, Balvenie and Kininvie) on one site, while Dufftown distillery and

Mortlach lurk just down the glen. Yet Dufftown's drams range from the light and malty Fiddich to the elegant honey and orange accents of Balvenie to the robustness of Mortlach. Though regionality may be over-simplified there is still, somehow a link with the area. Perhaps the first Speyside distillers tried to incorporate the local flavours of bracken, pine forest, honey and heather into their whiskies. The original distillery style was perhaps an expression of the personality of the distiller.

Tasting notes

Balvenie: A very subtle, elegant malt. Honey is the signature note here along with soft fruits and a hint of smoke. Magnificent.

Glenfiddich: The 12-year-old is an approachable, fruity, gentle dram, but the chocolatey 18-year-old is the best of the range. Look for even older bottlings.

The Glenlivet: A textbook light, flowery Speysider. The 12-year-old is charming while the complex 18-year-old is one of Scotland's finest malts.

Glenrothes: Ripe and rich yet delicately perfumed. Subtle, sweet and complex.

Macallan: Ex-sherry casks are the key here, matching the oily richness of the spirit and adding notches of clove, incense and elegant spices.

227

North of the Great Glen and onto the Islands

The north-east coast has long been a somewhat forgotten whisky region in terms of single malt, but things are changing. Glenmorangie from Tain, the best known globally, has been joined by Glen Ord in the Black Isle, which has been reinvented as the Singleton of Glen Ord. In addition, Dalmore is making a bid for the top-end luxury market, Balblair is exploring the "vintage" bottling approach, Old Pulteney is building a sterling reputation for itself, while Clyelish is establishing itself as a cult whisky. The only one which remains slightly under the radar is Teaninich. The north-east may be remote, but its distilleries have survived where so many others have failed for the simple reason that they make superb whisky.

This sense of whisky-making in isolation is common to the western isles. Lack of raw materials and brutal clearances put paid to most island distillers. There is a new, thriving, distillery on Arran, but, with the exception of Islay, island distilleries are few and far between. There is one each on Mull (Tobermory), Skye (Talisker) and Lewis (Abhainn Dearg).

Talisker is another of those places where the link between landscape, community and whisky is at its strongest. The distillery workers are crofters and fishermen, one has a sucessful oyster-farming business. Perhaps it is this strong link to the place, or its magnificent scenery that gives Talisker a taste that seems to be a distillation of its location.

The same could be said of Orkney's greatest whisky, Highland Park. Using heather-scented local peat, malting some of its own needs in the traditional way helps to produce a smoky, yet sweet dram. Its neighbour, Scapa, is exotically fruited and totally different and like so many of these remote malts, completely overlooked.

Tasting notes

Balblair A mix of fresh berries, melon and occasionally jasmine and elderflower. Older vintages show a richer and more topical edge.

Clynelish Honeycomb, cinnamon, an oily palate and a hint of smoke. Hugely underrated.

Dalmore One of the richest malts with bags of fruit, a curranty sweetness and a hint of peat.

Glenmorangie The two pillars here are tall stills giving a citric, fruity and minty spirit, which is then aged mainly in vanilla-rich American oak casks. The older the expression, the deeper and more chocolatey and caremalized the flavours become.

Highland Park (Orkney) Scotland's sexiest malt. Heather, honey, orange, fragrant smoke, soft fruits. Superb at any age, try the 18-year-old!

Pulteney Big, unctuous malt with beeswax, salt and peaches.

Scapa (Orkney) A hidden gem. Lusciously peachy, exotically fruity.

Singleton of Glen Ord Reformulated for the Asian market, Glen Ord's signature green grassy intensity is now coated in a mix of toffee, ginger and dark fruits from European oak casks.

Talisker Skye's sole legal distillery and a truly classic malt. Heathery peat and a cracked pepper note along with mellow cakey fruit. Massive, lingering and uncompromising.

Teaninich A rarely seen single malt (most of it goes to blending). Has a wonderful austerity with pine, tea, dried grass and a hint of smoke.

Blending and blends

Blended whisky is a mixture of malt whiskies and grain. The latter is often dismissed as nothing more than Scottish vodka, the filler that dilutes the malts, or the spirit which makes it go further. However, although grain whisky might be lighter than malt in style, it brings its own silky texture to a blend and introduces new aromas. Each grain distillery also produces a different spirit.

Another misconception is that blenders follow a strict recipe and will always use the same percentage of certain malts. While specific whiskies may always be present in a blend the volume may change. Blenders think in terms of blocks of flavour, the constituent parts of which may vary. Because distilleries do shut down a certain style of whisky, perhaps aged in a specific wood type, may not have been made 12 years previously. A blender must be able to make a consistent product with ever-changing components so that if one drops out it can be replaced by another or by a combination of two new ones. This knowledge of how whiskies can be combined, coupled with an understanding of the flavours produced by each whisky (including grain) at different ages and in different wood types, reveals the blender as an artist.

William Grant's Girvan Distillery: Produces clean, complex grain

Tasting Notes

LIGHT
J&B Rare Pale with a delicate nose: notes of citrus fruit and sweet hay.

Antiquary 12-year-old Sweet and succulent nose with golden syrup, luscious grain and toasty spices. Chewy, long and complex.

Ballantine's Finest Lifted with green grass, cucumber, pear drops and some backed apple notes behind. Delicate but with good softness in the middle of the tongue.

Cutty Sark A floral/fragrant nose with a soft buttery note, light red fruits and oaty maltiness. Creamy and grassy with a lemon lift.

Dewar's Delicate, malty start then lemon meringue pie, clover, honey, vanilla, a wisp of smoke and some spiciness.

Chivas 18-year-old Pears, apple, green grass and cereal on the nose. Some honeyed sweetness and malty weight on palate.

MEDIUM
The Famous Grouse A soft, fruity nose, with cereal, peach/apricot. The palate is chewy with sultana, walnut and a veil of peatiness.

Grant's Family Reserve Fragrant with honey, lime and a hint of peat smoke. The sweet grain is superbly balanced by the complex malts.

Bell's 8-year-old Spicy and nutty core with fresh-cut apple and a juicily thick marmalada-like palate.

HEAVY
Whyte & Mackay Cooked dark/dried fruits on the nose and a lovely silky finish.

Johnnie Walker Black Label Complex and elegant with peach, honey, vanilla, cream and rich peaty notes on the nose. The palate is also complex: sweet honeyed notes mix with sherry wood, leather, ripe fruits and fragrant smokiness.

Mix and match: Most malt distilleries produce for blends, not single malt

Irish Whiskey

Each country has its own idiosyncratic approach to the basic recipe for making spirits and Ireland is no exception.

It's worth remembering that although there may only be three whiskey producers and (at the time of writing) three distilleries in Ireland that this is far from being a small-scale boutique industry. Irish whiskey may not be the mighty global power it was in the nineteenth century but it has fought back from a pretty desperate period in the 1960s to be rightly accepted as a country which makes highly drinkable world-class whiskeys.

Intriguingly, the three distilleries each have their very own method of production, though all have the same aim – to make a style of whiskey which is softer and gentler than that made by their Scots cousins. What is equally surprising is that 30-odd brands of Irish whiskey (plus gin and vodka) are made in one distillery, Midleton. Built in 1974, this extraordinary plant is basically two distilleries rolled into one: one side making pot-still whiskey, the other making grain. The stills are all interlinked, allowing the master distiller to use any combination he wishes. There's a triple pot still: pot/column/pot; pot/column/column. When you consider the different combinations of malted and unmalted barley in each mash and the ability to collect distillates at different strengths you can appreciate how this plant can produce a myriad of flavours.

Triple distillation isn't the only thing which characterises the Midleton whiskeys. This is the home of single pot still, the whiskey style that first established Ireland as a world force. The use of unmalted as well as malted barley in the mashbill, plus triple distillation (in pot stills), adds an oily mouthfeel with a dry spicy/

Old Bushmills Distillery: The sole whisky maker in Northern Ireland

apple/blackcurrant character on the palate . The final element comes from a wood policy which utilizes a lot of first-fill American and European oak barrels. That's a lot of flavour being built in.

Compared to the complexities of Midleton, Bushmills (owned by Diageo) is slightly easier to understand. A classic malt whisky distillery, it sits on the north Antrim coast virtually in sight of Islay and Campbeltown. Triple distillation of unpeated malt gives a clover-fresh gentle spirit. The third member of the trio is Cooley which burst onto the scene in 1989 breaking Irish Distillers' monopoly. Aiming to produce a style that was substantially different, Cooley decided to not only double distil their whiskeys but even peat some of them. With every year that passes their whiskeys improve, benefiting the whole Irish industry in the process.

Tasting Notes

Black Bush Sweet toffee nose with touches of European oak, spice and dried fruit. Soft and richly fruity with a gorgeous silky texture. A classic.

Bushmills 10-year-old malt Clean and crisply malty with attractive clover and cream notes. Light, gentle and slightly grassy.

Bushmills Original Light and clean with a mix of crushed biscuit, bran and cut grass on the nose. Gentle, soft and amenable, especially with ginger ale.

Connemara single malt Cooley broke the mould when it introduced this – the only peated malt from Ireland. As the whiskey has matured so the fruity malt and the turfy peatiness have integrated with one another increasingly well.

Jameson Clean and quite malty nose with some pot still oiliness lurking in the background. Mid-weight, easy-going and attractive.

Jameson 12-year-old Noticeably more pot still here with added cumin and coriander, and more lush fruitiness: apricot jam and peaches. Tongue-coating stuff.

Kilbeggan Cooley's leading brand. Crisp and grassy with some grape and nutty cereal notes, then more coconut than a desert island. Lovely.

Power's The softest sexiest Irish whiskey of all, like peaches in honey. Slips down too easily.

Power's 12-year-old Even more outrageously fruit-laden, with more pot still whiskey in evidence.

Redbreast 12-year-old The epitome of pot still whiskey: an oily richness with a clean, mouth-watering bite from the unmalted barley. Spicy with fruitcake, lemon peel, dried and overripe fruits. Stunningly good.

Tullamore Dew A light-bodied, young mixing whiskey. Aromatic with green apple, pear and a gentle almond note.

On the road again: Irish whiskey is once more being rolled out around the world

Bourbon

Like all the great spirits of the world, bourbon draws its flavours from its surroundings. The first settlers in Kentucky, mostly Scots and Irish, were encouraged to plant corn (maize) and their knowledge of distilling allowed them to make whiskey from it. In those pioneering days anyone could make anything they wanted. Today the industry is more closely regulated.

Bourbon can be made anywhere in the US provided the mash contains a minimum of 51% corn, though it must not exceed 80% (then it becomes corn whiskey) To this corn is added a mix of "small grains" traditionally malted barley and rye, although there are some brands who prefer to use wheat. The ingredients of this mashbill are ground, cooked and then transferred to fermenters where yeast is added. Only rum producers are as obsessed with yeast as bourbon makers. Each distiller has its own strain, or strains, which impart different flavours to the spirit, thus helping to create the distillery character.

At this stage backset or sour mash is added. This is the acidic liquid residue left in the still after distillation which when fed into the fermenter helps to kill bacteria, balances the pH of the water and encourages a clean ferment.

After about four days fermentation the beer is first distilled in a column still or "beer still" and then passes through a second still known as a doubler. Only one distiller, Woodford Reserve, uses pot stills. Needless to say each distiller has its own variation on these basics: the composition of the mashbill, how much backset to use, the yeast strains, the speed and cut points of the distillate. The "white dog" as the new make is known is then filled into new, charred American oak barrels. It's here that bourbon acquires its signature rich reddish colour and sweet notes of vanilla, spice and honey. Most distillers age their bourbon in huge warehouses. Since Kentucky has hot humid summers the whiskeys in the top floors will move in and out of the wood more quickly than those on the cooler lower floors. Distillers therefore either blend together a cross-section from all the different floors, or as in the case of Wild Turkey and Maker's Mark, rotate the barrels from the top to bottom floors. This does not make the bourbon woody because by having an in-depth understanding of the flavours produced on each floor of each warehouse, the distillers can create a mature spirit with great complexity and elegance.

Kentucky's greatest exports: Horseflesh and bourbon

Tasting notes

JIM BEAM
Jim Beam White Label 80°
Light and spicy. Young and fresh.
A decent starter.

SMALL BATCH RANGE
Basil Hayden 8-year-old 80° Clean
and delicate with light and spicy rye
to the fore. Good balance.

Knob Creek 9-year-old 100°
Perfumed. Soft and fruity. Blackberry,
treacle toffee. Soft and powerful.
Less thick than Baker's.

Booker's 126.5° Huge and ripe:
spun sugar, apricot, lashings of
vanilla, orange crème brulee.
Perfumed with a floral lift.
Imagine flowers encased in
orange blossom honey. A big-
boned bourbon.

FOUR ROSES
Four Roses Small Batch The most
complex mix of yeast strains (five)
and mashbills (two), this small batch
has a great lemony rye accent mixed
with wild cherry, eucalyptus and
cinnamon toast.

WILD TURKEY
Wild Turkey 101° Big, fruity and
complex. Ripe, dark fruits: blackberry,

prune, caramelised fruit, leather,
chocolate. In time, liquorice,

molasses, chestnut honey. Huge
palate: treacle, chocolate mousse,
with a lift of rose petal. Thick layers
of honey, nut and balanced spicy
oak. This is what old-style bourbon
is all about.

Russell's Reserve 10-year-old
Spicier than 101° but with weight and
fragrance. Chewy weight with an
extra layer of dried spice. A complex,
serious, sipping bourbon.

Rare Breed 108.6° Even sweeter
than the 8-year-old 101° with an
added cedary note. More wood-
derived aromas and flavours (but this
is NOT woody) cigar box, hickory,
chocolate.

Kentucky Spirit single barrel The
most herbal and spicy of the range
with notes of molasses, chestnut
honey, creme brulee, rose and
tobacco. Huge and everlasting.
One to savour.

Wild Turkey rye Big and perfumed
nose. Huge, heavy palate then rye
blasts in. Powerful and a classic
balance between sweet and savoury.

MAKER'S MARK

Maker's Mark 90° Elegant. Runny honey, cherry, peach/apricot, butter icing/cream and fresh wild herbs. Ripe, soft, creamy and fruit-filled. Great balance and elegance.

BROWN & FOREMAN

Woodford Reserve Complex, honeyed and soft: orange blossom, tangerine peel, poached peach, mint, smoky oak. Ripe and soft, like orange honey dribbled on top of Greek yoghurt.

BUFFALO TRACE

Buffalo Trace 90° Rich and sweet with chocolate, cream, cigar box and honey. Soft and rounded.

Eagle Rare 50.5° Lush but spicy with vanilla, honey and black fruits. The 17-year-old is oily and aromatic: red peppercorns, coffee, coconut butter, plum cake. Spicy palate. One of the woodier ones.

Sazerac Rye An older rye with more oak influence, but there is still some prickly heat coming through with allspice, rye flour and clove. The palate has good acidity and a rich caramel underpinning.

W.L. Weller 90° Wheated bourbon which has a herbal/berried nose with caramelised fruits, leather. Soft and mellow. 19-year-old is an elegant marvel with mature spirit notes mixed with honeysuckle, gingerbread, pecan pie and chocolate covered cherries.

HEAVEN HILL

Elijah Craig 12-year-old Mature and elegant with cedar wood, old leather, spice boxes. The palate lifts into anise, mint and raspberry. Full bodied.

Old Fitzgerald 12-year-old A wheated bourbon with a smoky, charred nose. Deep: butterscotch, honey, chocolate and nutty oak. Lovely balance. One to sip with a good cigar.

VAN WINKLE

Van Winkle 12-year-old Rich, polished oak nose alongside pepper, cumin and nutmeg. In time Turkish delight. Big and soft with ripe berries and honey. Gentle but rich.

241

Tennessee rye and craft whiskeys

Ironically, most people's favourite bourbon, Jack Daniel's, isn't bourbon at all but until recently one of only two Tennessee whiskeys, the other being George Dickel. Both are made in subtly different ways. While Tennessee whiskeys start life in the same way as bourbon with a mashbill of a minimum of 51% corn, when the white dog leaves the still it is first filtered through a bed of maple charcoal instead of being put straight into new American oak barrels. This technique, also used by vodka producers, removes

Mr Jack: Small in stature, big in vision

impurities and buffs up the spirit. It speeds up what would normally happen over the first couple of years inside a barrel.

In much the same way as the American beer industry has been re-energized by the emergence of small local breweries, so craft distilling has opened up a new world of possibilities for the small-scale distiller. At the time of writing, there are around 200 distilleries making whiskey and experimenting with various techniques, grains, woods and smoking techniques. Names to watch include Balcones, Corsair, Hudson, High West and St George.

The other American whiskey making a remarkable recovery is rye. Made from a minimum of 51% rye, it was the most popular style of US whiskey pre-Prohibition and was the base spirit in such classic cocktails as the Manhattan. As America turned its back on its own whiskeys so rye fell from favour. A little was made but it had only a small following. Thankfully the recent arrival of top-quality, premium bourbons has stimulated a rye revival. It's an uncompromising style of whiskey, the grain giving an unmistakeable spicy, acidic, oily bite to the spirit which hits the back of the palate. Once tried never forgotten.

Tasting notes

JACK DANIEL
Jack Daniel's Black Label 80°
Very sweet and clean with a touch of liquorice, smoke and caramel. A good mouthful with a great sweet finish. Pretty young though and needs to be mixed

Gentleman Jack 80° An even sweeter version of the classic Black Label with added element of blackberry fruitiness and a sooty, rich finish.

DICKEL
This distillery, famed for making one of the finest and most goddamned drinkable whiskeys ever made, has recently reopened!

George Dickel No12 90° Spicy yet soft: apple pie, lemon cakes, honey with cloves,geranium and a light twang of rye. A spicy, complex fragrant/floral with apple, lime blossom, ginger/cinnamon and tobacco.

George Dickel Special Barrel Reserve 90° Softly fruited nose with butterscotch, caramel notes. Cinnamon, nutmeg and cumin on the palate with ripe fresh fruit: apple, orange/tangerine. Super-sexy.

George Dickel No. 8 An enigmatic nose that mixes lime blossom and smoky mocha notes. Light fruit on a palate that is both smooth and dry.

Canadian Whisky

Canadian whisky, like that of its southern neighbour, was first made by immigrants who arrived in the east of the country in the eighteenth century, but it was nineteenth-century English and European merchants like Molson, Worts, Seagram and Wiser who made it into a commercial venture, along with people such as Detroit-based whisky rectifier Hiram Walker who jumped across the border in the mid-nineteenth century.

Many of them originally used wheat as the base for their whiskies as well as rye, but as the prairies were settled and farmed, so corn became the dominant grain. Although many people still (wrongly) refer to Canadian whiskies generically as rye, that grain only plays a small—though significant—part in the overall blends and "true" rye whiskies such as those made by Alberta Distillers are unusual.

Rather, Canadian whiskies are single-distillery blends with all the whiskies in the final mix being made at the same plant. The foundation is a high-strength "base" whisky, which is most usually made from corn, although wheat (Highwood) and rye (Alberta) are also made. Some distilleries will make a number of different bases aged in different types of wood to widen their options. To these are added "flavouring" whiskies distilled to a lower strength to give

Hiram Walker: The founder of a great whisky dynasty

Tasting notes

Alberta Premium Dark Horse A blend of 12- and six-year-old rye with a little corn whisky. Bold, rich and prune-like with energetic spice and black cherry.

Canadian Club Some rye notes alongside crisp apple. Gentle and sweet on the palate with plenty of cream and toffee.

Crown Royal The sweetest of the major Canadian brands—masses of honey and crème brûlée backed with strawberry and plum. Light rye adds some balancing dryness.

Forty Creek Double Barrel Reserve A blend of corn, rye and malt whiskies finished in ex-bourbon barrels. Here you find maple syrup, coconut cream, red cherry and a mix of lemon and popcorn on the palate.

Seagram's VO Gentle and soft—and made for mixing with ginger ale—with banana split, butterscotch and firm rye on the finish.

Wiser's Deluxe Restrained rye to kick off with, a little sandalwood, nutmeg and anise mixed with apple and toffee. Perfectly balanced.

greater impact. These can be made of rye, wheat, barley or corn: again it is up to each distiller's recipe. A wide mix of woods—new, used, ex-bourbon, ex-sherry—will be used for maturation. Finally all these components will be blended into the final product.

Today, there are eight "classic" Canadian distilleries, with a number of smaller craft operations starting. A wide range of styles are produced, from punchy 100 percent rye to single malt, but at the heart of the Canadian style is an elegant, smooth, soft mellowness with subtle complexity.

Other Whiskies of the World

The last of the established whisky-producing countries is Japan, which, although a relatively recent arrival on the scene, has been distilling whisky since 1923. The Japanese distiller uses the same template as his Scots counterpart, with single malts and blends being produced. The style is, however, distinctly different to Scotch, with a heightened aroma, clarity of character and a lack of cereal dryness. The use of Japanese oak in some brands adds an incense-like lift to the whiskies. Also, because there are relatively few distilleries (eight making malt whisky at the time of writing) each has been set up to produce as large a range of whiskies as possible. This means that even a single malt will be a blend of different styles. All are highly regarded around the world.

The past few years have seen an explosion of whisky-making around the world. There are three new distilleries in England, one in Wales, while Brittany is establishing itself as a new Celtic heartland. Scandinavia has also caught the whisky bug, with distilleries in Sweden, Norway, Finland and Denmark. In fact, every country in Europe now has at least one whisky distillery.

The trend is global. There are two in South Africa, one in Taiwan, and a growing number in Australia—with the highest concentration in Tasmania. India too makes a vast volume of whisky—although much of it is distilled from molasses. However, there are a growing number of distilleries there conforming to the international definition of whisky as being a cereal-based, oak-matured spirit.

What is fascinating is that, although whisky-making is now truly international, each of these countries has adapted this template to create a style which speaks of its place of origin. The future is healthy—and varied.

Tasting notes

JAPAN
Nikka From The Barrel A high-strength blend showing grassy and herbal notes with touches of coffee.

Hibiki 17-year-old Suntory's premium blend. Generous and rich with a mix of cooked and dried fruits and hazelnut.

Hakushu 12-year-old Suntory's Hakushu makes a wide range of malts, but the bottled examples show a cool minty grassiness with touches of flower and bamboo.

Yamazaki 18yo Typifies Japanese whisky's ability to combine complexity with absolute clarity.

FRANCE
Glann ar Mor Hard on the water's edge in Brittany, Glann ar Mor uses old distilling techniques to make a robust yet aromatic whisky. One to watch.

AUSTRALIA
Lark Single Cask Bill Lark is the founding father of the modern Australian whisky industry. His Tasmanian distillery uses local peat, which gives an intense perfumed quality to his creamy, balanced whisky.

SWEDEN
Mackmyra1st Edition Though sticking to a Scottish template it asserts its 'Swedishness' by using juniper branches in the kilning of the barley and a small percentage of Swedish oak in the blend.

USA
Stranahan's Colorado Malt Whiskey Proof that America can makes its own single malt whisky, here's an understated, orange, malty, coffee-accented whisky which shows a delicious black-fruited sootiness on the plate.

Hudson Baby Bourbon From upstate New York comes this 100% aged corn whiskey that's brimful of sweet spice and rose petal.

St George From California comes this remarkable and intensely fruity single malt, which seems to capture the essence of mango and apricot and combine it with a crisp texture that softens into American cream soda.

Vodka

"It's true. I am a vegetarian, but I hear vodka comes from a potato."

Bette Midler, *Down and Out in Beverly Hills*

Vodka has made its name by being the perfect partner in any number of mixed drinks. Until recently it was regarded as light, flavourless, undemanding and malleable, but today we know there is more to vodka than that. A few years ago if you had asked for a vodka you would have been given an anonymous, interchangeable, brand, whereas now it is hard to keep up with the flood of new releases, particularly at the top end of the market. Although Smirnoff may dominate in terms of volume in the west, there are any number of vodkas from Eastern Europe and Russia which are re-establishing this spirit's historical credentials. Vodka is no longer just a cheap hit of neutral alcohol; it is a premium spirit.

The battle for vodka's soul these days is between brands that are wholly packaging led and those that prefer to speak of production-based quality. Some, happily, manage to straddle the two, among

them the brand that helped to kick-start the new age of vodka in the 1980s, Absolut. Inevitably, as the premium and super-premium vodka boom has gathered pace there have been some newcomers of dubious quality: drinks which are all about image and fail to deliver the goods when they hit the palate. The emergence of strong, independent economies in Eastern Europe and Russia has also finally allowed vodka producers to release brands that had been hidden from Western eyes for years. High-quality Polish, Russian, Estonian and Latvian vodkas have hit our shores, triggering a new premium revolution in the west. There are now top-class vodkas appearing from Holland, France, Canada and America, all of which taste of something.

How it's made

Vodka distillers have always aimed to make as pure a spirit as possible. This is partly because of location and partly because of fashion. Vodka's spiritual home, central and eastern Europe, has extremely cold winters and, since low-strength spirits can freeze, in order to transport it during those months it had to be as high in strength as possible. This involves redistilling: the more times you distil, the lighter in flavour and higher in strength the spirit will be.

Additionally, from the start vodka was a flavoured spirit, first as a base for medicinal herbs and then as a fashionable drink. Perhaps the fruits and herbs in some flavoured vodka recipes were initially added to mask the rough-tasting alcohol, but as distillation was refined the flavourings became the important elements in the drink and needed to sit on as pure and light a spirit as possible. Furthermore, the higher strength the spirit, the more effective it is in leaching flavours.

Technically, vodka can be made from anything containing starch or readily available fermentable sugars. Any type of grain will do, as will sugar beet, potatoes, molasses or grapes. "Classic" vodkas, however, are produced from wheat, rye and potato. National, or more precisely regional, styles emerged as distillers turned to the crop which was most readily available. So Scandinavian distillers

Shaken, not stirred: Suave he may be, but Bond didn't know how to make a Martini

used wheat, those in Russia used wheat but also rye, Poland used rye and potato. These definitions are less clearly defined these days. Wheat gives a light grainy delicacy to the spirit, rye a definite bite, while potato, contrary to popular belief, makes a vodka which is rounded, creamy and lush.

The key to vodka distillation is the removal of most, but critically not all, congeners. Vodka, after all, is not a neutral spirit, it must have personality and a subtle indication of the raw material it was made from. While distillation usually takes place in column stills, there are a number of high-quality pot still vodkas on the market. After distillation the vodka will be filtered, most commonly through charcoal, removing the aggressive edge of youth and replacing it with a milder, mellower flavour. What happens in just a few days would take a few years inside a charred barrel.

Polish Vodka

It is impossible to define a single specific character of Polish vodka, there are simply too many brands. Instead the best way to start to appreciate Polish vodka is to understand its history: this is a country that has made vodka for longer than anywhere else, including Russia. Poland was already exporting vodka at the end of the sixteenth century, by which time the spirit had ceased being used purely as a medicine and type of cologne and had started being flavoured with spices, fruits, berries and honey. The vodkas of this time were genuinely aristocratic spirits.

Indeed, only the gentry were allowed to make them – legally that is – and by the seventeenth century there were highly sophisticated distilleries in operation. By the mid to late nineteenth century improvements in distillation and filtration techniques meant that

Poles on the rocks: Who needs a fancy bar in order to appreciate vodka?

vodka distillers were not only able to produce the traditional flavoured styles but pure and kosher vodka as well.

Polish vodka was traditionally made from rye, wheat, barley and oats. Potatoes were used from the middle of the eighteenth century, becoming a significant component by the nineteenth.

Politics has always interfered with spirit production either through taxation or other forms of legislation. After 1945 the Polish industry was brought under the control of a state monopoly. Only with the downfall of Stalinism were the distilleries allowed to become independent and, although the politics of who owns what remains confusing, many were floated on the stock market. Some were snapped up by western drinks conglomerates, eager to get their hands on a new quality drink from Eastern Bloc, others are trying to go it alone.

The situation was complicated by distilleries changing distribution frequently and the Polish government apparently blowing hot and cold over the sale of some of its national assets to western drinks firms, but the privatisation has worked, allowing distilleries to not only promote and repackage many of their existing brands but to start looking at new ways to capture the imaginations of vodka drinkers the world over.

There has been a subtle change of emphasis in the marketing of Polish vodkas in recent years, with greater emphasis being placed on the base ingredients—mainly rye and potato—which, allied with a drive upmarket by brands such as Belvedere Chopin and Wyborowa Exquisite, has given a new gloss to an oft-misunderstood spirit.

The spirit of innovation which has always lain at the heart of Polish vodka is now beating harder than ever. While the cash-hungry plants could have easily flooded the market with cheap spirit, almost without exception they have chosen the quality route, allowing the rest of the world to finally appreciate the strength of Polish vodka. It's a full-time job just trying to keep tabs on what is happening, but a pleasurable one.

Tasting notes

RYE-BASED
Belvedere Dry and clean with a dusty rye edge that's mixed with dried lime and coriander. Cool and fresh. The palate mixes caraway and clean acidity.

Bols Lightly mineral nose. A pure, clean and soft palate that offsets a delicate sweetness with a hint of sootiness on the end.

Sobieski A top-seller in its home country, this rye vodka has a gentle nose with hints of rye tartness and fruits. Very clean, with a soft sweetness in the centre balanced by a sour, peppery rye finish.

Wyborowa Blue A classic old rye vodka which was the first Polish vodka to gain credibility in the West. With a mix of almond and pepper on the nose, the palate manages to mix an oily mouthfeel with zingy spices and a light touch of allspice.

Wyborowa Exquisite The firm's super-premium expression has a softer nose, with the sweet/sour rye bread accents being more restrained. The palate is considerably more crisp and dry, with greater nutty crunch

and higher levels of spice and an almost salty edge.

POTATO-BASED
Luksusowa Red Label Potato-based vodkas are another Polish speciality. A very gentle nose with a slight vegetal character gives way to the creamy/buttery palate typical of potato vodkas. Sweet with some fennel on the finish.

Chopin Gentle and discreet nose. While this has the umami-rich palate of potato vodkas, it is balanced with a clean peppery spice and a cereal-like crunch.

MIXED BASE
U'luvka Made from a mix of wheat, barley and rye, this has a lifted, quite aromatic nose with distinct graininess. The palate is almost perfumed, with a lime-like zest, a succulent mid-palate and a driving spicy finish.

Soplica A mix of wheat and rye is used here to produce a vodka which has a forward, aromatic nose with cumin-like spices. This discreet fragrant character continues in the mouth, where a soft mid-palate gives way to a zingy, energetic rye-accented finish.

255

Russian Vodka (and former Soviet republics)

The relationship between vodka and the Russian psyche is strong. Medicinal spirits were being made in Russia by the fifteenth century, and by the seventeenth century vodka production had become the preserve of the aristocracy, all keen to outdo each other on the purity of their, usually flavoured, spirits. Peter the Great "invented" (or at least had someone else invent) a vodka still and his recipe involved the production of a triple-distilled spirit, which was then flavoured with anise and redistilled once more. This was highly sophisticated distilling compared to what was going on worldwide at that time, but appears to have been the norm in Russia. With an understanding of charcoal filtration arriving in the late eighteenth century, the top distillers in Russia were making a high-quality spirit which would have been of considerably better quality than that coming from the whisky stills in Scotland or England's gin distilleries.

The Russian state has always had an ambivalent relationship with its national spirit. Even in the eighteenth century the industry was effectively split between the nobility, making and exporting top-quality rye and flavoured vodka, and state distillers producing crude spirit for the poor. By the time of the Revolution the overall quality had improved and vodka remained a handy political tool. Rather than hiking taxes, Stalin cut prices and upped production, keeping the country in a relatively docile alcoholic haze.

Although there is still concern about the levels of alcohol consumption within Russia—and the possibility of a Putin-led clampdown—Russia's reputation as a producer of high-quality premium vodkas continues to rise. The initial legwork was done by Stolichnaya, Moskovskaya and its premium variant Cristall. These days the range is considerably wider, with new entrants into the super-premium category such as Stolichnaya Elit, Kauffman and Beluga, some of which are priced to appeal only to oligarchs...

Ancient vodka bar: A drink for aristocrats from the word go

Tasting notes

Beluga Barley-based Siberian vodka with a firm, slightly nutty nose and hints of basil leaf. The palate is rich and smooth with a firm grain undertow and a lengthy clean finish.

Cristall (Russia) Pure, ultra-clean grainy nose. Elegant, delicate and one for sipping.

Etalon Hailing from Belorussia, this rye/wheat vodka is crisp and very clean with a light and scented nose akin to green apple and tree sap. The palate is soft and silky with a fragrant aniseed/liquorice note.

Green Mark Another 100 per cent wheat vodka. Once again the Russian oiliness is apparent on the nose alongside a light hint of fennel. The palate has some weight. Green olive in the middle, then a bone-dry finish.

Ikon Fresh and clean on the nose and, like Etalon, with a little pine edge. A focused and quite intense needle on the palate adds interest, while the finish brings out a touch of caraway and pepper.

Imperia The super-premium expression of Russian Standard (see below) is wheat-based and has a very clean, fresh nose. The palate is rich and textured with white pepper, anise and a hint of citrus. The finish is medium-length and clean.

Kauffman Luxury Vintage Unusual insofar as it is only made in years in which the distiller deems the wheat to be of suitable quality. Here you meet a clean, gentle nose with undercurrents of allspice and anise. The palate is ever so slightly herbal with a menthol coolness, leading to a long, clean finish.

Stolichnaya Elit The super-premium variant of the old classic is wheat-based and is triple-filtered. The nose is restrained and cool with a mineral quality. In the mouth, however, it has weight and depth, with a little sweet spot in the middle before the tight, fennel-like finish.

Zyr Produced from a mix of wheat and rye, here is a vodka which is lightly sweet on the nose with a touch of cereal. The mouth has the oiliness typical of Russian brands but with a firmness given by wheat underneath leading to a steely finish.

Side by side: Two of Russia's most famous exports: caviar and vodka

Scandinavian Vodka

Distilled spirits appeared in most European countries in the fourteenth century. Certainly by this time the Swedes were making a spirit (brannvin: "burnt" wine, though grain was also used) to be used both as a medicine and in the production of explosives. Just as in Poland and Russia, drinking spirits began as an upper class pursuit and slowly spread to the rest of the population who took to it with a passion.

By the mid eighteenth century there were around 180,000 stills in Sweden. Most would have been tiny home stills, but it gives an indication of how the knowledge of spirits production had spread and how people had acquired a taste for strong alcohol, regardless of how crude it was.

By the mid-nineteenth century, the state intervened and production was restricted to large licensed commercial distilleries equipped with column stills. One individual who challenged this state monopoly was Lars Olsson Smith, creator of the country's first rectified spirit in 1879. He began by selling his "Absolut Rent Brannvin" from his house just outside the Stockholm city limits, before increasing production and moving down to Skåne on the Baltic coast.

After the end of World War I, the Swedish government stepped in once again and the state monopoly, Vin & Spirit started controlling not just production of vodka, but also its legislation, importation and sales. The monopoly has since been broken up and Pernod-Ricard owns Absolut.

Spirit of the Mountains: Home distilling was popular in vodka's early days

The same pattern was repeated across much of Scandinavia. Finland and Norway both had tightly controlled state monopolies, but now vodka production has returned to private ownership (for example, Jack Daniel's parent company, Brown-Forman, now controls Finlandia).

Denmark remained free of such rigid state control, but is better known as a maker of akvavit, rather than vodka. All these

Scandic vodkas are linked by a cleanliness and delicacy that you obtain from well-distilled wheat. They are light, but not neutral, and while they may lack the complexity and range of flavours of the best from Poland, Russia or Estonia, they are nevertheless, quality products.

Tasting notes

Absolut (Sweden) Clean, light and neutral. Although a style icon, the arrival of other higher quality vodkas has rather exposed its lack of complexity and character.

Finlandia (Finland) An excellent wheat vodka, clean with hint of lime and citrus and a fresh bite on the finish.

Danska (Denmark) Strange bottle, which may slightly cheapen what is actually a very decent vodka. Made by the same firm behind Aalborg akvavit (and Cherry Heering), it is a whistle clean, pure spirit. It doesn't have quite the character and complexity of many from Poland and Russia but it is a high-quality everyday brand.

Fris (Denmark) Good weight, although it seems glycerol rich in texture. Like all these vodkas, the nose doesn't reveal much, this is all about palate weight.

Vikingfjord (Norway) A rarity, a Scandinavian potato vodka. Typically light and clean on the nose but good texture on the palate.

Other Vodkas of the World

The picture in the rest of the world is more confusing. Vodka hit the American mainstream in the late 1950s when drinkers discovered a clean, neutral spirit that slipped easily into orange juice giving it a bit of a kick. It was mild and odourless and suited the conservative post-War USA perfectly. As the trend for light spirits grew, vodka boomed. Eventually even Martinis were being made with it. Britain, as ever, took a few years to catch on but today it is the country's top-selling spirit, even in Scotland.

The danger for quality vodka was that copies made by western firms were there to satisfy an unsophisticated mass-market, turning vodka into a commodity. The public at large had not been exposed to the top Polish or Russian brands and did not know that western vodka was merely an interpretation of the east European original. Ironically, though vodka was made in Scandinavia the state monopolies were not interested in exporting their products.

Today, however, the picture is much different. Vodkas from outside its home territories are helping to develop the lucrative premium and super-premium markets. The niche first settled on by Grey Goose is now wider than ever and, while some brands are undoubtedly all image-driven, the ones which have stuck have done so because of inherent product quality. The new brands' heritage may not be as great as the vodkas from Poland, Russia and Scandinavia, but vodka connoisseurs can now satisfy themselves with assessing the differences between brands from Holland (Ketel One and van Gogh), Iceland (Reyka), New Zealand (42 Below), France (Grey Goose, Ciroc) and the US and Canada—not just in terms of their country of origin but their base ingredients and methods of production. Vodka, at this level, has got serious.

Tasting notes

Chase An English vodka made from potatoes, this has the typical buttery creaminess on nose and tongue that you would expect, but with a hint of fruit behind and a clean, spicy finish.

Ciroc French-made, grape-based, this is one of the most aromatically lifted of the new wave of vodkas with touches of vetiver, lemon and nettles. Sweet and almost fizzy spiciness on the tongue and a long citric finish.

Crystal Head The packaging (the clue is in the name) is distinctive, as is the acetone-heavy aroma with touches of bubblegum in the background. The palate is clean and quite firm.

42 Below New Zealand vodka made from wheat and with the anise/liquorice nose typical of that grain. The palate is fine with decent depth and a lightly peppery finish.

Ketel One Dutch vodka made from wheat distilled in column and pot stills, this is one of the fuller-bodied vodkas on the market. Lightly floral with a clean minerality and lime zest. The palate has dry cereal underpinning a silky mouthfeel. The crisp finish palate hints at charcoal.

Rain (US) Organic vodka from Kentucky. Soft and sweet with a hint of liniment and spice on the nose. Chewy, but beautifully clean and wheat-soft with apple on the finish.

Reyka Distilled in Iceland from wheat, this is a very soft and gentle vodka with a fleshy nose. The palate picks out subtle pear sweetness alongside liquorice and a tingling spiciness on the finish.

Smirnoff The biggest-selling "Western" vodka in the world, Smirnoff is distilled at various locations globally. It also often outperforms more pricey competitors at blind tastings. It is grainy on the nose, clean and plump on the palate.

van Gogh Blue Distilled in Holland from wheat, this has quite a weighty nose with little hints of the sweetness of a grain loft. A pastoral palate with good thickness in the middle of the tongue, it finishes with typical wheat-derived focus.

Flavoured Vodkas

As we've seen, flavoured vodkas are not a new invention: they were originally medicinal herbs or sweetening agents. However, as vodka became a drink rather than a tincture, the recipes became increasingly complex – thus revealing vodka's sophistication and its enduring link with the land.

An excellent example of this traditional style is Poland's Tatrzanska, which uses herbs and berries from the country's Tatra mountain region. Others include spicy hunter's vodkas, such as Russia's Okhotnichaya and the magnificent bison grass vodkas hailing from the Bialowieska forest.

You can find honeyed vodkas, including Krupnik, vodkas flavoured with plum, or wild cherry. Less traditional examples include fresh lemon, orange and cranberry vodkas and palate stinging pepper ones. The choice is seemingly endless.

Traditionally, flavoured vodkas are made by macerating the ingredients in the spirit or, as in the case of bison grass, by passing the spirit over the flavouring agent. Some, however, are made by blending distillates of the flavours with the vodka. Sadly, but inevitably, as soon as any trend appears there are always those who are too keen to leap on the bandwagon.

Today, almost every mass-market brand has to have its own variants, and every supermarket wants its own range. Sadly few, if any of them, want to invest in the time, skill and ingredients needed to produce quality and authenticity. The result is the proliferation of vodkas flavoured with concentrates, which are clumsy and poorly made excuses for the real thing.

Tasting notes

POLISH

Korzen Zycia A ginseng vodka with a peculiarly green/stewed nose.

Krupnik (honey and spice) Very old style of flavoured vodka. Rich, sweet and herbal. Try it warmed up.

Wisent Bison Grass (rye) One of the best – fragrant, elegant and gorgeously perfumed. It is free of the natural flavouring coumarin, to which the US Government objected.

Wisniowka (cherry) Concentrated cherry notes, off-dry, with a lovely kick halfway through.

Zubrowka (bison grass) Mown grass, lavender, flowers and spice. Complex, long and sophisticated. The greatest flavoured vodka style of all.

Extra Zytnia (rye vodka, apple spirit and fruits) Clean and spicy thanks to the rye with a perfumed delicate palate. Lovely balance.

DUTCH

Ketel Citroen Natural and juicy with some dusky floral notes

behind. Oily texture with delicate lemon all the way through.

Vincent Van Gogh Citroen Vodka Highly citric and zesty. Use carefully to give cocktails an extra layer of complexity.

Ursus Citrus Some nice citric notes, but lacks depth.

Ursus Roter A sloe vodka. Dark, but lacking the sweet, bitter interplay which would give it complexity.

Gin

"'The air! Isn't it wonderful?'
"'Yeah, it's like a shot of gin. It makes your blood race, your face numb and your spirits soar.'"
Katharine Hepburn and Humphrey Bogart,
The African Queen

One of the most heartening aspects of the revival in premium spirits and mixed drinks has been the re-emergence of gin. At long last it has managed to shrug off its old, staid, image and reintroduce itself as the quality spirit which kicked off the golden age of cocktails in the mid nineteenth century.

The prototype for gin was first distilled in Salerno, Italy, in the eleventh century as a juniper-based elixir used to aid kidney problems and even as a possible cure for the Plague. It was only when distillers in Flanders and Holland (such as Lucas Bols in 1575) began to distil commercially in the sixteenth century that it began to be taken as a drink rather than as a medicine or tonic. At the same time British mercenaries fighting in Holland against the Spanish acquired a taste for "genever" which they called "gin" (or "Dutch courage"), but it had to wait for King William, a Dutchman,

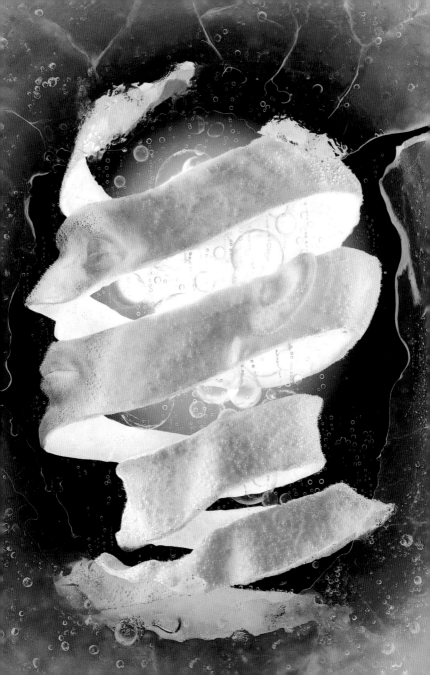

to ascend the throne in 1688 to become truly popular. The king banned imports of French goods and, deprived of their supplies of brandy, the English turned to this quirky spirit, previously only made in country houses and by apothecaries. While the gentry continued to drink rum and smuggled brandy, gin became the drink of the urban poor and at one point was cheaper to buy than beer, resulting in London being awash with badly distilled spirit, sweetened to hide its burnt taste. This sweet style (known as Old Tom) remained the prevalent type of gin well into the nineteenth century and is widely mentioned in cocktail recipes.

Gin's first break came when dry gins appeared, mostly, but not exclusively, from column stills. This was such a different drink from Old Tom that the middle classes took to it quickly, happy in the knowledge that they were consuming a different product. The new gin barons were men of standing and made good products: clear, dry, fragrant spirits that could be mixed. These new dry gins were distributed throughout the world via the Empire and, significantly, they appeared in America just as the first cocktail age was getting into its stride. Since vodka was unknown, gin and dry gin especially became the white spirit to use as a mixer.

Gin ruled, unchallenged, until the 1950s when vodka became fashionable. Gin makers found that new drinkers were rejecting old-fashioned spirits, preferring plainer tastes. They failed to recognize the challenge posed by vodka and watched, apparently paralysed, as the new, clean spirit stole their market share.

Gin suffered badly in Britain and the US from the late 1970s on as a new generation turned their back on "old" drinks and embraced vodka. In recent years, however, gin has undergone a remarkable renaissance, partly driven by an appreciation of pre-Prohibition

Serene: Four column stills in the still house at Tanqueray & Gordon

cocktails and also a search for a white spirit with flavour. In America, gin has become a spirit of choice for craft distillers, while in the UK new brands are emerging at a rate of around one a week. Gin, most definitely, is back.

How it's made

There are two ways to make gin. The simplest and cheapest is by adding essences to a neutral spirit (known as cold compounding) but the poor quality, confected product it produces isn't worth the money, even at its low price. The proper way to produce gin is by adding herbs, peels, roots and spices (botanicals) to a neutral spirit and redistilling it. Each producer not only has its own secret recipe of botanicals (see p273) but will distil in a slightly different way to everyone else.

The stills, traditionally are pot stills (though column stills are used). The neutral spirit, usually a wheat-based one, is first diluted (otherwise the still might explode) and the botanicals are added. Gordon's, Tanqueray and Plymouth add the botanicals shortly before the redistillation starts. Beefeater macerates its botanicals in the spirit for 24 hours before redistillation, while Bombay Sapphire and Hendricks use Carterhead stills which have baskets containing the botanicals suspended in the neck of the still. The vapour passing through the basket strips the aromas from the botanicals.

Distilling fixes the flavours and aromas of the botanicals in the gin, but it is a slow process. Nosing the young gin as it is collected indicates that not all botanical aromas appear at the same stage. First to be released are the lightest and most volatile citric aromas, then juniper begins to emerge along with coriander. In time the juniper note deepens and earthier, rooty notes of liquorce, orris and angelica begin to come through. This process is translated into the glass. Let me explain...

Since different aromas emerge at different times of distillation, they are held in the gin at different alcohol strengths. Your glass of neat gin contains a series of little trigger points which release their aromas when diluted. The most volatile, citric notes are the first to be released and appear to be triggered at around 40%ABV. This means when a distiller reduced its gin to below 40% ABV at bottling it loses these lighter, more fragrant aromas, producing a rather flat disappointing result. Try Gordon's at 40% and 37.5% to see for yourself. What the distillers save in money by cutting strength is lost in flavour. Noticeably the new gin brands, even supermarket own-label brands, have learned from this major mistake and are now being bottled at the proper strength.

Opposite: The spice of life: Without spices, such as nutmeg, gin would be very bland

Botanicals

The use of botanicals is the defining element in a gin's aroma.
Without them you produce a pretty bland vodka.

The use of spices in spirits has been common since the sixteenth
century: not only was there a thriving international spice trade
(controlled by the gin-making countries of Holland and England),
but certain spices were locally grown such as saffron in
Cambridgeshire and Suffolk and coriander in Sussex.

Botanicals remain the single most important element in making gin and each brand's precise recipe is only known to a select few people. As with blending any spirit, the quantity of botanicals isn't what is important, it is the way in which the aromas and flavours combine and play off each other which gives each brand its unique character.

All brands are based on juniper, usually sourced from Italy, which gives the drink its signature note of pine, heather, sage, lavender and camphor. Gin distillers will micro-distil samples of each year's juniper harvest before making their decision on which supplier, or suppliers, to purchase from. Without high quality juniper a gin will almost certainly fail.

Coriander seed, usually from eastern Europe and north Africa, gives a lemon or lemon balm note sometimes with a touch of pepper. Angelica, from Saxony, has a musky dry quality; there's bitter Seville orange peel from southern Spain and sweet orange peel as well. Lifted aromatic lemon peel comes from across southern Europe, the earthy, violet-accented orris root comes from Italy, while there are exotic additions from further afield: cinnamon and cassia bark from India, ginger from the East Indies, nutmeg from Grenada, cubeb berries from Java and grains of paradise from West Africa.

Not all distillers will use each and every one botanical. While all distillers tend to use juniper and coriander, each individual distiller favours his own special recipe: Gordon's, for example, adds ginger, cassia and nutmeg, Beefeater uses bitter orange, angelica root and seed, while Plymouth's seven botanicals include sweet orange peel and pungent cardamom. The aim is to produce a balanced, complex, aroma with its own individual signature.

Tasting notes

Beefeater Lifted and quite intense nose, which leads on a piney juniper and citrus. The palate is very fresh and dry with a heather note.

Berry's No 3 A fresh, very clean nose with good juniper, some cardamon, gentle florals, ginger and citrus notes. The finish becomes dry and rooty, adding weight and seriousness.

Bombay Sapphire Light and clean with lots of delicate fragrant aromas: blossom, cut flowers, citrus. Low on juniper. Delicate and gently spicy on the finish.

Gordon's At export strength this shows good juniper, some lemon notes, sage and a spiced finish. At 37.5 per cent all of the lifted aromatics disappear.

Hendrick's From Scotland. The additions of cucumber and rose to the gin base come across early, backed with very light violet and a hint of juniper.

Monkey 47 Made in Germany's Black Forest to a very complex (47-strong) botanical mix, this has an intense, lifted herbal and exotic nose with camomile, spruce, juniper and rose. The palate is zesty and pure with a creamy texture.

Plymouth Light oiliness on the nose alongside angelica, sage and orange blossom. The palate has great impact and complexity with a long finish.

Sipsmith A boutique London dry gin (and made in London). Quite a floral nose mixed with clean juniper and bergamot. The palate is clean and crisp with a lemon edge on the finish.

Tanqueray The biggest of the old London gins and the simplest in terms of botanicals. Heavy on juniper and oily in texture with a delicious violet earthiness on the finish.

Dutch gin

The original gin distillers had a ready market for their genever. Indeed in the late seventeenth century Diderot described the Dutch as "living alembics, distilling themselves". It was the Dutch who created Cognac, who controlled much of the world's spice trade, made rum in the Caribbean and perfected the art of liqueurs at home. Yet genever remained the country's spirit.

Genever has as much to do with whisky as it has to do with the British style of gin. All of its various styles have as their base a cereal spirit called "moutwijn" (malt wine) which can be made from malted barley, wheat, rye or corn distilled to 47%ABV. Different mashbills will give different flavours and vary depending on the distiller.

To this will be blended different percentages of a neutral grain spirit which has been redistilled with botanicals (the same technique as used in British gins). Again, the botanical mix is up to each individual distiller, with juniper a requirement, but not necessarily the dominant player.

In blending the two spirits together, three styles of genever can be made. The first is "oude" (old style) which emerged in the nineteenth century. This must have a minimum of 15 per cent moutwijn—but most contain considerably more. It has to be a minimum of 35%ABV and contain no more than 20 grams of sugar per litre. They can be aged for at least a year in a cask of less than 700 litres in capacity. The two types of spirit can be aged separately and then blended.

"Jonge" (young style) genever appeared in the 1950s. They have much the same regulations but can only have 10 grams of sugar per litre and they are not aged. Generally speaking they contain less moutwijn and have a simpler botanical mix.

Tasting notes

Bols Corenwyn (40 per cent): Light gold in colour. Very rich and malty on the nose, with deep juniper aromas mixed with red fruits and almond.

de Kuyper Genever (40 per cent): Rich and malty with oily juniper undercurrent. Rich in texture, clean nutty finish.

Bokma Royal Dark (40 per cent): More delicate than most genevers, gently junipery with a subtle smooth character.

Bokma Volmout (40 per cent): Highly malted but with a crisp attack on the palate.

Bokma Vijf Jaren (40 per cent): Rich elegant with juniper oil well in evidence. Full unctuous feel and restrained wood.

There is also a style called "Corenwijn" (corn wine) which must be made up of a minimum of 51 per cent moutwijn, be a minimum of 38%ABV and have the same maximum levels of sugar as oude. These also can be aged in the same fashion as oude. Some can rest in a cask for 20 years or more.

In addition you will find flavoured genever and some which are 100 per cent column still distillates. The latter are known as "graanjenever".

Genever, like British gin, has suffered badly in recent years, but its fortunes are reviving once more as consumers turn back to spirits with heritage and, most importantly, flavour.

G&T, anyone?

The quintessential English mixed drink was born out of necessity. It was during the days of the Empire when the officers stationed in India were suffering terribly from malaria. They knew that quinine was a relatively effective antidote but the problem was it tasted extremely bitter. Mr Jacob Schweppe, a purveyor of soft drinks and mineral waters, created the first quinine-laced tonic water which was a much more palatable way of taking their medicine. It was further improved when they added tonic water to the increasingly fashionable gin. (Naval officers, faced with the same dilemma, took their quinine in the form of Angostura bitters added to gin.)

The G&T remains a classic long drink, but there are some essential rules to bear in mind if you want to achieve the full mouth-watering fusillade of aromas.

TO MAKE A CLASSIC G&T

1) Use a gin of 40% ABV or above. Not only can you taste the difference between brands, but a one made with a 37.5% gin is a miserable experience.
2) Use a tall glass and fill it two thirds full of ice. Add a squeeze of lime (not lemon).
3) Pour in a generous slug of your gin and stir.
4) Top up with freshly opened tonic water. (2 parts tonic to 1 of gin). Only use 1-litre bottles if you intend to use them in one sitting. Try to use premium tonic such as Fever Tree.
5) Cut a wedge of lime and run it around the inside of the top of the glass then drop it in. Enjoy.

It: The g&t remains the most uplifting, deliciously sexy mixed drink

Rum

"Give a man a fish and he'll eat for a day. Teach a man to fish and he'll sit in a boat and drink all day."

Anon

Beneath rum's apparently benign image lurk tales of depravity and despair. Rum's story takes in slavery, piracy, the American revolution, the rise of organized crime and anti-Communist politics. It makes every other spirit's story seem rather bland and uneventful.

Sugar cane arrived in the Caribbean with Columbus who planted it in Hispaniola (now Dominica Republic/Haiti) and Cuba during his second Atlantic voyage. Sugar was seen as the new gold by many of the settlers and as they began to grow rich on Europe's subsequent sugar addiction so their slaves began to consume a distilled drink made from the by-product of the proceeds, molasses. Known by a variety of names: kill-devil, brebaje, guildhive, taffia, and rumbullion, seventeenth century accounts of colonial life in the Caribbean all agree it was ferocious stuff and, by and large, was drunk by slaves, overseers and field workers.

Rum's first major export market was to the colonies on America's east coast. Rum, not whisky, was America's first commercial spirit (the first rum stills on the US mainland appeared in the first decade of the eighteenth century) and it has been argued that it was in the rum taverns of Pennsylvania that the first notion of an independent American identity took form.By this time rum punch had become the fashionable drink on the London literary scene and along with brandy was the middle class drink. If there had been such things as yuppies in those days they would have been rum drinkers.

Rum's fortunes have always been tied to the fortunes of the sugar trade and as a result the industry fell on tough items during the nineteenth century when sugar beet began to be grown in Europe. A falling demand for Caribbean sugar meant a reduction in rum distilling and by the end of the nineteenth century rum was lagging behind whisky and gin. Even the "rum runners" of the Prohibition era brought in relatively little rum and although this period heralded the arrival of a new wave of Cuban cocktails, rum never quite overthrew its rivals – except in France where it was the most popular spirit until the 1970s. Only one firm managed to break free, Bacardi. As the sugar industry has consolidated so rum distilling has been concentrated into fewer (and larger) plants, many of which are among the most sophisticated in the world.

Attitudes to rum have changed, mainly as a result of a decline in the bulk market and the creation of distillers' own brands. With their destiny finally in their own hands, rum-makers have created a new wave of excitement among bartenders and consumers internationally. Rum's golden age is beginning.

Bay Rum Still: St Thomas, US Virgin Islands

How it's made

Sugar cane is a giant, vigorous grass which like all green-leafed plants converts its glucose into sucrose but atypically doesn't then store it as starch. There are a host of sub-species and strains of cane, each suited to a particular climate or soil, important when you realize that each island – and each region within each island – can have slightly different climatic conditions. In turn this means that each island's cane juice varies slightly in terms of sugar and acidity levels.

After the cane is harvested (any time between February and June) it is transported to the processing plant where the canes are chopped into smaller lengths and fed through a series of rollers which squeeze out juice. The liquid is then run into holding vessels and clarified: traditionally by adding lime but now done in centrifuges and filtration plants. Now the juice is ready to be turned into sugar and then molasses. Only then can rum-making start – unless you are doing it the French way in which case cane juice will suffice.
To make sugar you have to boil the juice until it crystallizes, but

283

there is a point when no more sugar can be extracted and the producer is left with a thick sweet syrup: molasses. Now the distiller can get to work. The molasses will be diluted and then pumped to fermenters where yeast is added (though some rums are still naturally fermented). Some distillers, especially those in Jamaica, will also add the acidic residue from the previous distillation (dunder), a sour mashing technique which helps fermentation and raises the ester levels.

The length of ferment, the temperature and the type of yeast will all have an impact on what aromatics are produced, but a general rule is that light rums are made from short ferments and in column stills, while heavier rums ferment for longer and are distilled in pot stills. Both types of still can be found in the same plant. Some distilleries, again especially in Jamaica, still use a device known as a retort. The column stills range from one of the last wooden Coffey stills in the world to interlinked four- and five-column stills allowing one distilley to make a huge variety of flavoured spirits.

White rum will be reduced in strength, filtered and normally bottled immediately, while aged rums will then go into used oak casks, mainly ex-Bourbon barrels. In the Caribbean's humid climate the spirit quickly extracts high levels of tannins and colour from the wood meaning that rum can get woody relatively quickly. Some rums are taken off-shore to mature more slowly in Scotland and England. When the same type of rum is matured in two different climates, the resultant flavours can differ enormously.

Finally a blend of different ages of rums and often different types of distillate is assembled. Caramel and other additives can also be added, but purists would question the practice of masking one of the world's most elegant sipping spirits.

Barbados

Barbados can lay claim to be the home of commercial rum. It was here that the first reference to "kill-devil" was made in the mid-seventeenth century, only twenty years after cane was first planted on the island. It soon became one of the most famous rum-producing islands and one of the few whose rums were requested by name: "Barbadoes Water". Over three million gallons were exported to England in 1776. This infers not only that the Bajan style had a good reputation but that it was being made to a specific type virtually from the word go. By the end of the nineteenth century every sugar plantation would have had its own distillery. Barbados has always been know for an elegant, fruity

Tasting notes

Mount Gay Lifted and sweet nose with some banana/toffee notes and a hint of smoke. Very clean, elegant and long.

Mount Gay Extra Old
Toasted wood, some coconut, orange and banana. Positive wood on palate, but balanced by sweet, complex layers of fruit flavours.

R.L. Seale 10-year-old From the Foursquare distillery, this is a rich, elegant and balanced rum with a mix of dried mango and apricot

and a palate of dried flowers, Seville orange and a hint of chocolate.

Mount Gilboa
A triple-distilled pot still rum, this shows more weight than you normally expect from Barbados. Lightly oily on the nose with vanilla, laurel, ginger, sandalwood and a smooth sweet, peachy, honeyed palate.

Doorly's XO A sweet rich nose full of ripe fruit and soft honey. Soft and elegant. Stunningly good.

style of rum, and as with every island these days, produces everything from strong, clear, overproof to rich aged pot still. Consolidation of rum production has been steadily proceeding since the start of the twentieth century.

These days there are only two distilleries on the island. The best known is Mount Gay, which makes the eponymous brand and Mount Gilboa. The West Indies Rum Refinery is home to brands such as Cockspur, while Foursquare's mix of column and pot stills and radical (for rum) approach to wood makes R. L. Seale, Doorly's and others. The newest, St Nicholas Abbey in the north of the island, is developing a cane juice distilled rum from its own plantation.

Jamaica

The Jamaican trade was built on the back of the trade with the Navy and the privateers (or pirates depending on whose side you were on) who guarded the island in the early days of the colony. By 1893 there were 148 small distilleries, making Jamaica, after years of vying with Barbados, the producer of the best quality rums. In more recent times as rum has fallen from favour and the sugar industry has collapsed it has struggled, though today things are beginning to look up.

The best known Jamaican distillery (and one of the oldest producers in the Caribbean) is Wray & Nephew which was founded in 1825 by John Wray. The firm owns the prestigious Appleton Estate, a brand which proves categorically that rum can age superbly well.

Jamaican rums are typified by a full flavour and a pungent, fruitily intense, high ester character. Jamaican rum was traditionally divided into four classes, each graded according to the ester

Tasting notes

Wray & Nephew Overproof Rotten banana, heavy, oily and pungent. Oily in mouth, full and flavoursome. In time, a citric edge unveils itself. Clean and a weighty base for cocktails.

Smith & Cross A nose which combines typical Jamaican pot still intensity with some cacao, nutmeg, allspice and blackberry. The palate is ripe with cigar notes and a powerful citric undertow.

Blackwell Black and Gold Made for the founder of Island Records, this is a thick, dark, sweet rum with notes of toffee, dried coconut and citrus. Low in the pot still impact.

Appleton V/X Slightly vegetal with banana esteriness before raspberry compote fills the nose. Good grip mid-palate before rounding out for a long, pleasant finish.

Appleton 12-year-old Immediate vanilla/toasted coconut wood on the nose. On the palate, it's smokily complex and mellow. Very good.

Appleton Estate Master's Blender's Legacy Elegant and refined with a sweet honeyed nose that touches on crystallized ginger, light leather and cinnamon. The palate has crème brûlée, roast plantain and nutmeg.

content and, as well as being bottled on the own, were highly prized by British, German and South African blenders.

The adherence to this style and a belief in pot still distillation cost Jamaican distillers dear when the world decided that rum should be a light-tasting beverage, but ironically it is this big, complex style which the new rum aficionados want to drink. Try and find the classic old-style single still rums from either Long Pond or perhaps Monymusk.

Cuba

Although Cuba was responsible for bringing rum into the modern age, it had been a latecomer to the art of turning molasses onto spirit. Established by the Spanish in the sixteenth century as a staging post rather than a sugar colony, it only began making rum commercially—and only in small quantities—in the mid-eighteenth century. All that changed a century later, when industrialized sugar production began. With it came rum distilling with the most modern of equipment—specifically column stills. As a result, the Cuban rum-makers pioneered light rum—now the most widely made style in the world. The first large modern distilleries were built in the 1840s in Havana, Matanzas and Cardenas, all of which were encouraged by the government to produce a rum which was substantially different to the others on the world market. By the turn of the twentieth century brands such as Matusalem and Havana Club were being exported to the US and Spain, but it was another Cuban brand, Bacardi, which had already started out on its global domination.

Havana in the 1930s: The birthplace of modern bartending

Tasting notes

The Havana Club range starts with the clean, limey, gently sweet and hay-like **3 anos**. Things become richer with the **7 anos**, which shows darker fruits, coffee, dark chocolate. Newer arrival **Selection de Maestro Roneros** is for me the pick of the bunch—complex, elegant with citrus to the fire, light tobacco, dried flower, sweet fruits and a long finish. The **15 anos** is the big brother of the 7 anos but is slightly drier with more clean oak on show.

During Prohibition Cuba was perfectly placed to slake the thirsts of Americans and tourists and bartenders flooded into Havana. Already a centre for innovations in mixology (the Daiquiri was perfected here in 1896) the Prohibition years brought a new surge of creativity and a sucession of rum-based drinks named after Havana regulars like Garbo, Dorothy Gish and Mary Pickford.

Bacardi ceased to be made in Cuba in 1959 when Castro nationalized the sugar industry and the firm's holdings. The most widely seen post-revolution brand is Havana Club, but there are other distilleries in Cuba making their own brands up to the 1980s.

Havana Club now specializes in aged rums produced by a complex blending regime involving different degrees of dilution of column still rum with high-strength aguardiente to create different base flavours. These are then aged for different lengths of time. Some are also re-blended and re-aged, allowing the "maestro roneros" a huge range of different flavours to work with. Other Cuban brands, such as Varadero and Santiago, are now becoming more widely available internationally.

Trinidad and Guyana

Trinidad, in common with every other island, made rum almost as soon as the first cane was harvested and by the time the British wrested the island from Spanish control in 1797 it was making large quantities (though of pretty foul stuff.) Until the nineteenth century, though quality had improved, not much was exported, or if it was, was used only as a blending component. The Trinidad style has always been light and attractive.

The island has long been home to Angostura, the producer of the world's most famous brand of bitters and, since the demise of the government-owned Caroni, the sole rum distiller on the island, the result of the decline of the sugar industry in the Caribbean. When that happens there is less molasses and distilleries are forced to close, resulting in consolidation of production into larger units. Although there is only one distillery in Trinidad, the approach is the same as in other innovative large plants in Poland, Ireland or Canada. They might not be as touchy-feely as a pot still plant making small volumes of spirit, but neither is it churning out a bland, anonymous product. Technological advances allow the distiller to make as wide a range of different distillates as he wishes.

Much the same happened in Guyana, where the sole distiller, Demerara Distillers, has preserved the highly individual "marks" originally made at each sugar estate by moving the stills—including the famous wooden pots and an ancient Coffey still—which created these rums to a central site. The Guyanese style has always been rich and powerful. While Jamaica perfected high ester rums, Guyanan distillers perfected the deep bassy Demerara style. Today everything is made at Demerara Distillers, seen at its best in the firm's brand, El Dorado – a complex blend of rums from the distillery's remarkable collection of different stills.

Tasting notes

El Dorado 15-year-old Deep, ripe and resonant. The aromas tend towards those of brandy. Highly complex with touches of Demerara sugar and some balancing wood.

Port Morant 20-year-old Dry and subtle with superb balance between the,rich, Demerara style and some crisp wood arrested flavours.

In the Navy: British sailors collect their grog ration

French Antilles and Haiti

The French not only spell rum differently: rhum, but make it in a different way. In Guadeloupe, Martinique and Marie Galante rhum agricole is made not from molasses but from sugar cane juice. This, the Antilles distillers argue, makes their rhums more complex because there is a higher amount of sugar in the base material.

It is produced under regulations similar to those governing Cognac and Armagnac. Rhums can be divided into two types: rhum agricole which is made from sugar cane and rhum industriel which is made from molasses. Within the agricole designation there are a variety of sub-categories (again like Cognac): white overproof; paille, a pale straw-coloured rhum aged for a short period in wood; then vieux and hors d'age which are aged for longer; and at the top of the scale vintage (millessime) rhum. These can all be made in pot, single or linked column stills, and the barrels used for aging must be less than 650 litres in capacity (rhum is usually aged in ex-cognac casks although increasingly ex-bourbon barrels are used). The use of cane juice gives this style a fresh vegetal nose with a peppery finish—most obviously in the white version. Ageing removes the green aspect of youth, replacing it with a delicate finesse quite different to molasses-based equivalents.

There are other cane rums made in the Caribbean, the best of which, Barbancourt, comes from Haiti and has been made by the Gardiere family since 1862. It's not the easiest brand to find but, to my mind at least, is one of the great rums of the world.

Tasting notes

Neisson l'Esprit Blanc From Martinique and bottled at 70%ABV, this is a classic example of the pure rhum agricole style. Vegetal and grassy with some lemon, raspberry and—even now—sweetness. The palate is smooth with light white pepper and flowers.

JM 1998 An example of a vintage rhum agricole from Martinique. The vegetal notes have given way to cooked apple, plantain, marzipan, mint and flowers. Light grip from the oak, some tingling spice and, finally, white pepper once again.

Trois Riviere Vintage 1990 Ageing in ex-bourbon casks has added a more lush, rounded character to this Martiniquean rhum agricole. There's a hint of cane but more vanilla, milk chocolate, banana and mango.

Clement Canne Bleu A single varietal/plantation rhum agricole from the south of Martinique. The most remarkable element here is how fruits are already coming through the grassiness. The palate is very silky.

Rhum Rhum PMG Liberation 2010 An aged rhum agricole made on Marie Galante in pot stills, this has a complex nose of mandarin orange, passion fruit and espresso, and a palate which hints at cardamon.

Karukera Rhum Vieux From Guadeloupe, this aged rhum agricole is rich and set on the nose with a heavy floral aroma which is mixed with ginger, vanilla, guava jam and a little hint of cherry.

Barbancourt Reserve Special From Haiti's best-known distillery, this is a very elegant pot still rhum which mixes stone fruit, cane syrup, oak and liquorice. The palate is gentle and sweet with light tannins and sweet spice.

Bacardi

Bacardi is more than a brand, it is a global phenomenon. The biggest spirit brand in the world, it is made in Puerto Rico, the Bahamas, Mexico, Spain, Venezuela and Brazil, among others. Founded (in 1862) in Cuba by Spanish émigré Facundo Bacardi who had arrived in Cuba as a teenager thirty years earlier, it was

Don Facundo Bacardi en famille: Head of a great spirits dynasty

among the first rums to be distilled in a column still and its light, soft style immediately captured drinkers' attention. Bacardi's growth from small family rum to mega-brand is an astonishing success story which has resulted in Bacardi being the only spirits brand which has transcended its category. How many people who ask for a Bacardi and coke know that they are ordering a rum?

Tasting notes

Bacardi Carta Blanca The white rum which started it all remains a classic of its style. Light and clean with hints of white mushroom, blue cheese, delicate spice and a soft almost creamy palate.

Bacardi Reserva A gold rum which shows evidence of oak ageing in the amount of caremelized fruits and vanilla of the nose. Light in nature with some guava and golden syrup.

Bacardi 8-year-old Lifted and honeyed showing some more depth.

Light touches of orange peel, apricot and banana. The palate mixes sweetness with a minty spiciness.

Bacardi Oakheart A spiced variant. Heavy on the vanilla, cinnamon, nutmeg with a slightly powdery palate. Big impact and slightly sweet.

The Bacardi family had the vision to realize that a mass-market spirit brand needn't be tied to one distillery. By the 1930s, it was producing its rum in Mexico and Puerto Rico as well as Cuba, and by the time that Fidel Castro nationalized its assets it was registered in Nassau. Just over a century after the family arrived they were forced to leave Cuba. It was perfect timing as the US market was about to demand lighter-tasting spirits. It hasn't looked back.

As the world has woken up to the qualities of rum, so Bacardi has been able to return to its roots and discuss its heritage. This move, as well as giving drinkers a new perspective on what was a familiar brand, has helped build the category as it moves into a new era.

Rum from the rest of the world

If there's sugar cane in the fields, rum production won't be far away. That has been the rule for centuries and it holds firm today though it is only when you start searching for other rums that you realize how many there are. The Caribbean has fine quality rums from the Virgin islands (the huge Cruzan operation is there), St. Lucia, Grenada, the Dominican Republic and Paraguay. Many of these are made from sugar cane syrup rather than juice or molasses and have been aged, sherry-style, in a solera system. Soft and lush rums come from the Central American countries of Nicaragua (Flor de Cana) and Guatemala (Zacapa). Rums from South America not only include the Demerara rums from Guyana, but more delicate offerings from Venezuela (Pampero/Cacique) and Paraguay (Papagayo) while the Brazilian cane spirit, cachaca, is in volume terms one of the biggest-selling spirit styles in the world.

Production line: If there is cane in the fields this won't be far away

Tasting notes

Black Tot The last of the authentic rum served daily (until 1970) to every member of the British Navy. Deep and treacle-like with leather, walnut and grilled peppers. The palate is thick with lots of cassis and eucalyptus.

Brugal Anejo The biggest seller in the Dominican Republic, this aged variant shows sweetness, kiwi, peach, bubblegum, nutmeg and vanilla.

Chairman's Reserve From St. Lucia, this is a highly approachable aged rum with soft vanilla and mango nose and a palate that touches on white chocolate, lime and toasty oak.

Flor de Cana from Nicaragua is a classic "Latin" style. Light and sweet, a gentle mix of mashed banana, peach and flowers and a citric finish.

Zacapa from Guatemala is aged at high altitude in a highly complex solera-style system utilizing many different types of cask. This has a nose of raisin, tropical fruits, jam, tobacco and ginger.

Appropriately enough, since it is in this part of the world where sugar cane originated, the Philippines makes a huge amount of good rum (Tanduay, Manila). There are rums from the cane fields of Mauritius, India and even a rum from Nepal. Australia meanwhile weighs in with Bundaberg produced from cane grown in Queensland.

In addition, Britain has always specialized in blending rums for brands such as OVD, Lamb's, Black Heart and Captain Morgan, while wine and spirit merchants like Cadenhead, Bristol Spirits and Berry Brothers & Rudd specialize in high-class single estate "early landed" [UK-matured] rums. Germany has its rum verschnitt – destination for much high-ester Jamaican produce – and there's a similar style in South Africa. That's just the tip of a sweet iceberg that thankfully is becoming better known and appreciated.

Brandy

"Claret is the liquor for boys; port for men; but he who aspires to be a hero must drink brandy."

Samuel Johnson

Some educated guesses can be made as to who made the first brandy, but the truth is we don't know. It is certain that the Moors were distilling in southern Spain in 900AD, but they used their al-ambiqs to make perfume not liquor. It is possible that Christians were allowed to turn their wine into brandy, but there is no hard evidence. Equally it may be that there were grape-based spirits being made in monasteries in Italy, but again there's no documentation.

The earliest record of brandy production comes from Gascony in 1411, which suggests that the secret of distillation came to this southern French region from across the Pyrenees. Armagnac, as the brandy became known, began to be exported by the seventeenth century, with the Dutch as the main purchasers. It wasn't an ideal trade. Armagnac is far from the sea and the nearest port, Bordeaux had a tendency to silt up. In time, the

Dutch looked elsewhere and found the perfect site north of Bordeaux at La Rochelle, where there was access to the sea and from where they were buying salt. The Charente made an acidic, light white wine perfect for distillation and the first record of brandy being produced around the town of Cognac was in 1638.

The Dutch needed brandewijn ("burnt wine") to make the drinking water on board the ships of their huge mercantile fleet potable. They also needed to fortify table wines in order to stabilize them. All in all they demanded huge supplies of brandy. In the Charente, and more specifically close to Cognac, they found a region perfectly suited for the production of high-quality spirit. The climate and soils were just right, there were forests for barrels and there was that all-important sea route. Cognac rather than Armagnac became the drink of the northern European bourgeoisie, and by the nineteenth century it was the world's premium spirit.

Armagnac, meanwhile, had to wait until the building of railways to gain proper access to the lucrative northern markets, but production boomed in the nineteenth century, by which time Armagnac distillers had made a significant stylistic switch from the traditional pot still to a small continuous still. Then came phylloxera, the vine disease which wiped out the French vineyards. Brandy production stalled, but Cognac fought back and made the luxury end of the spirits market it own.

Armagnac meanwhile has shrunk, while what was probably the original European brandy, from Jerez, has remained a Spanish speciality. Quality brandy finds itself at a crossroads. It is expensive and quality hasn't always kept pace with the price. Today however, smaller houses are offering top-notch, well-priced alternatives to the offerings from the main houses. A new chapter is beginning.

Cognac

To understand what makes Cognac such a great spirit you have to understand the French concept of "terroir": how the typical characteristics of a wine (or brandy) result directly from the effect the soil, climate, altitude and exposure to the sun has on the vine. If Cognac didn't have so many distinct terroirs then the master blenders of the region would not be able to draw on so many diverse spirits. It all comes down to how much chalk there is in the soil. Bands of chalk run through the region, with the main two quality zones (crus): Grand and Petite Champagne having the highest concentration.

Grand Champagne, lying to the south of Charente, has the most chalk and makes eaux de vie which are elegant, subtle and refined, but which need time to open. Petite Champagne is the semi-circular zone which arcs around the southern part of Grand

Cognac Chateau: The timeless, serene face of Cognac

Courvoisier's Paradis: An aptly named store

Champagne. Although twice as large it only produces the same volume of eaux de vie as its neighbour and the spirit is slightly less intense but more floral and fruity. If a Cognac is made up with from these two crus it can call itself Fine Champagne.

The small region of Borderies lies on the north bank of the Charente opposite the western area of the two Champagnes. Here the maritime climate has more of an influence as does the higher percentage of flint and clay in the soil. The result is a rich, full-bodied almost waxy distillate which adds richness and guts to a blend.

These three regions are encircled by Fins Bois which supplies the bulk of Cognac and is unfairly dismissed as a result. There are chalky strips running through the clay which dominates most of the cru. Vineyards on this chalk produce a more delicate, refined spirit than the normal quick-maturing, robust style. It is however dangerous to generalize: in this vast area there big differences between east to west and north to south – so stick to producers not regions.

Fins Bois is itself surrounded by Bons Bois and here quality begins to decrease, although good spirit can be made if there is some chalk in the soil. The final cru is Bois Ordinaire whose vineyards are planted on sandy soil and have to cope with a cool, Atlantic climate, which is not an ideal combination. A little brandy is more here these days.

The proof that terroir exists lies in the fact that all these regions make their substantially different eaux de vie in the same way and from the same variety – the late-ripening, high acid Ugni Blanc. Acidity is necessary in brandy production for a number of reasons. It acts as a natural preservative making it more difficult for the wine to oxidize (after all you can't add sulphur to a wine you're going to distil) and has an impact on the aromas and flavours produced by distillation. In addition, the lower the strength of the wine, the easier it is to concentrate the flavours in distillation.

All Cognac is distilled in elegant alambic Charentais pot stills, comprising a boiler with an onion-shaped head and a long thin neck that swoops into the condenser. Some firms use a preheater to gently raise the temperature of the wine. The amount of lees left in the wine will also vary, depending on which style of eaux de vie is to be produced. A wine with heavy lees will give a long-lasting, richly-flavoured eaux de vie, while one destined for a young blend will usually have only light lees. It's a matter of balance: the absence of lees can make the distillate hard and thin, while too much makes it heavy.

Tasting notes

VSOP
Rémy Martin VSOP
Fruity and relatively full-bodied:
berries, caramelized fruits light toffee
and oak. Quite sweet with cinnamon
half way through. A very sound
commercial style.

Jean Fillioux – La Pouyade
Light with hint of lily, apple blossom,
white fruits, grapefruit skin and
chamomile. Superb balance
and elegance.

**Léopold Gourmel
– Premières saveurs**
The nose has lime flower/privet
blossom with a little touch of
honeycomb and a drying note of
almond. The palate has vanilla fudge,
and a balancing chalky dryness.

**Château de Beaulon 7 ans
– Folle blanche**
Aromatically it has a pleasant hint of
damp earth, slightly paper like,
orange zest. Has some depth.

XO
Camus – XO Borderies
A modern-style, turbo-charged XO
made for the hip-hop market: fat and
robust with caramel toffee and sweet
orange. Oak, chocolate and lilac.

François Voyer XO – 40%
The nose is light and seems
(relatively) young: dried flowers,
pot-pourri. Herbal with hints of bay
and lemon thyme and faded roses.
The palate is soft and complex with a
light touch of honey, macadamia,
and soft fruits.

Prince de Polignac – XO Royal
Waxy, this time with fruitcake added.
Berry fruits, marmalade.
Fat, nutty and solid.

Courvoisier XO
Another of the big modern camp,
this time with added bitter chocolate,
coffee grounds and dried strawberry.
Liquorous, and fruity.

VERY OLD
Davidoff – Classic The nose is all
chocolate garnish, lavender with light
rancio. Very masculine. The palate is
chewy and supple with robust earthy,
leathery flavours.

Famille Estève, Réserve Ancestrale
Autumnal on the nose: chanterelle,
moist autumn earth, mulch. Deep
weight. Good rancio and elegance.
Orange and apple cider and a
hint of dried fig. The palate is deep,
rounded and quite fleshy.

Hennessy Paradis A deep nose: Darjeeling tea, dried citrus peels, moist gingerbread cut with cigar box. Lightly earthy with some rancio notes. Some coffee. Complex. Well-balanced.

Martell – Grand Extra A big, bold and accessible nose with the house waxiness next to ginger in syrup, gentian. Balanced and nutty and while it might not be massively complex it is extremely well made.

Delamain – Vesper Complexity from the word go. Meddles with heavy rose petal, hickory sweetness, hints of sandalwood, nutmeg, prune. Soft in the mouth, it only really reveals its layers on the mid palate. Semi-dried fruits, wet orchid, light tannin. Seductive yet slightly haughty.

A.E.Dor - vieille réserve N°6 Pollen, kumquat, lime and freesia. Light and clean with a touch of vanilla and lemongrass. The taste is sweet and quite vinous with ripe fruit. A powdery floral note hangs in there giving a crisp balance. Gossamer light and very subtle.

The spirit is distilled twice and, as ever, each house will have its own specifications on when to start and stop collecting the heart of the run. Normally the new spirit is then placed in new 350-litre Limousin oak barrels for one year before being decanted into used barrels, where it remains for anything from twenty to thirty years. By this time the rancio aroma (an odd-smelling combination of nuts, mushrooms and blue cheese) will appear. These ancient Cognacs will eventually be decanted into glass demijohns and stored in the appropriately named Paradis.

The humid riverside climate of Cognac is perfect for this slow maturation, but it is worthwhile trying vintage "Early Landed" Cognac which has spent all its time maturing in cellars in England. Here the wood has virtually no influence and you can "taste the vintage". It helps to remind you that Cognac is a wine and its production is something of an art.

Armagnac

Armagnac is divided into three regions: Bas-Armagnac, Tenareze and Haut-Armagnac. The best quality spirit comes from the first two. Bas-Armagnac has a sand and clay soil giving a supple, relatively quick maturing eaux de vie. Tenareze which arcs round Bas Armagnac's eastern border is higher and has increased amounts of chalk, producing a rounded, aromatic, fruity style capable of great ageing.

Producers can use up to 12 grape varieties but the majority use Folle Blanche, Ugni Blanc, Colombard and a hybrid called Baco 22A. As Armagnac has a more moderate climate than Cognac the grapes are higher in potential alcohol when harvested (around 9%ABV) though they still have good acidity. Ideally distillation should take place as soon after fermentation as possible to preserve the lightest aromas.

Distillation is where Armagnac differs the most from Cognac. The vast majority of distillers use the traditional alembic armagnaçais or column still. In principle this is no different to any other column still, but the biggest difference between the stills used in Armagnac and the majority of column stills used around the world is that they're tiny. Because of this the strength of the distillate is low, much lower than Cognac. This is where much of Armagnac's rich, pruney fruitiness and earthy rich character comes from. It takes a highly skilled master craftsman to make an elegant spirit at this strength.

Pot still distillation, while legal, is controversial and most producers prefer to stick to the traditional method, though ironically the first Armagnacs in the fifteenth century would have been made in pot stills. Traditionally Armagnac was aged in the local Monlezun oak, which it is claimed gives an extra richness to the spirit. However, due to commercial expansion most producers use Limousin or Tronçais wood. As in Cognac the new spirit will first be aged for about a year in new barrels before being decanted into old ones. As it ages, the spirit will be regularly decanted into progressively older and often larger barrels in order to cut down on the impact of the wood but still allowing a slow, steady oxidation. After a maximum of 40 years in wood the few Armagnacs which are left will end up in glass jars in Paradis.

The fact that Armagnac is made from a low-strength spirit means it takes time in the barrel for those rich flavours to break down. However, because most of the larger producers hope to achieve as quick a commercial return as possible, they release young brandies and add caramel and boisé (a mix of wood shavings and brandy) to it in order to give a semblance of age. As a result the spirit

Gascon vineyard: Remember, Armagnac is a wine

Work of art: Still life in Gascony

tastes like a young brandy with added caramel and wood shavings. Virtually every producer will distil wines from different regions and varieties separately and won't blend the eaux de vie until the Armagnac is ready to be bottled. This alows producers to release vintage Armagnacs (only recently was Cognac allowed to do the same) Be careful though. As in wine, "vintage" doesn't automatically equal great and blends are often the better option.

Armagnac isn't Cognac nor intends to be. Instead, this proud, strangely isolated part of France shows its individuality in the glass: aromas of beech woods, prunes, dates and mellow fruit. Rich, slow maturing and elegant, it is one of the world's sadly forgotten spirits.

Tasting notes

JANNEAU

Janneau 5-year-old Pale amber. Light roast hazelnut nose with some green herbal woody notes. Soft in the mouth with clean fruit.

Janneau 8-year-old Soft, rich and almost oily on the nose with some spicy wood. Walnut veneer and earth on the palate. Very sound.

Janneau 15-year-old A haunting aroma filled with a mix of dried roses, apples, cinnamon, butterscotch and nuts. An oily weight; the spirit long and full with touches of nuts and prunes.

Janneau VS Very young and fiery on the nose. A hint of coffee, but rather green. A sweet attack and nicer than you'd imagine.

Janneau VSOP Clean and light with perhaps a touch of sandalwood. Easy, commercial and pretty in its own way.

Janneau XO Perfumed woodsmoke and earth with a hint of plum on the nose. Good weight on the palate. Chewy, long, full and fat.

Janneau Reserve Complex and elegantly scented, with nuts, plums, prunes and a touch of violet and woodland fruit. Rich weight with a touch of rancio and a clear bell of fruit ringing out. Pruney richness on the finish.

Janneau 1984 Green plums and rather too spirity. Quite high acidity. Fierce and too young.

Janneau 1976 Refined with earth, nut and a undertow of elegant beech wood mulch. On the palate the fruit is soft and plummily rounded with a grip of chilli pepper on the finish

Janneau 1966 Pulpy, ripe fruit, with a whiff of musk. Deep, smoky and subtle. Quite high-toned with gorgeous length.

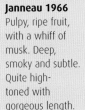

Brandy de Jerez

Although brandy may have been made in Andalusia since 900AD, even the locals didn't drink it until relatively recently. Instead the brandy of Jerez was used to fortify the local wine: sherry. Even when the brandy was shipped in barrel to England, Scotland and Holland it was still used as a fortifying agent rather than drunk on its own. So much brandy was shipped to the Netherlands that the best eaux de vie used in the production of Brandy de Jerez is still known as holandas.

It was only in the nineteenth century that brandy itself started being aged for commercial sale on its own by sherry producers. The first brand, Fundador, only appeared in the nineteenth century. It proved to be a huge hit in Spain, but the rest of the world has been slow to catch on.

The wine for Brandy de Jerez doesn't come from the region itself but from the plains of La Mancha and most is distilled in the town of Tomellosa.Based on the bland-tasting Airen (and occasionally the better quality Palomino) the base wine is stronger than those of Cognac or Armagnac, giving a fatter, softer spirit. The base wine is either distilled in a column or pot still giving three types of distillate: holandas

Barrels of fun: The ancient solera at Osborne in Jerez

(a pot still spirit at between 60 and 70%ABV) and two aguardiente: one of less than 85% ABV, the other between 86% and 94.5%. By law the final blend must contain more than 50% of spirits below 86%. A rule of thumb is that the better the brandy the more holandas is used.

The brandies are blended immediately and shipped to Jerez where they are aged in a solera. This consists of a series of butts, each horizontal tier of which contains brandies of the same approximate age. If you wish to bottle a brandy you take the amount you require, never more than two-thirds of the volume in the cask, from the oldest tier and then replenish those barrels with the same volume of brandy from the next oldest and so on back down the scale. Because the casks are never emptied there will always be some of the original brandy in the cask. It doesn't speed maturation up, but is a way of blending old and younger spirits, allowing consistency and increasing the interaction with wood.

The problem is that demand has been so high in Spain that the brandies, particularly at the lower end of the price scale, have been passed through the solera system a bit too quickly. The end result is that you get a young brandy with a veneer of age on it which then has to be heavily adjusted. Speed is OK when you are making fino sherry but not when you are making a brandy. It takes time for a young spirit to break down in cask. Stick to the Gran Reserva brands would be my advice.

Producers are allowed to adjust the spirit by adding colouring and sweetening agents: usually caramel, or PX sherry. Badly adjusted brandies are poor examples of what can be a rich, robust style. The best examples are ripe, sweet and characterful.

Tasting notes

SOLERA RESERVA
Senor Lustau Burnt, more than a touch of PX, some complexity and crispness from young spirit.

Magno Smooth, but not complex. Rich with a hint of plummy fruit. Soft in the mouth. Simple and attractive.

Fundador Young, nutty, clean and quite simple.

SOLERA GRAN RESERVA
(1=Dry 5=Sweet)
Lepanto (1) Clean, nutty and dry, but gently subtle. Fresh finish. Very good.

Osborne Dali (3) Quite complex on the nose. Clean wood on show. Smooth, sweet as a nut. Very long and rich.

Carlos 1 Imperial (3) Soft, rich plummy/figgy fruit. Very soft to start, followed by lifted, delicate top notes. Long and clean.

Carlos 1 (3) Rounded, with walnut/ Dundee cake notes on the nose. A chewy and clean taste with a good range of flavours and soft, vanilla fruit.

Conde de Osborne (3/4) Medium intensity on the nose. A full, sweet, raisined impact with a clean grip.

Señor Lustau (4) Subtle, soft and elegant on the nose with a hint of burnt Madeira-like fruit. Very soft on the palate, but with a decent grip.

Gran Duque d'Alba (5) Full and sweet; nothing more than raisins steeped in alcohol.

Cardenal Mendoza (5) Coffee beans on the nose. Rich and deep with a chewy complexity and a fresh dry finish.

Tequila

"Actually it only takes me one drink to get drunk. The trouble is I can't remember if it's the thirteenth or fourteenth."

George Burns

Although distillation didn't arrive in Mexico until the time of the conquistadors, the basis for mezcal (pulque, the fermented juice of the agave) was already being drunk by the indigenous population as part of shamanic rituals. When the art of distillation arrived, many of these traditions were simply transferred to mezcal and tequila. Even today the spirits are used to bless the land, as folk medicines and are often only consumed on important feast days.

And although the first spirit made in Mexico was probably rum rather than mezcal, the latter followed soon after, even though it was illegal under Spanish law (in an attempt to force settlers to drink only Spanish brandy). It wasn't until the eighteenth century that commercial distilling took place, by which time it had been noticed that quality appeared to be highest in what are now the lowlands of the tequila DO. It was here, in 1785, that the Cuervo

family bagan to produce its "mezcal wine" at the La Rojena distillery. What we know as tequila was born, though it wasn't until after 1945 that this Mexican speciality began to be seen in export markets, getting a massive boost with the invention of the margarita (still America's most popular mixed drink) in the 1950s.

That said, it was always regarded as a wild, slightly unhinged, spirit. It wasn't until the 1980s that tequila began to acquire a respectable air with the launch in the US of Chinaco, a 100 per cent agave tequila. By the 1990s, its reputation among the world's savvier drinkers was assured. Producers started to concentrate on 100 per cent blue agave examples, delicate, often wood-aged spirits, which showed that the plant could make an elegant spirit. Even more amazingly, top-notch mezcals (usually seen as tequila's rougher cousin) also began appearing. Premium tequila boomed.

Tequila's rapid rise was dented at the start of the millennium with a crisis in supply caused by a lack of agave, exacerbated by a disease which affected the plant. Today, however, I believe that it is the most exciting spirit category in the world. The idea of tequila as the rough shoot-'em-up liquor has virtually disappeared and in its place has come an elegant sipping spirit with its own character, its own terroir and identity, inextricably linked to its place of birth.

How it's Made

Tequila is a distillate of the blue agave, one of over 200 strains of this family of desert lilies which grow throughout Mexico. The agaves are harvested when they are mature, which will vary depending on the plant, the soil and the terroir, but on average this will be between eight and ten years—by which time the heart of the plant weighs on average 35 kilos (sometimes much more).

There are sub-regions within the denominated region, but it is easier to split it into two: the Lowlands (aka Tequila Valley) and the Highlands (Los Altos). The former's sandy soil gives a tequila which is forward and robust. Los Altos, higher with iron-rich soil, gives a tequila with more fruit, sweetness and elegance. Once the agave is ready for harvesting its leaves are hacked off, exposing the central starchy core known as the piña (pineapple) which, when distilled, will produce about 2½ litres of tequila.

Once in the distillery the rock-hard piñas are cooked either in autoclaves or in brick ovens. Agave is not starchy, but instead high in compounds called fructans which need to be changed through cooking in order to be available for fermentation. The cooking also creates caramelized flavours and makes the agave easier to mill. They are then crushed (in pits or with shredders) and the sweet juice drained off and put into fermenters.

The agua de miel is then diluted with water (each distillery jealously guards its own supply) and yeast is added. The strain will depend on the house style: some use industry yeasts, others have their own strain, some ultra-traditional firms rely on a wild yeast ferment. Some producers add accelerators to speed up the process which can be as short as 30 hours or as long as 72 hours. The pulque is then double distilled in either copper or steel pot stills.

There are five classes of tequila. Silver/plata/blano can be aged up to 60 days either in cask or in tank. Gold/oro/joven abogado is a plata tequila with up to one per cent of its volume being made up with colouring—either spirit caramel, oak extract or aged tequila. Glycerine and sugar are also permitted. Reposado has been "rested" for a minimum of two months and up to one year in wood. Anejo is aged in oak casks of less than 600 litres for a minimum of one year and up to three years. After three years in

Tasting notes

Calle 23 Blanco Gentle and fruity with light lemon, white pepper, hot earth, vanilla, agave and lychee. Soft, quite light and gentle, it finishes with sweet fruits, flowers and a dusty earthiness.

Olmeca Altos Plata Refined and fruity with lifted floral notes, lime blossom citrus, stewed fruit and pineapple. Good Altos agave sweetness on the tongue.

Sauza Tres Generaciones Plata A solid silver tequila with light notes of fruity agave and a forward, tingling palate with hints of white pepper.

Tapatio Blanco Typical Altos fragrance and finesse on the nose that drifts into grass, prickly pear juice and long pepper. The palate is rich and long with a delicate nutmeg hint on the end.

Herradura Anejo The brand which, they say, started this class of tequila— way back in the 1960s. The oak has pumped up the agave notes and added pine/cedar and a toffee element, hints of mango and banana split.

Jose Cuervo Reserva de la Familia Anejo Bottled in small batches, this shows rich cask-driven aromas of coffee, date and chocolate, backed with semi-dried fruits and a light edge of charred wood.

Ocho Reposado Sweet and spicy with a mix of cinnamon, almond milk and pear on the nose. The palate is gentle with good fresh agave notes, and builds in fruitiness as it finishes.

Patron Reposado Very light oak influence. Light herbal/vegetal notes, capsicum, clay. The oak provides a mix of sweet spice and coconut but doesn't obscure the gentle agave character.

Don Julio Anejo Silky, smooth anejo with a fresh agave nose of pomelo, orange, light pepper, stewed pear and honey, and balanced vanilla-rich oak.

7 Leguas Extra Anejo Clear oak-driven aromas here with cherry, sap, vanilla and white chocolate on the nose. The palate shows positive pear-like fruitiness.

Arette Gran Clase An unusual experience in tequila, this is a single-barrel release so there will be variations on its very citric, green olive character. Quite minerally with a little mint. The cask kicks in with lots of cream, liquorice and cinnamon.

the same type of cask it becomes extra anejo. These wood-influenced tequilas appeal to whisky and cognac lovers, but if you wish to experience the true flavour of agave go for high-quality plata or reposado.

Under the law, tequila can be made with a minimum of 51 per cent of the sugars in fermentation coming from blue agave. The other 49 per cent can come from other sources—cane syrup being the most common, or corn syrup—but not from other types of agave.

Mezcal

Tequila is a mezcal from a designated region. This does not mean that all other mezcals are poor quality spirits. Mezcal is made wherever agave grows, which is just about everywhere in Mexico. What makes each mezcal different depends on a number of factors: the type of agave, which can range from the giant agave to the rare tobala and espadin.

Production, with a few exceptions, remains rustic, although in 2005 a "norma" (set of regulations) was created for mescal, establishing seven designated states where it could be produced. The piñas are roasted (giving a smoky edge to the spirit) then crushed in a pit and left to ferment naturally. After that it is distilled twice in either a clay, copper, or ceramic still.

The days of mezcal being a rough, rubbery spirit are on the wane. The work done by the producers of Sotol (itself a designated type) and producers such as del Maguey has ushered in a new, quality-oriented era, but one where the artisanal creativity of the producers has not been diluted.

Anise and Absinthe

"A glass of absinthe is as poetical as anything in the world. What difference is there between a glass of absinthe and a sunset?"

Oscar Wilde

An important ingredient in early medicines, anise lives on in the national drinks of Lebanon, Turkey and Greece as well as specialities of Italy, Spain and southern France. As an ingredient it is best known as the main flavouring agent in pastis, Pernod and absinthe, but it is also used in ouzo, raki, sambuca and the huge variety of Spanish anise liqueurs.

Its most notorious manifestation is as one of the main flavouring agents in absinthe. Absinthe was first made commercially by Henri Dubeid and his son-in-law, Henri-Louis Pernod, adapting an old mountain cure-all recipe which took its name from artemisia absinthium (wormwood), its second major ingredient. It rose in popularity when French soldiers were given it as a remedy for malaria in the Algerian war of 1840. They brought the taste back with them and soon everyone was drinking the Green Fairy.

Absinthe's high strength and peculiar form of intoxication made it a drink extolled by artists and writers such as Degas, Lautrec, Verlaine, Baudelaire and Rimbaud and it became the LSD of the Belle Epoque. French society was scandalized and absinthe was soon being blamed for all of society's ills, even as the cause of a degenerative brain disease "absinthism". Wine producers, seeing their sales plummeting joined the absinthe backlash and in a fervour of moral rectitude it was banned in 1915. In France and Switzerland that is... This wasn't an unexpected turn of events given that the most popular drink in the country was an often poorly made high-strength spirit. It was alcohol which was the problem, not absinthe.

Pernod licked its wounds and in 1920 launched a new sweet, lower-strength, wormwood-free brand. In 1932, Paul Ricard launched his pastis (a Provençal dialect word meaning "mixed") a bone dry southern speciality made to slake workers' thirsts. Absinthe was no more... or so we thought.

In the late 1990s, Czech versions began to appear in the west and it was discovered that absinthe had actually never been banned in the UK. Now Spanish, Balearic, Swiss, French (Pernod has released a version of its Original), Andorran, Czech, Portuguese and Brazilian examples are available. Some are very good, but on the whole the mistakes of 100 years ago seem to have been repeated resulting in the market being flooded with poorly made, high-strength drinks, designed to carry the drinker into a state of oblivion.

The absinthe made by Pernod was based on anise and wormwood but also contained fennel seed, nutmeg, hyssop, angelica and other herbs and roots. The infused spirit was then redistilled, à la gin, and given an extra dose of wormwood. It is this ingredient which is at the root of the peculiar, trippy, intoxication you get when drinking true absinthe. Wormwood is high in a chemical called thujone which is in the same family as THC, the active ingredient in cannabis which induces hallucinations. While new French and Swiss absinthes will be (virtually) thujone-free, the best from Andorra and Spain follow the original recipe. The poorest modern versions simply add colourings and essences to approximate the flavour. More importantly, they don't louche.

Star anise: The essential ingredient for aroma flavour and louche behaviour

Louching is that magical moment when water is added to any anise-based drink and it goes milky. This is because anethol, the essential oil of star anise, isn't soluble when diluted and forms an emulsion.

Pernod louches, as does pastis, but don't get the two confused. Pernod is built in three blocks: star anise and fennel are distilled to produce anethol which is then blended with neutral alcohol and the distillates of a variety of aromatic plants. Meanwhile liquorice is macerated and blended with another herb-flavoured alcohol. The two components are then blended, sweetened and coloured.

Pastis is different and is, essentially, produced by maceration rather than distillation. Ricard uses a base of anethol and liquorice-flavoured alcohol in which a secret mix of spices and aromatic herbs is macerated for up to 72 hours. It is naturally dry and unsweetened.

There are other, better, examples. Janot steeps its flavouring agents in alcohol for twelve weeks, while the magnificent Henri Bardouin, made by the last distiller in Forcalquier, the centre of Provençal herb cultivation, is the most complex with scents of anise, liquorice, dried herbs, cinnamon, cardamom, pepper, tobacco, flowers, clove and dried peels. It makes Ricard taste flat and one-dimensional.

Ouzo and raki can be made in a variety of ways. Some ouzo producers use pot stills to redistil aniseed and other flavouring agents as with gin, others distil anise and fennel seed and then blend the result with alcohol. Raki, the national spirit of Lebanon and Turkey, is produced from grape pomace which is then flavoured with aniseed. Ouzo and raki are as dry as pastis but have more delicate flavourings.

Almost every Mediterranean country makes an anise-based drink. In Italy and Spain they tend to be liqueurs such as sambuca, anise itself and the Basque speciality pacharan. Pacharan is made by blending together alcohol which has had sloe (blackthorn) berries macerating in it, sugar syrup, anisette and other fruits. Some firms, the makers of Etxeko, for example, use an eaux-de-vie distilled from the previous year's spent sloes as the macerating alcohol, rather than the more common neutral alcohol. Pacharan can vary from sickly sweet (such as Zoco) to dry, richly coloured and complex (La Navarra, Etxeko are good examples).

Tasting notes

PASTIS

Henri Bardouin Glowing yellowy-green when louches. The aroma has anise, liquorice, cardamom, dried herbs, pepper, cinnamon, tobacco, a hint of clove, flowers and dried peels. Complex, moreish and beautifully balanced.

Janot Product of long maceration and a more complex mix of botanicals. Anise dominant with a herbal lift.

Pastis 51 Best of the big commercial brands and one of the cleanest and crispest examples.

Ricard Dry and liquorice dominant with light spices. Clean and refreshing, but not hugely complex.

ABSINTHE

Un Emile Clear as water, but dusty like a dry wood, herbal and exotic with a bitter finish. Milky louche with a gold spot in the centre. Clean and slightly herbal. Dry.

Verte de Fougerolles Pale olive green. Lightly dusty with camomile tea, fennel. The louche is slow and more jade like. Sage, Japanese green tea, angelica. Complex, yet elusive.

Vieux Pontarlier Francaise Superieure. Pale green with a swirling, opalescent louche. When neat has a tight bitter note but when diluted with water dripped through sugar allows a lifted and herbal, spicy quality to rise along with camphor and moss.

La Fee. The brand which ushered in the new age of absinthe is solid green with plenty of anise, dry leaves, some herbal note, lemon and liquorice.

Other Spirits of the World

Although these days the global drinks market is dominated by a few major categories there are still some wonderful, relatively specialized, spirits which the true drinks hound should seek out. Here are some of them.

Grappa and Pisco

Every winemaking country makes brandy and while you can find superb examples from South Africa, the USA and Armenia the one grape brandy the cocktail enthusiast should get hold of is pisco. Although best known as a Chilean speciality, the Peruvians claim they were the first to make it – and they do have a town called Pisco.

Chilean pisco is made in the Elqui valley in the far north of the country from three strains of the Muscat grape along with small amounts of other aromatic varieties, such as Torrontes, Moscatel de Alexandria and PX. Producers often give the wine a short period of time on skins to achieve a greater aromatic intensity. It is not, as commonly thought, a pomace spirit like grappa but distilled in pot stills and can be sold under four designations: Seleccion (30%ABV) Especial (35%) Reservado (34%) and Gran Pisco. While Seleccion is usually kept in stainless steel tanks the others are aged in wood which can give the older examples a pale pinkish hue. The best – look for

Grappa: No longer an Italian spirit, but Italian style personified

ABA – are gorgeously fragrant spirits filled with the aromas of jasmine and light citric fruits and are a great cocktail base. Peruvian pisco is divided into Pisco Fur (single grape variety), Aromatico (as the name suggests) and the unusual Pisco Verde, which is made from partially-fermented grapes. Bolivians know the drink as Singani and their version is mainly a distillate of Moscatel de Alexandria.

The other most significant wine-based spirit is best sipped on its own. Made from the skins left over after fermentation it is a spirit that's produed in virtually every winemaking country. Known as marc in France and orujo in Spain, it reaches its greatest heights in Italy where it is called grappa.

For years grappa was the heart starter that was slipped into the first espresso of the day – a rustic, earthy, slightly greasy spirit that immediately promised a hideous hangover. Then, as Italian wine transformed itself in the 1970s, so distillers decided to pay greater attention to what had been the runt of the litter. Firms such as Nardini, Nonino and Poli revolutionized grappa production by, quite simply, taking care over how they distilled it.

Now there are wood-aged and even peated grappas appearing. Every grape variety is distilled, each top estate has its own grappa. It might still be an acquired taste but it is a classy one to acquire.

Calvados and fruit brandies

The Normandy apple brandy is further proof of artisanal distillers being able to embrace the essence of any ingredient which came to hand. The first record of Calvados production was in 1533; these days it is governed by its own appellation regulations, which cover permitted varieties (over 40 of them) the nature of distillation and ageing. Over 40 varieties of apple and pear are allowed and each distiller will have his own particular blend. The fruit is crushed and then fermented, usually with natural yeasts. In the Pays d'Auge only pot stills can be used, but the rest of Calvados uses column stills. Ageing takes place in oak barrels or large vats.

Calvados can have a slightly aggressive character when young, but as it matures it softens and mellows into a truly glorious spirit filled with the scent of apple, clove and raisin. Search out the smaller distillers and ultra-rare 100% pear versions. Excellent cider brandy is also made in England and in the Channel Islands.

The production of fruit distillates (eaux de vie in France) is a speciality of Alsace, Southern Germany, Switzerland, Austria and north east Italy. Production varies depending on the fruit. Stone fruits are lightly crushed but the stones are rarely cracked – with the exception of kirsch production where the almond flavour given by cherry stones is desired. Fermentation is a long, natural one giving a fruit "wine" of around 5%. Soft fruits are even lower in alcohol so are macerated in alcohol before being redistilled. Traditionally stone fruits are double-distilled and then left to mellow in glass jars. Wood is rarely used.

Every fruit, wild or cultivated, is distilled and while Poire William is the most widely seen example, mirabelle is more charming. Questch made from plum is richer and similar in style to the slivovitz made in the Balkans and Southern Poland. There are fruit spirits made from raspberry, quince, blackberry and even holly berries and rosehips. Austria weighs in with its own specialities, including juniper, greengage (ringlottenbrand) and rarest of of all, adlitzbeere, made from the fruit of the wild service tree. All are pure essences of their root ingredient.

Campari: Effortlessly stylish old chap

Classic Distillates

BITTERS

Spirits were originally produced to benefit health and there is one branch of the family – bitters – which remain rooted in this ancient purpose. Because of this "drink it, it will do you good" aspect they are regarded with a certain amount of suspicion in the US and the UK. Some are so bitter that drinking them is hardly pleasurable, while others make tremendous aperitifs or digestifs and essential additions to any home bar.

The bitter ingredient is always vegetal in origin and can come from one or more of the following: quinine/chinchon, angelica, gentian, bitter orange, rue, nux vomica, artichoke, wormwood, bitter aloe or rhubarb root. The potion is then often given a lift by the inclusion of aromatic herbs and spices, similar to gin.

"MEDICINAL" BITTERS

These are best taken in small quantities and in one gulp and though claimed to be an aid to digestion, the only use I've ever found for them is as a highly effective cure for an extreme hangover. The best known is the explosive slightly peppermint-accented Fernet Branca. The German duo Jagermeister and Underberg are equally effective with the former having a slightly sweeter anise flavour, while Underberg is simply bitter tasting.

Cocktail staple: Campari is essential for any bar

DIGESTIF BITTERS

The best Italian examples are Averna and Montenegro which are given a boost with sweetened wine. Cynar, whose bitterness comes from artichokes, is relatively light and sweet. Worth trying are Unicum from Hungary and Melnais Balzans from Latvia; both are sweet with the latter having an extra resonance. Spain also has its own versions of these: Chinchon is the most widely seen and occupies a position half way between a bitters, a liqueur and an anise drink. Better tasting, on that cusp between sweet, herbal and bitter, is Calisay which also uses chinchon bark as its bittering agent along with herbs, bitter orange and wormwood.

APERITIF BITTERS

Campari, one of the world's classic drinks, dominates this group of bitters. A gorgeous rich pink colour with lifted aromas of orange and spice, it is one of the great cocktail ingredients as well as a refreshing aperitif. Punt e Mes is halfway between a bitters and a vermouth, as are the French-made Dubonnet and St. Raphaël. France's best bitter-based brand is Suze which gets its kick from gentian.

COCKTAIL BITTERS

There are some bitters which are so intense they only need to be added in minuscule quantities to drinks. The best known is Angostura, created as a cure for malaria but now an essential addition to any bar. It is not the only one of its kind, however. Search for the sweeter anise-flavoured Peychaud from New Orleans or the magnificent Abbot's or Elby orange bitters. If you are in Peru try their variant on the Angostura theme, Amargo. Experiment with them. They can turn an ordinary drink into something special.

Akvavit and schnapps

Akvavit is a Scandinavian variant of flavoured vodka and is one of the great northern white spirits, despite being hardly known outside its native region. Like vodka it is produced from a highly rectified spirit often made from potatoes, though wheat is also used. The difference between akvavit and flavoured vodkas is that the latter have flavouring agents steeped or infused in the spirit,

while akvavit is redistilled with its botanicals. The main flavouring agent is caraway seed but dill, fennel, cumin, orange peel and others are also used, and while akvavit is normally dry there are some delicious sweet versions.

The most widely seen brand is Aalborg Taffel which is clean, light and a great introduction and just one of 15 akvavits made by the firm. Aalborg Jubilaeums is aged in wood and has dill and coriander added as well as caraway and is a more complex drink. Brondum is light and bone dry, perfect as a base spirit for home-made flavoured spirits, just macerate fruit or peels in it.

Caraway: The main botanical flavouring agent used in making Scandinavia's Akvavit

Akvavits are great food spirits and the most recent arrival, Dild, is as the name sugests heavily accented with dill, and is made to be drunk with shellfish and sushi. Norwegian aquavits are equally impressive with the top brands coming from Lysholm and Løiten.

All are subtle, fragrant, mouth-watering and strangely exotic spirits which really should be drunk ice cold as a shot, ideally with food. Confusingly though the labels say akvavit/aquavit they are referred to as "schnapps", from the Old Norse snappen, meaning to gulp.

To make matters even more confusing what people refer to as schnapps in Germany is in fact korn, an ordinary grain distillate that's often flavoured, while in Austria schnapps is what we normally refer to as eaux de vie.

Vermouth

For thousands of years people have been flavouring wines and spirits with herbs, spices and roots. It is the basis for many spirits, and liqueurs, but the most widely consumed example is the fortified, wine-based drink: vermouth. This takes its name from the German for its original main flavouring compound, wormwood (wermut). The Latin name for this plant is artemisia absinthium, which makes vermouth a second cousin to absinthe. The fundamental difference between them is that while absinthe uses a distillate of the thujone-heavy leaves, vermouth uses the "harmless" flowers.

There are three main styles: Provençal (typified by Noilly Prat), Savoie (Chambery) and Italian (Martini & Rossi, Cinzano) of which the first is by far the most complex.

Noilly Prat is a blend of Picpoul and Clairette wines which have been aged for a year in the open air before being blended and having some fruit essence and mistelle (grape juice and alcohol) added, along with the addition of an all-important mix of herbs: camomile, cloves, coriander, bitter orange, nutmeg and cantuary which are allowed to macerate in the mix. No Martini should be without a splash of this.

Savoie vermouths are more delicate having had no weathering, the Alpine climate makes this impossible, but the best, Dolin Chambery is a subtle and delicious drink and its wild strawberry version Chamberyzette should occupy every bar. Equally good and in the same weight category is the Bordeaux version, Lillet, beloved by Ian Fleming – and his creation, James Bond.

Italian vermouths are created in a slightly different fashion, with flavourings rather than maceration being used. The Italian style also tends to be a little heavier and sweeter than the French style. That said, the best red vermouth (actually halfway between a bitters and a vermouth) is Punt e Mes which balances fruit, oranges and herbs with its light bitterness. Look for its premium variant Antica Formula.

Use Punt e Mes to get a different spin on a Manhattan. Dubonnet and St. Raphaël are its French equivalents but are softer and a little sweeter on the palate.

Martini and Rossi: Vermouth has been an essential part of the home bar for over 100 years

Liqueurs

"A woman drove me to drink and I didn't even have the decency to thank her."

W.C. Fields

Although liqueurs can lay claim to being the earliest of all spirits, they still remain a strange and rather disparate group, ranging from classics like Chartreuse and Drambuie to such modern best-sellers as Baileys and Malibu. It's a category so large and so specialized that it is impossible to list them all here. Liqueurs often come in fancy and colourful bottles and are often made to a secret recipe with the story of their unusual origins attached. Taking their name from the Latin liquefacere "to dissolve" they are a group of sweetened spirits where the ingredients rather than the base spirit takes centre stage.

The greatest have a direct link to the ancient alchemists and apothecaries. The original recipe for Chartreuse doesn't just specify what ingredients to use, but by what phase of the moon they should be harvested. These are the medicines our ancestors would

Chartreuse: The secretive and silent stillhouse

have been given, first by monks, then by wise women and healers. It was only with the arrival of sugar and the greater availability of herbs and spices that liqueurs became social drinks, perfected by the great Dutch firms of Bols and deKuyper and the French Cusenier. By the mid-nineteenth century liqueurs were hitting their stride and many of the major brands: Cointreau, Grand Marnier, Benedictine, Disaronno were founded at this time. They were both sweet sticky things to sip at the end of a meal and great flavouring agents for bartenders.

In recent times liqueurs have become rather passé. As wine drinking has increased, people have stopped taking a liqueur at the end of the meal. They haven't disappeared, but changed. These days, gentle cream-based drinks such as Baileys have taken the place of the more complex old brands, but it is worth searching for the latter style. Those old bartenders knew what they were doing.

MACERATION
The ingredients are placed into the base spirit (usually a neutral spirit but whisky and Cognac also are used) to allow their flavours to leach out. This can take days, weeks or even months. Some brands will macerate different groups of ingredients together, while others will add them throughout the macerating period. Equally, some firms will force the alcohol through the flavouring agents, while others use gentle heating (infusion) to break down the flavour compounds.

DISTILLATION
While fruits will impart all their flavour druing maceration, seeds, nuts, peels, roots and herbs are usually redistilled after a period of maceration to extract any remaining flavours and fix them in the spirit. The bulk of top liqueurs use redistillation for all or part of their brand. Some will keep their botanicals separate and redistil each one individually before blending, while others will combine them. Occasionally the distiller will take some of the major aromatic components, add some water and distil the mixture in order to capture their concentrated essential oils.

CONCENTRATES
These are industrially produced additives which can be added directly to the spirit.

FINISHING/ADJUSTING
It is common for many liqueurs to be aged in large wooden casks after blending. This allows the flavours time to marry but doesn't impart any wood influence. After any ageing the liqueur is sweetened with sugar syrup, or sometimes honey, and adjusted for colour. Caramel, saffron, turmeric, carrot or vegetable dyes are used. Then it's time for filtering, cold stabilisation and bottling.

Herbal liqueurs

This group contains some of the oldest spirits known to man and were originally created to cure illness. The only one which has fully retained this link is the extraordinarily powerful Elixir de Chartreuse the most concentrated "liqueur" of all – few others come close to its complexity. Made by Carthusian monks since 1603, it is a concoction of around 130 flowers, herbs, roots and spices, though how it is made is known by only three monks. At 71%ABV, the Elixir is best taken on a sugar cube and is a wonderful cold cure. Most widely seen is Green (55%ABV) with its extraordinary, intense bouquet. Yellow (like the other two, aged for eight years in casks) is lighter and softer and more honey-accented – but my personal favourite is the VEP a sort of turbo-charged Green.

Benedictine also has religious overtones being first made in 1510 by Don Bernardo Vinvelli in the monastery of Fecamp. Its precise recipe is a secret but it is made by assembling five separate batches of botanicals. The batches are aged separately, blended and married before being sweetened. Softly sweet and herbal, but not cloying, it is among the best.

The roots of herbal liqueurs lie in Italian monasteries but the Italian flag is flown these days by relatively new arrivals: there's the sweet fennel/mint Strega and its similarly-coloured sister Galliano.

Fruit liqueurs

The most common fruit liqueurs are based on orange peel. Curaçao is made from bitter orange peel mixed with other citrus fruits, blossoms, leaves and roots and redistilled to collect essential oils and then blended with alcohol. Triple sec will normally use sweet orange peel or, in the case of Cointreau, mix it with bitter orange and other citrus fruits. The peels are macerated and double distilled. Less well known is the Andalusian speciality Ponche which combines three local ingredients: Seville orange peel, sherry and brandy along with herbs and nuts.

Estonia may not be known for its orange groves, but it does make a fascinating orange peel liqueur, Vana Talinn: a blend of essential oils of orange and lemon peel mixed with a macerated extract of cinnamon and vanilla, blended with high-ester Jamaican rum.

South Africa has the rather lovely van der Hum which uses tangerine as well as orange peel, macerated with nutmeg and other spices in brandy before redistillation. The beautifully balanced Mandarine Napoleon uses the essential oil of tangerines blended with Cognac which brings it close to the most complex orange-based example, Grand Marnier. Bitter orange peel is macerated in brandy, redistilled and then blended with aged Fine Champagne Cognac, sugar syrup and herbs before being aged.

Seed and nut liqueurs

The production of liqueurs from nuts and spice is a spin-off from herbal liqueurs which, instead of being a complex melange of different herbs, tend to rely on a single, strong note. The oldest commercial example is Kummel which is made from caraway seed (the oldest cultivated spice in Europe) and is a Dutch and Baltic speciality. Caraway is also the main ingredient in Akvavit and the sweet, Gdansk speciality vodka Goldwasser, which contains infusions of aniseed, caraway, citrus peel and flakes of gold.

There are plenty of anise liqueurs as well: the sloe-berry flavoured Pacharan, the sweeter Anis del Mono and the Italian classic Sambuca.

Nuts are also used, most notably in production of Amaretto which is based on an infusion of bitter almond oil and crushed apricot pits.

The Spanish speciality Madroño is made from the fruit of the strawberry tree (arbutus unedo). The same base is used for the Portuguese Medronho, sweetened Brandymel, a Corsican version, Liqueur a l'Arbouse, while in Sardinia it's used to make a dry eaux de vie and a liqueur.

Hazelnuts are used for Italy's Nocino and the sticky Frangelico, while, at the risk of appearing overly contrived coconut is the main flavour in Malibu and other better brands like Koko Kanu or Cruzan Coconut.

Whisky liqueurs

The vast majority of liqueurs use a neutral spirit base, but a few mix with a richly flavoured liquor. The Cognac-based Grand Marnier is a good example, as are the whisky-based liqueurs such as Drambuie, Glayva, Southern Comfort and Wild Turkey.

Drambuie and Glayva both hark back to the style of drink made when whisky was first distilled in Scotland. Then it was common practice to add heather blossom and other aromatic plants to the whisky to hide what was probably a rough spirit. Drambuie therefore taps into an ancient past and in many ways bears a closer similarity to what the Highlanders would have drunk than to the malts we know today. That said, the tale of how it was a recipe given by Prince Charlie to the Mackinnon family must be taken with a very large pinch of salt. Whatever the truth, it's a fine liqueur, a mix of herbs macerated in an aged blended whisky then sweetened with heather honey. You get notes of clove, nutmeg, heather and thyme with a cinnamon finish. Glayva is more orangey than Drambuie and a touch sweeter.

Oranges and peaches are the main note in Southern Comfort which came into being when, allegedly, a New Orleans bartender added spices and fruit to improve the Red Eye he was being shipped from Bourbon county. In recent years Wild Turkey has released a honey liqueur which tastes like, well, Wild Turkey with honey added.

Creams

The arrival of cream liqueurs was the first major innovation in the world of liqueurs for over a century and helped to revive a waning category. It was kicked off by Bailey's Irish Cream which came into being when Gilbey's in Ireland was stuck with a surplus of spirit. Someone – and many people have claimed to be that person – decided that instead of just redistilling it they'd try to make a bottled Irish coffee. The result was an international hit. Baileys is the polar opposite of Chartreuse, it has no heritage, no ancient artistry is involved, it's hardly what you could call complex. It is however a triumph of modern drinks-making technology. Producing a dairy-based alcoholic product which doesn't curdle or split in the bottle is no mean feat.

Baileys created a new category, plenty of which are cheap copies which smell as if the milk is on the turn. The mid-market is filled with mild-mannered alcoholic milkshakes which cause no offence but are far from exiting. Even old brands seeing a new niche decided to have a go and Creme de Grand Marnier and Tia Maria both appeared and, as far as I know, disappeared soon after.

There are exceptions. I tasted a white chocolate one a few years back which was like an alcoholic Milky Bar while the South African Amarula, made from distilled fruit of the marula tree is probably the best of the bunch.

Cremes and emulsions

Although related to fruit brandies, creme liqueurs don't use the stone of the fruit and are usually produced with concentrates rather than by macerating the main ingredients, although some brands like Himbergeest and creme de menthe do use essential oils. Cremes are sweeter, lower in alcohol and more brightly coloured than fruit brandies, and can be used in much the same way as syrups like Orgeat or Grenadine. The sector is dominated by Bols, de Kuyper and Cusenier. By and large, these drinks aren't intended to be drunk on their own.

Coffee-based liqueurs are an exception to this rule. This small category is dominated by two brands: Kahlua and Tia Maria. The former is a mix of cane spirit, Mexican coffee and vanilla, while Tia Maria is a blend of Jamaican coffee and spices infused with Jamaican cane spirit and a little chocolate. It's sweeter than Kahlua and has less body. This select band has been joined by Toussaint which claims to be Haitian, but is in fact made by a Trinidadian based in Flensburg. For me it's the best of the bunch, with lots of bitter notes in the nose and a much drier flavour.

For emulsions, read advocaat. Dutch firm Warninks claims to use 60 million egg yolks a year, which are mixed with grape spirit, sugar, vanilla and an emulsifying agent. Thick, yellow, claggy and sweet it can be drunk on its own but quite why anyone would want to do so is beyond me.

Champagne

"There comes a time in every woman's life when the only thing that helps is a glass of champagne."

Bette Davis, *Old Acquaintance*

Sophistication may be the byword for a classic cocktail, but there is nothing quite like the sparkle and glamour of Champagne for kicking off a celebration. The sound of the cork bursting out of the bottle signals the start of a party, just as a starter's pistol heralds the beginning of a race. And those bubbles which tickle the nose and tantalise the tastebuds keep the party in full swing, transporting the alcohol through your bloodstream in no time at all. Whatever the case, no home bar should be without a decent supply of the world's favourite sparkling wine. Champagne is the essential component of many a cocktail: the Champagne cocktail itself, a **French 75** (see p. 103), or the classic, **Buck's Fizz** (see p. 71).

There are a few golden rules to bear in mind once we have a bottle of sparkling in our clutches to ensure the wine is in tip-top condition. For starters, make sure it is well chilled, (colder than a

white wine) but not frozen like a fizzy popsicle. Aim to hit a balance between producing a refreshing glass and being able to actually taste the quality of the wine. Never put Champagne or any other sparkling wine in the freezer to chill it down quickly. You run the risk of the bottle exploding.

Secondly: open the bottle correctly. There's no point in taking the Formula One racing driver approach by shaking the bottle up before opening. Handle the bottle with care: first remove the foil, then with one hand cup the cork and remove the metal cage holding it in place. Slowly turn the bottle and not the cork, easing the capsule out. You'll feel the pressure against your hand, so take it slowly, controlling the cork until it comes out with a soft sigh. Finally, pour the wine into the flute glasses and not the bowls that you see in old Hollywood movies. A fluted glass helps preserve the bubbles (or mousse.)

The sparkling wine produced in the Champagne region in northern France is known as Champagne, anything else, even if it is made in exactly the same fashion must be called a sparkling wine. The Champagne region is a land of chalk hills and a cool climate: ideal conditions for making a light, quite acidic wine which has considerable finesse. Champagne, the drink, can be made from three types of grape: Pinot Noir which gives the final blend weight, body and a strawberry like fruitiness; Pinot Meunier chips in perfume, while Chardonnay gives freshness and notes of flowers, lemons and light fruits.

The grapes are harvested when they still have good, quite high, acidity and are made into wine. Each vineyard will be vinified separately and the master blender will then nose and taste each one to make his blend. This is an art in itself. Blending is hard enough: involving having a mental map of how various flavours sit together, but blending highly acidic young wines which most of us would assume are almost identical is a phenomenal task.

Once the blend is assembled the wine is put into the bottle with some sugar and yeast, sealed and allowed to ferment for a second time. The action of the yeast produces carbon dioxide which

Hidden depths: Billions of bottles are stored in the cool chalk caves of Champagne

cannot escape and is held in the wine as bubbles of gas. Although the yeast eventually dies its work isn't finished. The dead cells – known as lees – continue to interact with the wine, adding flavours of bread, brioche, nuts and even chocolate. The longer left on the lees, the richer the resulting Champagne will be. When the producer deems the wine ready for sale the bottles are plunged,

Tasting notes

There are various terms you should understand when buying Champagne.

Brut means dry.

Extra Dry is slightly sweeter than Brut.

Demi-Sec is medium-sweet.

Blanc de Blancs means the Champagne has been made solely from white grapes, i.e. Chardonnay, producing a clean, light fresh style.

Blanc de Noirs means the Champagne has been produced from red grapes only: i.e. Pinot Noir and Pinot Meunier, giving a richer, more strawberry-accented result. The wine isn't red in colour as red wines get their colour from the skins of the grapes. Since Champagne is normally, but not exclusively (see below),

vinified without its skins, the resulting wine is white.

Rose Champagne is made by blending a little red wine (from Pinot Noir/Meunier) with white. It is pale pink, has an aroma of soft red fruits and is exceptional.

Vintage Champagne is the product of a single year's production and will bear the date on its label. It is similar to Port insofar as vintages are only made in the very best years. These are wines which will also need more time in the bottle after purchasing in order to appreciate their complexities to the full. Allow them the best part of a decade.

Champagne is pricey because it is a labour-intensive business, because the grapes are expensive to buy, and most of all because the houses that

neck down, into a cold bath which sends all the leesy gunk into the neck. The bottles are quickly turned right way up again, the cap is removed and a pellet of frozen wine and lees is shot out. This is replaced by a mix of wine and sugar, the amount of the latter depending on whether the wine is to be dry or sweet. The bottles are then recorked and the wine is ready for drinking.

produce them like to maintain Champagne's status as the world's premier sparkling wine. Although it is, admittedly, an expensive wine to produce, the high price tag often reflects the house's feeling that their wine justifies higher expenditure. Let your own palate decide: a rule of thumb is that at the lower end of the market, the wine is young, green tasting and acidic. Great houses, unsurprisingly, tend to produce the great wines; Moët is solid and reliable, Lanson is making a comeback, while Laurent-Perrier, Roederer and Taittinger are always excellent. Disappointingly, Bollinger has been a little poor recently as has Mumm. Charles Heidsieck offers the best value, while Billecart-Salmon and Laurent-Perrier both make a stunning rose.

Champagne from small independent growers can also be great value. If you want to splash out then go for a prestige cuvée, but be aware that these are hugely expensive. Dom Perignon is a lovely wine as is Roederer Cristal, though my favourites are Guiraud's Cuvee Louise, Salon le Mesnil (a rare, single vineyard Champagne), Pol Roger's Winston Churchill and, of course, Krug. Taste the latter and you'll never drink any other Champagne again – but don't use it for cocktails!

Sparkling Wine

Virtually every wine-making country produces wine using the same method employed in the Champagne region – a second fermentation in the bottle (look for method traditional on the label) – and many are challenging Champagne in terms of quality and price. The fact that major Champagne houses, such as Moët and Mumm have established offshore winemaking facilities only goes to show that as long as the grapes are good and grown in cool climate regions then the quality will follow.

Australia makes an elegant and increasingly complex style, particularly in the Yarra Valley, though New Zealand with its cooler climate has the edge in terms of quality. There are some sophisticated examples from the cooler areas of California and South Africa, while Spain's Cava is always reliable once you accept it has an often earthy character.

There are other ways of getting bubbles into wine: the transfer method involves taking a wine after its second ferment in the bottle and decanting it into a large tank, removing the lees, then adding a sugar solution.

Wines such as Asti are made by a bubble-producing technique in which the wine is fermented in pressurized tanks to which yeast and sugar are added. The result lacks the richness and deep complexities of bottle-fermented wines, but these qualities are not expected in an Asti Spumante. The oldest method, which predates the technique perfected in Champagne involves bottling the wine before it has finished its first fermentation and is still fizzy. Because the wine has not fermented fully it is naturally sweet and the fizz is more foamy. Clairette de Die is the best known example. There are also the cheap and cheerful examples which have simply had a blast of gas added to them. One look at the price tag will tell you which ones they are and these are best avoided.

As for sparkling red wines, these cause most people – apart from Australians who have perfected the style – immense and irrational problems. For some reason we have difficulty accepting that a red wine can be fizzy. Often made with Shiraz, though you can find sparkling Cabernet and Grenache, red sparkling wine is usually rich, often sweet, very spicy and fairly alcoholic. They are well worth trying.

Wine pouring: High quality fizzes are bubbling up

Wine

"A meal without wine is like a day without sunshine, except that on a day without sunshine you can still get drunk."

Lee Entrekin

Though it may seem unlikely, the reason cocktails have become so popular is because the mass market has become so interested in wine. It wasn't that long ago that buying a bottle of wine was a rare treat; when the range of labels on show was an endless list of mysterious names, and when the people in the industry closely guarded the secret world of wine by making sure that none of us could enter their elite club. Those days have gone. Wine has, finally, been democratized and across America and the UK a new generation has learned that wine, while a complicated and fascinating subject, is essentially a drink to be enjoyed. The fact that wine is now accessible doesn't mean it is simple and bland. Instead it has become comprehensible. It's all about flavour.

The shift came with the arrival of wines from Australia, California, New Zealand, Chile and South Africa. These were full of fruit and

packed with flavour; wines which told you what grape they were made from on their label. As people discovered flavour in wine so they began to want the same quality in their spirits and in time in their cocktails. Finally the world of drinks is singing to the same tune, one where flavour and quality are the dominant notes.

White Wine Varieties

These days, we buy wine according to what grape it has been made from as opposed to its country of origin. Rather than look specifically for a French or Italian maker, we tend to base our decision on the flavour, such as a buttery, fragrant Chardonnay or a crisp and refreshing Sauvignon Blanc. Here then is a quick guide to what flavours you should expect from the world's major grape varieties.

CHARDONNAY

This variety is the world's most popular white grape and it is easy to understand why. After all, Chardonnay is the most amenable grape on the planet. While other

Margaret River: Australia's greatest region

grapes can pose problems to winemakers with their taut acidity or tendency to get overripe and bland, Chardonnay will do almost anything the winemaker wants it to. The downside of this is it can easily become bland, boring and overoaked, though barrel-fermented examples are the most complex! Think of it this way: Chardonnay makes the lean acidic white wine behind the greatest Champagnes, yet also produces the soft, rich, nutty, peachiness of a good Californian. It can be made austere and unoaked as in Chablis, or fat, buttery and richly oaked. It comes in a myriad of different styles ranging from the oceans of easy drinking, slightly fat wine from warm irrigated areas across Australia and the Central Valley to some of the greatest, most complex, long-lived white wines of all.

France makes the world's greatest white wines from Chardonnay. They come from the soils of Burgundy. However because Burgundy is divided and subdivided into a mass of appellations, each of which make a subtly different wine, with each producer often owning a few vines in each of these mini zones, it is confusing. It's best to stick to a producer you can trust, rather than buying according to the name of the appellation. Burgundy is one of those places where knowing a reputable wine merchant is very handy. Don't be put off though. These barrel-fermented whites which are racy and lean when young, gain in complexity as they mature picking up notes of nut, honeysuckle and elegant fruit. Superb.

The rest of the world is still trying to reach these levels of complexity. The best Australian Chardonnays tend to come from cooler climate regions such as the Yarra, Adelaide Hills and the Clare Valley, though the warmer Margaret River makes sublime examples. California, too, is going cooler and, though the style is richer and softer than that from Europe, the wines are becoming

increasingly elegant with less reliance on oak. Oregon and
Washington State make excellent examples as well. For good value,
top quality and often characterful Chardonnay stick to Chile.

RIESLING

This is the only variety that can challenge Chardonnay in terms of
complexity and longevity. Despite its tarnished reputation, Riesling's
trump card is its naturally high acidity. Young Riesling is all green
apples and citrus fruit (lime is the signature aroma in Australia). With
time that austere shell cracks and honey, baked apple and flowers
emerge. The acidity is still in evidence however, allowing Riesling to
last for aeons. When the grapes are left on the vine, the sugar levels
increase giving the resulting wine extra honeyed richness and, should
it be attacked by the magical fungus of botrytis cinerea (noble rot)
expect luscious apricot depth. Even the sweetest examples retain that
acidity however. Germany remains Riesling's spiritual home. Go for the
top single estate wines from the Mosel, Rheingau or Rheinpfalz and
be amazed. Alsace makes a richer, more powerful version which is
equally long-lived and a wonderful food wine. Australian Rieslings
(look for Clare or Eden Valley on the label) are fresh and limey when
young and are the perfect partner for Thai food, while Rieslings from
New Zealand and Austria are also worth seeking out.

SAUVIGNON BLANC

Behind the eastern Loire's greatest wines lies the Sauvignon Blanc
grape. It produces the bone-dry, crisp, gooseberry-accented wines of
Sancerre, Pouilly-Fume and Menetou-Salon. It is also the major
player, with Semillon in Bordeaux's elegant, dry whites and that
region's superlative noble-rotted sweeties: Sauternes and Barsac. In
New Zealand, Sauvignon Blanc acquires an extraordinary intensity:
all cut grass and green pepper but with a luscious tropical fruit note
as well. South Africa makes equally excellent examples. Sadly,

American winemakers' fear of bone dry whites means that most US examples tend to be bland.

SEMILLON

These are far from the only white varieties. Be brave and seek out Semillon, Sauvignon's partner in Bordeaux, but at its best as a solo player in Australia's Hunter Valley (unoaked and long-lived) and Barossa Valley (oaked and lemony) and the ripe pear and gorgeously silky textured examples from Washington State.

Sancerre: The flinty heart of Sauvignon Blanc

VIOGNIER

Trendier still is Viognier, the shy-cropping grape that only a few years ago was barely clinging on in the northern Rhone and which is now the trendiest thing to be sticking in the ground. This is a flavour bomb of a grape all lilies, super-ripe peaches and vanilla pods. The trouble with this variety is that it needs to be fully ripe to show its full range of flavours yet as soon as it gets overripe it becomes bland and alcoholic. These days many Californian winemakers are switching attention to Marsanne and Roussanne, two other aromatic Rhone whites which hold their acidity better.

Red Wine Varieties

CABERNET SAUVIGNON AND ITS BORDEAUX COUSINS

These days, the world of red wines is dominated by Cabernet Sauvignon, the rich, black-fruited grape which has its spiritual home in the French wine region of Bordeaux. Cabernet has small berries with thick skins and since all of a grape's colour and most of its tannins are contained in the skin it is no surprise that a Cabernet-based wine will be dark in colour and high in tannin, the latter allowing it to age superbly well. A good Cabernet will have

aromas of blackcurrant, blackberry and briar fruits, the sort of big punchy aromas that today's wine drinker wants. That means that Cabernet, like Chardonnay, has spread itself across the globe, producing wines which fall broadly into two camps: the serious wines with high tannins which are intended for longterm ageing and the upfront, sweet, bramble jam wines for instant gratification. Most of the top winemaking countries have a foot in both camps.

Bordeaux remains the dominant player and no other region has managed to craft Cabernet into wines which give such superb silky elegance. That said, California is giving Bordeaux a run for its money. Though the wines tend to be denser in terms of fruit and slightly sweeter with softer tannins, Stags Leap and the highest hillside sites of Napa and Sonoma are making high-class,

Sonoma Valley: Its hillside vineyards are among the best for Cabernet

Heard it through the Grapevine: Sangiovese grapes in Italy's Montepulciano region

elegant examples. Washington State makes excellent Cabernet
where black cherry is the dominant note, but every country can be
said to have a clutch of great examples: Margaret River and
Coonawarra make the best in Australia, while Waiheke Island has
proved that New Zealand can hold its own. Chile and South Africa
are also now making rich, top-quality examples. Like most grape
varieties, Cabernet works best in a blend. The Bordelais realized
this years ago and have always included Merlot and Cabernet
Franc in their wines.

Merlot is more fleshy than Cabernet with slightly lower tannins
and a soft, plummy aroma. It lends weight, softness and opulence
to a Cabernet blend and is the major player in the wines from
Pomerol and St Emilion. Because it has less tannin than Cabernet it
has become a hip red variety in the US. Once again, Washington
State is the place to seek out bargains, while California makes

some magnificent, if huge, examples. The best place to start with Merlot without breaking the bank is Chile, though much of what was thought to be Merlot is in fact a different variety called Carmenere. If you smell green peppers in your Chilean "Merlot" then this is what you've got.

The last of the Bordeaux triumvirate is Cabernet Franc which is unjustly overlooked. A perfumed grape: think red fruits, dusty raspberries and violet, it gives a lift to Bordeaux blends and produces remarkably long-lived wines in the Loire. It is gaining recognitions as a single varietal: watch out for South African examples. A word too about Malbec, the grape Bordeaux forgot, which has become Argentina's dark star.

PINOT NOIR

The red wine world is divided into two camps: those who love Cabernet and those who prefer Pinot. When you pick up a bottle of Cabernet you know what you are getting. With Pinot, on the other hand, you have to be prepared to wade through a mass of mediocrity before you discover that elusive bottle of greatness. It is worth the search: Pinot noir is one of the world's great red grapes. In fact it is the the world's greatest red grape! It has a dimension that no other red variety can emulate: fragrant yet funky, silky and sensual, yet with a strange earthy quality.

Burgundy is where Pinot Noir is at its greatest, but don't think that a Burgundian label is a guarantee of quality. You have to get to know who the top producers are, what vintages to pick and be prepared to pay for the privilege. In Burgundy they have had thousands of years to work out which sites, which soils and which clones will produce the best results. No other country has yet come close. Most non-Burgundian Pinots have captured its fruity quality (though this can be jammy rather than pure) but lack its the depth. That said, New Zealand is improving fast, as is South Africa, while Santa Barbara has overtaken Carneros as California's finest site. In good years Oregon comes up with the goods as well.

OTHER REDS

Suited to the palates of big wine lovers, Syrah is a warm-climate variety which comes in two stylistic camps: the sooty, earthy, lusty Syrahs of the northern Rhone and the black fruit, pepper and alcohol of the Shiraz style in Australia. This is a wine which is all about power and weight and delivers an upfront blast of concentrated flavour.

Red Rhone varieties are ideal for today's flavour-led consumer, so look out for Grenache (Garnacha in Spain where it is behind Priorato) which gives immense spice and Mourvedre (Spain's Monastrell) with its flavour of baked black fruits. Zinfandel is also in this same general style. Its flavour is reminiscent of earthy wild fruits picked from the hedgerow with surprising lifts of rosemary and roses.

Some of the lighter, juicier flavours are also worth rediscovering, such as Gamay, the fruity variety used to make Beaujolais a versatile wine which is great both with food as well as on its own. Two overlooked Italian varieties are Nebbiolo and Sangiovese. Nebbolio is Italy's answer to Pinot Noir and the grape behind Barolo and Barbaresco. At its best, this late-ripening grape with its high tannins and high levels of acidity, is a wonderful mix of savoury and sweet, floral, yet tarry. Sangiovese is at its greatest in Tuscany where, if yields are kept low, it gives a wine with ample cherry and red plum flavours as well as a fresh acidity which doesn't just help it age well, but makes it a cracking food wine. It is this slightly bitter edge which makes Italian wines so magnificent with a meal.

Choosing Wines

Despite the huge selection of wines available, choosing a wine is still a daunting prospect. You have to ensure that the wines you select match the foods they accompany, appeal to all your guests, and are of a good quality without breaking the bank. Faced with a vast array of labels on the shelf, most people prefer to play safe and stick to the wines they have tried and tested. Buying a known property is a pretty sensible way of getting round the dilemma, but a safe Chardonnay can become boring time after time. Work out your ideal style and look for variations on it.

Oysters: Stick to Chablis...or vodka

Matching wine with food is not that difficult providing you follow two broad guidelines. There are many books dedicated to the subject of pairing wine with food, all of which suggest you should drink what you like, yet offer various, and often complicated, "ideal matches". To simplify matters, first consider the origin of the dish and choose a wine from the same region.

365

Dishes from Alsace, Burgundy or a region in Italy can be matched easily with corresponding wines. In fact these dishes were invented to suit the wines. If the meal's origins are not clear, then choose a wine to suit the flavours on the plate, especially sauces. If you think of red wines in terms of black or red fruit then things are easier still.

If you are having a bold main course with a rich sauce then go for a bold, black-fruited wine to complement it. Beef is great with Cabernet, and Syrah/Shiraz. Lamb is a little lighter and more perfumed so go for a mix of red and black fruits in the wine: a lighter Merlot, red Rioja, or a Chianti. Pork is softer and slightly more bland so go lighter again: try Valpolicella or Beaujolais. For game dishes you need punch and savoury qualities so go for a southern Rhone variety. Red Burgundy is excellent with duck, salmon and firm fleshed fish like turbot. If you're relaxing with pasta and a tomato-based sauce then any juicy red-fruited wine is perfect, while barbecued foods require gutsy blacker fruits. Curries are surprisingly good with sparkling wine.

The same rules apply with white wine. The lighter the dish the fresher the wine should be. Seafood needs acidity: Sauvignon Blanc or Chablis. Thai food is best with Riesling, Chinese with white Burgundy, good Italian whites, such as Gavi, with simple grilled fish. When it comes to chicken think of the sauce rather than the meat and choose accordingly.

Cheese is a trickier area. In fact it is a complete nightmare because no one wine will go with every style of cheese. Goat's cheese is perfect with young Loire whites (after all goat's cheese is a speciality of the region) while mature hard cheeses are best with peppery, low tannin reds. Blue cheeses go well with botrytized Riesling and Sauternes; it or peaty whisky.

Sherry

Unfashionable it may be, but sherry remains one of the world's greatest wine styles. Its fall from grace is entirely down to a poor image rather than anything to do with the quality of the wines which are among the most complex you'll come across. Once you have discovered sherry you will come to appreciate a wine that ranges in style from the lightest, driest most refreshing aperitif to the richest and sweetest after-dinner drink you could ever wish for.

Sherry can only come from a small triangular area in deepest Andalusia. Here, around the town of Jerez, the rolling chalk hills are home to the Palomino grape variety. While this grape makes a rather mundane wine, it's what happens afterwards that counts.

Producers first decide whether a wine is destined to be a fino or an oloroso. If it is the former, the wine is lightly fortified and then put into a barrel where it immediately begins to grow a film of yeast (flor) on its surface. This seals the wine from the effects of the air and ensures it is fresh and clean, while the yeast adds its own nutty, bready notes. Unusually, fino doesn't stay in the same barrel. Instead it is moved through a solera. Imagine a block of barrels six high and six wide. Each horizontal row contains wine of the same average age with the youngest on the top row. To bottle sherry, wine is taken from the bottom row, then topped up with the same volume of younger wine, from the row above it and so on back through the system. This means the wine is not just being blended but that every bottle has the same character. In fino this regular movement ensures that the flor stays alive.

Olorosos are slightly different. A richer, more full-bodied style, they are fortified to a level where flor cannot grow and then aged in a solera where they are moved less frequently than a fino. This allows the wine to oxidize, mature in colour and develop a richer, nuttier character.

There are three further classic styles. Manzanilla is a fino which is aged in the seaside town of Sanlucar de Barrameda. Because the marine climate produces a thick layer of flor this is the lightest, most fragrant style of fino. Amontillados are finos whose flor has been allowed to die and some oxidation has occurred. There's also the thick, sweet, treacley PX made from dried Pedro Ximenez grapes. Pour it over ice cream.

All true sherry is dry. Finos are like fresh almonds with hints of green olive, amontillados are toasted almonds and hazelnut, while oloroso are have a note of walnut. All share an intensity of flavour unrivalled in the world of wine.

Port

People are often confused by the difference between port and sherry. Other than one coming from Portugal and the other from Spain, there's one fundamental difference. Sherry is a fully fermented wine which is then fortified and is therefore dry. Port is a wine whose fermentation is stopped by the addition of alcohol and is therefore sweet. Traditionally, in port-making, the grapes would be harvested and then pressed by foot in large stone baths called lagares. (The best ports are still made in this labour-intensive way.) It sounds unhygenic but is in fact the best way to extract the maximum amount of colour from the grapes without making the resulting juice too tannic. The frothing dark ruby juice is then half-fermented before the yeasts are stunned into submission by the addition of alcohol. The fortified wines are then subdivided into the different categories.

At the top of the tree is vintage port, the production of one year, which is made only in the very best years. Vintage port is aged in the bottle and shouldn't be drunk until it is at least a decade old. It also needs to be decanted as it has a thick sediment.

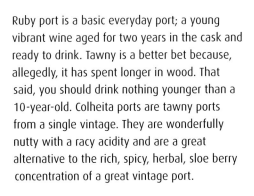

Single quinta port is also from a single year, but rather than being a blend of different vineyards (quintas) comes from a single property. This tends to mature more quickly than vintage port and is cheaper.

Late Bottled Vintage (LBV) is a wine which has been aged in the barrel for four years and then bottled. It is best drunk six years after bottling. If the label reads "Traditional" then it should be decanted.

Ruby port is a basic everyday port; a young vibrant wine aged for two years in the cask and ready to drink. Tawny is a better bet because, allegedly, it has spent longer in wood. That said, you should drink nothing younger than a 10-year-old. Colheita ports are tawny ports from a single vintage. They are wonderfully nutty with a racy acidity and are a great alternative to the rich, spicy, herbal, sloe berry concentration of a great vintage port.

Other Fortified Wines

Winemakers have been adding spirit to their wines for thousands of years, initially to preserve them in transit. While port and sherry remain the two best known examples of this genre, there are other fortified styles which are worth seeking out.

Madeira comes from the eponymous island off the coast of north west Africa. It is even more unfashionable than sherry, which is baffling because it occupies a niche halfway between the richness of port and the dryness of sherry. Great Madeira has a naturally high acidity and can last for centuries. It is high time it was rediscovered.

Muscat, or to be precise Liqueur Muscat, is a newcomer compared to these other Old World classics, hailing from the baked red earth of Rutherford in the Australian outback. Made from the Brown Muscat variety and aged in a type of solera, it is a thick, complex wine which tastes like burnt orange peel and Christmas pudding.

Montilla is wrongly perceived as a poor man's sherry. Like sherry it hails from Andalusia, close to Cordoba. The extra heat makes it a fatter style (indeed amontillado means "in the style of Montilla"). If it is to make any sort of a breakthrough it will come via people discovering its magnificent PX wines which beat those of Jerez hands down.

Marsala, from Sicily was, allegedly, invented by an Englishman when he fortified the local wine in order to ship it back to Britain. Sadly these days it is mostly left at home in a kitchen cupboard. Today there are only two producers making any sort of quality examples of Marsala.

Hills are alive: The steep terraces of Madeira produce one of the world's great wines

The last of the fortified family are vin doux naturel, from France. The best known white, Muscat de Beaumes de Venise, is a Rhone speciality. Light and honeyed, it's rather one-dimensional. Better are the red VDNs from Banyuls, Rivesaltes and Frontignan. Rich, powerful and sweet, they go perfectly with chocolate.

Tonics and juices

Without fruit juices, cordials and carbonated mixers the world of cocktails would be a poorer place. Where would a Collins be without the addition of soda. How would the British Raj have fought off malaria – and given the world a new drink – without the addition of Mr Schweppe's quinine-laced tonic water? How would we soothe our hangovers without ginger ale in a Horse's Neck? Without lemon juice, sours would not exist. The arrival of juicing machines gave birth to a whole new family of long drinks.

Even humble water has its place in the success story of the cocktail. If frozen water didn't work its strange magic then a cocktail simply would not be a cocktail. Mineral water has its place in the home bar too. It can lightly dilute Scotch or bourbon, opening up its complexities.

Tonic water and mixers

The humble soda water, known as "charged water" in the nineteenth century, has been with us since the tail end of the eighteenth century. This was a time when it had become fashionable for the (British) middle classes to travel to the country's various spa towns to take the waters. This was no new phenomenon. As long ago as Roman times, impressive complexes at spa towns, such as Bath, were built because of the beneficial properties of their waters.

In the eighteenth century man-made carbonated "spa waters" were produced for medicinal purposes. One of the main pioneers of this new type of drink was Jacob Schweppe, who saw a commercial opportunity in flavouring the water with a variety of herbs, spices, barks and extracts – a non-alcoholic version of what apothecaries had been doing with spirits for centuries.

Schweppe's most famous invention was a "tonic water" made specifically for countries where malaria was rife. The secret ingredient was quinine and he used a lot of it. So much in fact that the best way to drink tonic water was to dilute it with gin. Today, it contains far less quinine and more sugar, yet remains the mixer no one can be without.

Soda water is another essential mixer, as are other everyday carbonated mixers such as ginger ale, which is at its best when mixed with either Scotch or bourbon.

Juices

If there is one thing which separates today's cocktails from the nineteenth and early twentieth century classics it is in the extensive use of fruit juices. That's not to say that fruits weren't used in earlier times, for without orange, lemon, lime and grapefruit juice, cocktails just wouldn't have existed.

There is one simple rule when it comes to using juice: make sure it is always freshly squeezed. The superiority of freshly squeezed juice over the pre-packaged alternative is obvious and will give the drinks you make added quality. Although many recipes call for "the juice of one lemon" not every lemon contains exactly the same amount of juice, so it is wise to measure the fruit juice accurately rather than just squeezing away.

The more cocktails you make the more you'll need a good juicer to squeeze your own juice. This handy device not only makes excellent health drinks – and allows you to experiment with different combinations of fruit and vegetables – but also opens up all manner of unusual possibilities. One bar in London used its juicer to make a sweet potato juice which was then, believe it or not, used in a bourbon-based cocktail.

Cordials and fruit syrups are also useful items to keep behind your home bar. The best known is grenadine, which is made from pomegranate and is an essential ingredient in rum punches. Rose's Lime cordial is essential for drinks such as the Gimlet, while

Fresh fruit: As a garnish it adds a certain something to a cocktail.

the more elusive, yet wonderfully exotic orgeat (made from almond sugar and rosewater/orange blossom water) lends your drinks an air of sophistication. Use lightly alcoholic fruit cordials such as cassis (blackcurrant) and mures (blackberry) to give a rich, concentrated fruitiness to drinks.

Ice

Ice is the forgotten element in the creation of a mixed drink. After all, it was the arrival of commercial ice-making in the US which triggered the first cocktail boom in the nineteenth century. Low-cost ice let bartenders to start experimenting with new "fancy drinks". Remember, one of the first definitions of a cocktail was a cold drink.

Ice doesn't just cool down a drink, it alters it, lowering the temperature and allowing the flavours to fuse. As the cocktail ingredients drop in temperature the ice also begins to melt, causing the drink to dilute. Shaking lowers the temperature quicker than stirring, while the finer the ice, the faster the chilling process. Remember that the longer you shake over crushed ice, the greater the rate of dilution. Time comes into play as well as temperature.

If you want your drink at a temperature of 0°C, then the amount of dilution should be the same whether you use crushed ice or cubes: the crushed ice just gets you there quicker. When a film of ice forms on the outside of the shaker you've hit the right temperature. When Constante Ribalagua used his electric blender to make the first frozen daiquiris in Havana, he was using technology to cool down the drink more efficiently and not – as most bartenders seem to forget – to make it more dilute.

It is a personal decision whether you shake or stir. The main difference is simply aesthetic. Shaking gives cocktails a haze, while stirring keeps them clear. Many people prefer their Martini or Manhattan stirred for this very reason. Make sure your ice is clean: chlorinated water makes chlorinated ice cubes. One of the most undrinkable things imaginable is something like a Tanqueray & tonic which has been mixed with ice cubes made from stinky tap water.

Hair of the dog

The easiest way to avoid ever having to refer to this chapter is to not drink too much. However, we've all overindulged at some stage in our lives and suffered the inevitable hangover – the shakes, the headache, the sweats, even a complete loss of memory in some cases. Most hangover symptoms are caused by your body producing too much insulin, resulting in low blood sugar levels. The one part of your body which isn't dried up and screaming for liquid is your brain, which has swollen and is now rubbing against your skull. Apparently, people over the age of 60 don't suffer from as intense a headache as their brains have shrunk, but that's not much consolation if you have 30-odd years to wait. Before a party or even while you're there, there are some things you can do to minimize the effects of one drink too many:

Consuming a glass of milk or a tablespoon of olive oil before you start drinking helps line the stomach and slow down the uptake of alcohol. Drinking plenty of water to slow down the dehydrating effects of alcohol is an even better idea. Alcohol inhibits the release of antidiuretic hormone (ADH) which allows water in the urine to be reabsorbed into the blood. Without ADH we release more water in our urine, thus dehydrating our bodies.

Drink a glass or more of water for every cocktail. If you forget, then drink a pint of water before you go to bed, or if you can't face any more liquid, then at least have one in the morning.

Hangovers come in all shapes and sizes. The type you experience largely depends on what you have been drinking: the more congeners in the spirit, the more vicious the hangover. Be especially cautious of brown spirits like Scotch, bourbon and brandy. Know whether you are sensitive to certain alcohols and compounds within alcohol. Many people get depressed on gin, while others are hopeless after only three pints of beer. Knowing what you can and can't tolerate is another way of preventing a truly bad hangover.

If you forget to carry out any preventative measure before a night of drinking, you can try drinking a cola or eating a fried breakfast in an attempt to raise your blood sugars, but even doctors have to admit that the best way to get rid of a hangover is to turn to a hair of the dog or, literally, "the hair of the dog that bit you."

Here are some personal favourites:

1) The Bloody Mary (see pp 64–5). There is something about spiced up tomato juice and vodka that just works. The tip is to plan ahead: make jugs of the mix the night before a party.

2) Underberg bitters (those tiny bottles of magic wrapped in brown paper) seemingly blast a hangover out of your ears. What they do in actual fact is get you drunk again, thus numbing the pain of the hangover in the process.

3) If the hangover isn't too bad try a Horse's Neck (see page 115). The ginger ale is great for any residual heartburn and raises the blood sugars, bitters have a tremendous settling effect on the stomach, while bourbon provides the requisite hair of the dog.

4) Pick yourself up with a sour. They freshen the mouth and clear the head. If you want to go gently into the dawn then try a Collins, but remember the best way to fight a hangover is to attack it not to try and persuade it to leave.

5) Try a Campari and orange. The Campari provides the medicinal benefits of bitters, while the orange juice provides a much needed shot of Vitamin C; the whole ensemble tastes wonderful.

Bloody Mary: Vodka, tomato juice, Worcestershire sauce, tabasco – the Hair of the Dog

Glossary

ABV The alcoholic strength of the spirit measured as a percentage part in relation to the liquid as a whole (i.e. 40% ABV is 40% alcohol, 60% water). Compare "Proof".

Aguard(i)ente Spanish/ Portuguese term for spirit. In Spain and Portugal it refers to grape brandy; in Brazil and Mexico it is sometimes used to refer to a young sugar cane spirit.

Alambic/Alembic Old term for a pot still.

Alambic Armagnaçais Traditional small continuous still used in Armagnac.

Alambic Charentais Traditional Cognac pot still.

Alquitara Spanish term for a pot still and a pot still distillate.

Analyser The first column of a multi-column still.

Anejo Tequila/mezcal that has been aged in the barrel for more than a year.

Agave Family of Mexican desert lilies used to produce mezcal and tequila.

Age Statement The age on a bottle of spirits referring to the youngest component in the blend or vatting.

Angel's Share The term given to the spirit which evaporates from warehoused barrels. Known as "Duppies Share" in Jamaica.

Aqua Vitae The original term for spirits. Its meaning: "water of life" has been translated into Scottish Gaelic uisce beatha; Irish Gaelic usquebaugh; and Danish akvavit.

Assemblage French term for blending.

Backset (also Setback or Sour Mash) In North America, the acidic residue from the first distillation which is added the mash tub and/or the fermenter, totalling no less than 25 percent of the overall mash. It is used to stop bacterial infection and to lower the pH in the fermenter allowing an even fermentation.

Bagasse The fibrous stalks of sugar cane, sometimes used as fuel for rum stills.

Batch Distillation Another term for pot still, or discontinuous distillation. The first distillation produces a low-strength spirit which is then redistilled and separated into three parts, heads, heart and tails of which only the heart is retained.

Beading A simple method of assessing a spirit's strength. When a bottle is shaken, bubbles (beads) form. The bigger they are and the longer they remain, the higher the strength.

Beer North American/ Caribbean term for fermented 'mash'.

Beer Still North American term for the first still in the distillation process.

Blending (1) The mixing of different types of spirit (e.g. rye, Bourbon or malt with grain); (2) The assembling of different ages of the same spirit. In both definitions the aim is to produce a consistent style.

Boise Extract of oak chips and spirit used to colour and flavour young brandies.

Bonne Chauffe The heart of the second distillation in Cognac which must be no more than 72 percent ABV.

Botanicals The herbs, peel, etc. which give flavour to gin, the most important being juniper.

Bouilleur French term for distiller.

Brandewijn Dutch term for grape spirit (burnt wine) which evolved into brandy.

Brouillis (also premier chauffe) The spirit collected at the end of the first distillation in Cognac.

Cask Strength A spirit which has not been reduced by water to the standard strength.

Chai Above ground warehouse used for ageing Cognac and Armagnac.

Charcoal Filtration Technique (used in Tennessee whiskeys and vodka production) which involves passing new spirit through vats or tanks containing granulated charcoal. This removes impurities and imparts a mellow roundness to the spirit.

Charring The firing of the inside of a barrel. The flame opens up cracks in the surface of the oak allowing easy penetration by the spirit and also releases sugar compounds which aid flavouring and colouring of the spirit.

Chill Filtration A filtering process done by lowering the temperature of the spirit to remove compounds which could cause clouding. It also has the effect of removing some congeners.

Condenser The equipment which turns the alcoholic vapours into liquid form. Traditionally this was a spiral of copper immersed in cold water, these days heat exchangers are used.

Congeners The chemical compounds found in a spirit which are formed during fermentation, distillation and maturation. They contain many flavour-carrying elements. The higher the alcoholic strength of a spirit, the fewer congeners are present.

Cold compounding Method of adding concentrates of flavours to neutral spirit. A cheaper method than maceration and infusion, but giving a cruder end product.

Column Still (also Beer, Coffey or Continuous still) Most commonly used in continuous distillation. They work by forcing pressurised steam up the column where it meets the descending alcoholic wash, vapourizing the alcohol and carrying it up to be condensed.

Distillation The technique of extracting alcohol from a fermented liquid by heating it. Because alcohol boils at a lower strength than water the vapour can be collected and condensed, thus concentrating the strength.

Doubler North American term for the pot still used for the second distillation.

Dram Scottish, Irish and Caribbean term for a glass of spirit.

Enzymes Organic catalysts which convert non-fermentable starches into fermentable soluble sugars. Grains such as malted barley and rye contain such enzymes and are added to other cereal crops to for this process of conversion or saccharification.

Esters Flavour-giving chemical compounds produced by the reaction of alcohol and acids during fermentation and maturation that appear soon after the start of distillation.

Eau-de-vie (1) French term for young distillate (brandy); (2) French term for spirits made from fruit.

Faibles Low strength solution of distilled water and Cognac used to dilute maturing brandies.

Feints (also Tails/Low Wines) Scottish/Irish term for the unwanted end part of the second distillation. They are collected and redistilled.

Fermenters Large vessels made either of steel or wood where the mash is turned into beer or wash.

Foreshots See "Heads"

Fusel Oil A heavy congener.

Fut/Fut de chene French term for a barrel of less than 650 litres.

Heads (also Foreshots/High Wines/Tetes) Term for the volatile first runnings from the still during second distillation. They are collected and redistilled.

Heart (also Coeur/Middle Cut) Term for the potable central fraction of the spirit in batch distillation which the distiller keeps.

Holandas Young Spanish brandy produced from a pot still (alquitara).

Infusion Process of extracting flavour from ingredients by gentle heating.

Maceration The process of steeping ingredients (fruits, herbs, etc.) in alcohol to extract colour and flavour.

Malt (1) A grain, usually barley, but also rye, which has been stimulated artificially into germination and then halted by drying ('Malting'). The malt is high in sugars and enzymes. (2) Common term for a single malt whisky.

Maltings Building where malting takes place.

Marrying Process Where recently blended spirits are placed in a large vat before bottling. The technique allows the different distillates to homogenize.

Mash The sweet liquid produced after hot water has been flushed through the base ingredient in the Mash Tub/Tun to extract the fermentable sugars prior to fermentation.

Mash Bill North American term for the percentage make-up of ingredients (corn, wheat, rye, barley) being used in mashing.

Middle Cut Whisky term for Heart.

Molasses The thick black liquid that is left after sugar has been crystallized. It can then be used to make rum, rhum industriel, or neutral alcohol.

Mouth Feel Term used for the shape and texture of the spirit in the mouth when being tasted.

Neutral alcohol/spirit Spirit of above 95.5% ABV containing little or no congeners.

Nose The aroma of the spirit.

Oak The most common type of wood used for casks used in maturation. Oak is strong, watertight wood which allows light oxidation. It also imparts a range of colour and flavour components to the maturing spirit. Different types of oak will give different effects.

Overproof Rum terminology for high-strength, unaged rum.

Paille French rhum that has been aged for less than three years.

Paradis Cellar containing the oldest and rarest brandies.

Peat A soft fuel made from compressed and carbonised vegetable matter – usually heather, wood, grass and occasionally seaweed. Its smoke, known as peat reek, is very pungent and when used in drying malted barley imparts its phenolic aroma to the malt.

Pina Term used to describe ripe agave.

Pomace See vinaccia.

Pot Stills Stills, usually made from copper used in batch distillation.

Proof American measurement of alcoholic strength. A 100°proof spirit is 50 percent ABV.

Rancio The rich, pungent aroma with hints of mushrooms, cheese dried fruit, nuts which is created by the oxidation of fatty acids during extended maturation of a brandy. It usually appears after 20 years or more.

Rectification Purification of a distillate by redistillation giving a high-strength distillate with very few congeners.

Reflux The process in which the shape or control of a still forces alcohol vapours to fall back down the still to be redistilled. The end result usually produces a lighter spirit.

Reposado Tequila/mezcal that has been aged in barrel for less than 11 months.

Retort A vessel used in batch distillation containing either the heads or tails of the previous distillation. The alcoholic vapour passes through the bottom of the retort heating the liquid and causing a second distillation.

Rhum Rum from French-governed départements (such as Martinique and Guadeloupe). Rhum agricole is produced from sugar cane juice; Rhum Industriel is made from molasses.

Ricks The wooden frames that hold maturing American whiskey.

Solera Predominantly Spanish method of maturation and fractional blending, most commonly seen in Jerez and used for sherry and Brandy de Jerez.

Sour Mash Another term for backset. A Sour Mash whiskey must contain 25% backset, the use of a lactic bacteria soured yeast mash which has been fermented for a minimum of 72 hours. All Kentucky and Tennessee whiskey is sour mash.

Stillage The non-alcoholic residue at the bottom of a still containing solids – which are processed for animal feed – and acidic liquid which in North America is used as backset.

Thumper A type of doubler containing water through which the alcoholic vapours pass.

Toasting The process of lightly heating the inside of a barrel releasing sugars in the wood. A more gentle process than charring.

Vatting Scottish/Irish term for the mixing together of malt from one distillery, or more. A "Vatted Malt" is a blend of malts from more than one distillery.

Vieux French term used for long-aged spirits like rhum or Calvados.

Vinaccia (also Pomace) The skins left after a wine has been fermented which when distilled produces grappa.

Vintage Term referring to a spirit produced from a single year.

VS (aka ***) French term for the youngest grading of brandy, usually spirits which have been aged for a minimum of two and a half years.

VSOP French term for the second quality grading of brandy, referring to a spirit which has usually been aged for a minimum of four and a half years.

Wash The fermented liquid which is ready to be distilled.

XO (also Extra/Extra Vieux/Napoleon/ Reserve) French term for the top quality grade of a spirit which has usually been aged for a minimum of six to seven years but normally considerably longer.

Yeast A micro-organism of the fungi family which feeds on sugar converting it to alcohol and CO_2. Yeast also imparts flavour compounds to the liquid.

Cocktails by spirit

The following pages contain a list of all 602 cocktails featured here, itemized by base spirit or category. Many of the cocktails contain more than one spirit, or fit in more than one category, so they appear more than once.

Whisky

(Scotch/Irish/bourbon/rye)

Gin

All types

Vodka

Including flavoured vodkas

Brandy/ Cognac

All types including Calvados

Rum

All types, including Cachara

Tequila

All types

Champagne
And Sparkling wine

Hot Cocktails

Creamy Cocktails

Includes cream/ crème liqueurs, ice cream and cream (milk) as ingredient, float, or topping

Non-Alcohoic Cocktails

Other Cocktails

Cocktails using none of the above ingredients

Index

Cocktail recipes in the A–Z listing are indexed by spirit, PP386–95.

INDEX

INDEX

INDEX

ACKNOWLEDGEMENTS

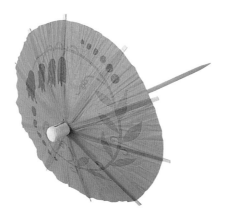

Special thanks to mixologist extraordinaire **Ryan Chetiyawardana**, A.K.A. Mr Lyon, who supplied the twenty-first century cocktail recipes, and to **Rebekkah Dooley** of the Callooh Calley Bar in Shoreditch.

The publishers also would like to thank the following people and companies for their assistance in the compilation of this book: **Ivan Jones**, **James Duncan**, and **Karl Adamson**, photographers; **Corinna Thompson** and **Natashia Bartlett**, Oddbins Ltd; **Chris Edwardes** and **Miles Cunliffe**, Blanch House Hotel; **Caroline Fraser Ker**, copy editor.

The publishers would like to thank the following sources for their kind permission to reproduce pictures in this book.

Advertising Archive: 335; **Allied Domencq:** 215; **Bacardi & Co Ltd:** 288, 294; **Baileys:** 344; **Anthony Blake Photo Library:** 16-17, 323; **Brown Forman Ltd:** 242; **Gerrit Buntrock:** 65, 93, 135, 137, 139, 147, 153, 169, 183, 187; **Leo Burnett:** 269; **Cephas:** /Stewart Boreham: 271; /Mick Rock: 301, 308; **Cooley Distillery:** 235; **Corbis:** /Paul Almasy: 347; /Tiziana& Gianni Baldizzone: 251; /Jonathan Blair: 296; /Alexander Burkatowski: 321; /Michael Busselle: 359; /Dean Conger: 253; /Eric Crichton: 332; / Richard Cummins: 381; /DiMaggio/Kalish: 8-9; /Owen Franken: 365; /Fukuhara: 353; /Mark Gibson: 283; /Rose Hartman: 259; /Charles O'Rear: 360; /Tim Page: 35; /Royalty Free: 376; /Brian A Vikander: 261; /Michael S Yamashita: 273; **Courvoiser:** 302; **Mary Evans Picture Library:** 291; **First Drinks Brand Ltd:** 345; **Getty Images:** /Per Eriksson: 299; /Andy Lyons: 239; /Photo Disc: 15, 279; **William Grant & Sons:** 231; **Hiram Walker & Sons:** 244, 245; **Irish Distillers:** 236; **Plodimex:** 257; **Polish Vodka Website:** 267; **Remy & Associates:** 311; **Rex Features:** /Stewart Cook: 22; **Scotland in Focus:** /R Weir: 225; **The Seagram Company Ltd:** 218; **Speyside Distillery Co Ltd:** 216; **Thinkstock:** 355; **Trentino D.O.C./R & R Teamwork:** 326; **United Distillers and Vintners:** 249; **UTo Nederlande B.v:** 277; **Johnny Walker:** 233